AI FOR EQUITY

This book brings an important and balanced perspective to the conversation on AI – highlighting both its risks and its potential to drive meaningful change. The EQUITAS framework is especially compelling and actionable.

— *Marta Tubielewicz*, Procurement Leader

This is an important book that all leaders must invest time to read. We know that AI adoption is moving from approach with caution to rapid implementation – but we must not lose human perspective as we seek advancement. I commend Jenny and Leah-Sunshine for reminding us of what still matters.

— *Samuel Kasumu*, Former Special Adviser to the Prime Minister, NED, Founder and Author

AI for Equity is a collective call to action to resist the current trajectory of AI and join those making technology which serves everyone equitably. Jenny and Leah-Sunshine Garrett's conversations with experts reveal that a future with AI does not have to be feared; instead, it is an opportunity to create a tool which reflects humanity not as it is, but as it could be.

— *Kyra Wilson*, University of Washington

This book drew me in right from the first paragraph. It is equal parts thought-provoking and empowering. This mother–daughter duo's strategic resistance to accepting things as they are makes this a must-read for anyone who understands and acknowledges the power of AI, and believes it can be redirected to counteract bias and improve our society.

— *Surya Ramesh*, AI Consultant, Educator, Mom

AI governance is not a technology problem. It is a leadership problem. This book names that truth with evidence, humanity, and a framework every board and senior leader needs to sit with. It belongs in every boardroom conversation about the future.

— *Albana Vrioni*, Executive Director, Women on Boards Albania; Founder, Vrioni Consulting

Most books about AI ask you to think differently. This one asks you to act. The most radical thing it does is also the simplest: it listens to practitioners, communities, and people whose knowledge has been sitting outside the room where AI decisions get made. Jenny and Leah-Sunshine Garrett have written the book the field has been waiting for without knowing it.

— ***Karen Blake MBE Hon. FBAASc*, Former Co-CEO, Tech Talent Charter; Honorary Fellow of the British Science Association**

Most AI strategy conversations stop at capability and skip the harder question: whose interests does the system serve, and what governance exists to ensure it? This book does not skip it. Twelve practitioners across four continents, grounded in real work, making the case that equitable AI is a design problem, not a technology problem. The EQUITAS framework gives leaders somewhere concrete to start.

— ***Markus Bernhardt PhD*, Founder, Endeavor Intelligence; Author, The Endeavor Report; Keynote Speaker, San Francisco**

AI for Equity is, simply put, a seminal work. Leah-Sunshine's aptitude for systemic pattern recognition maps out the interconnectivity across the continuum of domestic violence and abuse against women and girls, unapologetically refusing to treat instances as isolated incidents. Meanwhile, Jenny, with the meticulousness of a literary detective, drills down into the core of design, adoption, and deployment concerns with a rare precision that is a privilege to observe. Both have a wonderful, collaborative way of not catastrophising but championing - not just mitigation techniques – but actual, practical, grounded, and genuinely positive solutions. I could not recommend this book more highly.

— ***Cecilia Jastrzembska*, Senior Policy Advisor, Co-Founding Member, UKAI Women in AI, Political Journalist, Award-Winning Keynote Speaker**

AI FOR EQUITY

Creating a More Equitable Society for All

BY

JENNY GARRETT OBE
Jenny Garrett Global, UK

AND

LEAH-SUNSHINE GARRETT
Dawn Intelligence, UK

emerald
PUBLISHING

United Kingdom – North America – Japan – India
Malaysia – China

Emerald Publishing Limited
Emerald Publishing, Floor 5, Northspring, 21-23 Wellington Street, Leeds LS1 4DL.

First edition 2026

British Library Cataloguing in Publication Data
A catalogue record for this book is available from the British Library

ISBN: 978-1-83742-857-1 (Print)
ISBN: 978-1-83742-854-0 (Online)
ISBN: 978-1-83742-856-4 (Epub)

CONTENTS

Acknowledgements ix

1 The Dawn of Equitable AI: Why This Book Exists and What It Asks of You 1

2 The Mirror of Bias: How AI Reflects and Amplifies Inequity
In conversation with: Dr Mona Ashok, Associate Professor of Digital Transformation 17

3 Understanding the AI Landscape: Power, Promise, and Peril
In conversation with: Christian Ortiz, Founder, Justice AI 33

4 Designing for Fairness: Principles and Frameworks for Ethical AI
In conversation with: Jazz Rasool, Director, AI Coaching Alliance 51

5 AI as a Shield: Combating Gender-based Violence
In conversation with: Sumathi Menon, GenAI Educator and Regional Lead, Women Defining AI UK 69

6 AI for Inclusive Talent: Fairer Recruitment and Career Pathways
In conversation with: Dan Gallagher, Founder, Verityn Index 85

7 AI and Neurodiversity: Enhancing Work and Learning
In conversation with: Twan Wildeboer, TEDx Speaker, Innovator and AI Practitioner 103

8 Bridging the Health Divide: AI for Equitable Healthcare Access
In conversation with: Dr Keshav Malhotra, Embryologist and Reproductive Health Specialist 123

9 Empowering Communities: AI for Social and Economic Development
In conversation with: Dr Pauldy Otermans, Co-Founder, Otermans Institute 139

10 Dismantling Socio-economic Barriers with AI: Access, Redistribution, and the Difference Between Them
In conversation with: Sam Samarasinghe, Founder, Delenta | Anna Jones, Founder, RefuAid and Merit 157

11 The Human–AI Partnership: Leadership, Accountability, and Collaboration
In conversation with: Rod Brown, Founder and CEO, S/BES LLC 173

12 Building the Future of Equitable AI – A Call to Action: Curiosity, Creativity, and the Human Operating System
In conversation with: Finbar O'Hanlon, Innovation Strategist and AI Practitioner 189

13 Conclusion: Twelve Voices, Seven Commitments, One Choice 203

About the Authors 219

The Twelve Voices 221

Lexicon 225

Index 235

ACKNOWLEDGEMENTS

This book belongs to 12 people more than it belongs to us.

Dr Mona Ashok, Christian Ortiz, Jazz Rasool, Sumathi Menon, Dan Gallagher, Twan Wildeboer, Dr Keshav Malhotra, Dr Pauldy Otermans, Sam Samarasinghe, Anna Jones, Rod Brown, and Finbar O'Hanlon – thank you. Your work is the book. We were simply the people lucky enough to ask the questions.

We wrote this in months, and every one of them made equity feel more urgent than the last. That urgency is on every page.

We kept it quietly to ourselves for most of that time. Then, we mentioned it at a podcast festival and the room gave us a round of applause before we had said anything more than the title. That was the moment we understood how much it was needed.

To the team at Emerald Publishing, the listeners of the AI for Equity podcast across 40 countries, and the readers who gave their time to review early drafts – thank you for believing in this, following this, and making it better.

To the team at Jenny Garrett Global and Dawn Intelligence – thank you for keeping everything running while we disappeared into manuscripts and transcripts. The juggle was real and you made it possible.

To our families – thank you for the space, the patience and the love.

Leah-Sunshine:
Writing this book in my early 20s was one of the hardest things I have done – not because of the work itself, but because of what it asked of me. I had to push the limits of what I thought I was capable of. I had to learn how to hold my voice steady when I wasn't sure it was strong enough. I had to juggle work and life and

relationships and friendships and somehow keep all of them intact. Some days, I did not manage it. But, I grew more in this process than I expected to, and I came into my own in ways I didn't see coming.

To my partner, thank you for being my rock. To my friends (you know who you are), thank you for listening, for proofreading when I couldn't read it anymore, for sitting with me while I rambled about the challenges and the wins, and for never once being surprised that I was doing this. You went from listening to me read poetry at university to holding this book in your hands. That means everything.

To my Great Granny – this book is not just mine, it is yours too. Your bravery, your courage, your resilience, and your words are always with me. You show up in my dreams, and every time you do, you are telling me to keep going. So I am.

And to the reader – keep being curious. Even when you think you have reached the edge of what there is to know about AI, I promise you there is more. There is always a way to be more equitable, always a way to learn more. This experience taught me I can do anything I set my mind to. It also taught me that my mum really is my best friend.

Jenny:

The hardest part of writing this book was the pace. AI moves so fast that every day brought something new – a conference, a conversation, a moment in nature – that sparked another idea, another angle, another thing that needed to be in these pages. Finding the focus to finish while running a business, travelling and trying to stay current felt impossible at times. But I have wonderful coaches and confidantes in my circle who kept reminding me that my words matter and that I have something to say.

And the parents – so many parents – who said they wished they could do something like this with their own child. That stopped me every time. Because I almost didn't ask. I almost assumed she would be too busy, too independent, too her own person. And she was all of those things. And she said yes anyway.

Completing the MIT AI Strategy and Leadership Programme before we started this book gave me the foundation to think about

AI the way senior leaders need to – not as a technology question but as a leadership question. That collision is what this book is built on.

What I did not expect was how much this process would change me. I started this book as a leadership developer who was learning about AI. I am finishing it understanding that they were never separate. AI and equity, leadership and technology, my professional expertise, and this new landscape – they are one integrated argument. That shift happened in these pages.

And I discovered Leah-Sunshine as a peer. Not just my daughter, not just my co-author, but someone whose thinking genuinely surprises me and changes mine. She creates new neural pathways in me. I did not expect to say that about my own child. I am so proud of her. Her writing challenged me to write better. Her unapologeticness challenged me to be bolder. She gets to the same places I get to, but how she travels there is completely different. That difference made this book better than I could have made it alone.

My grandmother, Rosemarie, would have been so proud. Two generations writing books. At one point, there were four generations of women in our family alive at the same time. We keep stepping it up. She had a voice but did not always get to share it. We are sharing ours for her.

Writing this together added a new branch to our relationship – one we did not know was missing until it grew. We are both proud that both our voices are in it equally. We believe that fairness powered by AI is possible. This book is our evidence.

Jenny Garrett OBE and Leah-Sunshine Garrett

1

THE DAWN OF EQUITABLE AI: WHY THIS BOOK EXISTS AND WHAT IT ASKS OF YOU

> *In the Fifth Industrial Revolution, humans and machines will dance together, metaphorically. Gauri and Van Eerden (2019)*

This book began with insomnia. On the first morning of 2025, one of us could not sleep. Jenny's smart ring told her what she already knew: the night had been restless. But the anxiety was not the formless kind that comes and goes. It had a shape. It had a name. Artificial intelligence was reshaping the world, and the people most likely to be harmed were the people least likely to be in the room where the decisions were being made.

I have built my career on instinct and on asking tough questions. For 20 years, I have helped organisations build inclusive workplaces, challenging the biases that humans carry into boardrooms, hiring panels, and promotion committees. I have sat across the table from leaders who genuinely believed their organisations were fair, only to discover that the systems they trusted were anything but. Now, a new system was emerging, one that could make those same biases faster, more confident, and harder to see.

In the weeks and months that followed, the evidence kept mounting. Research consistently showed that AI was not fixing bias but amplifying it. Hiring algorithms penalised Black candidates even when qualifications were identical. Language models associated female names with family and domesticity, male names with career and leadership. In Canada, Air Canada had been found legally liable after its customer service chatbot gave passengers incorrect advice about bereavement fares – a small case that pointed to a much larger accountability gap.

The pattern was clear. AI did not fix biases. It turbocharged them. The same biases I had spent trying to surface in leadership meetings throughout my career – the assumptions about who looks like a leader, who sounds like an expert, who belongs in the room – were now being encoded into systems that operated at scale, at speed, and without the self-awareness that a human being, on a good day, might bring to the decision.

But somewhere between the alarm and the headlines, something shifted. I have never been the person who accepts the worst-case scenario as the only scenario. The headlines told one story. But I have spent my career finding the people who are writing a different one. I reached for my laptop and typed an email to my daughter.

THE EMAIL THAT STARTED EVERYTHING

Leah-Sunshine is in her 20s. Recently graduated and already building Dawn Intelligence, an advisory intelligence platform that provides AI-powered briefings to UK public sector bodies, using data to identify patterns of harm across communities. She was not discovering AI, but living inside it. Having used AI tools throughout her degree, built her business on them, and understood intuitively that the same technology being celebrated in corporate boardrooms was quietly reproducing the inequities she saw on social media every day.

Leah-Sunshine was already living inside the data I was only just discovering. By the end of 2024, over a third of employees were using ChatGPT daily. The job market she had graduated into was contracting, with millions of roles lost globally to automation – the risk falling disproportionately on women, people of colour, and workers in the global south. Private investment in AI had topped $100 billion globally, with the United States and China capturing the overwhelming majority, and computational power concentrating in the hands of a small number of corporations at an unprecedented rate. I was reading about this world. Leah-Sunshine was building in it.

My email said, Let's start a podcast. Let's find the people using AI to make the world a better place. We'll call it AI for Equity.

Leah-Sunshine replied within the hour. Excited by the research, curious about how working together as mother and daughter would feel, and already living the reality I was just discovering.

> *I hesitated. I had just been made redundant. I was coding Dawn Intelligence's portal, and I wasn't sure what the next two weeks looked like, let alone what we might be starting. Part of me sensed that this was going to be something big. Part of me wasn't sure I was ready. But something in me said: just do it. I pressed send before I could talk myself out of it. After I replied, I started to get excited. Before, I was nervous.* – **Leah-Sunshine**

Neither of us knew it at the time, but this was the beginning of the book you are holding. What started as a mother emailing her daughter before breakfast became a podcast, then a research project, then a global conversation with practitioners on four continents, and finally the book you are reading now. The journey from that email to this chapter took just over a year. In that time, AI moved from a topic of curiosity to a question of urgency. The window for shaping its trajectory narrowed. And the people we found building equitable AI told us, consistently and from every corner of the world, that the window was still open. But not for long.

THE HYPOTHESES THAT CHANGED EVERYTHING

Most people, confronted with the evidence we were gathering, would have stopped. Written a manifesto about regulation. Started a petition. Leaned into fear.

We did something different. We held two hypothetical ideas up to the light and refused to put them down.

First: if AI could accelerate bias, perhaps it could also accelerate fairness.

Second: if AI could reflect our biases back to us, perhaps we could finally address them.

These were not comfortable hypotheses. They required us to hold two contradictory truths at once: that AI is already causing harm, and that it might also be the most powerful tool we have ever had for undoing harm. That tension runs through every chapter of this book. We never resolve it. We do not think it should be resolved. We think it should be held, examined, and used to drive better decisions.

This was not naive optimism. It was strategic resistance. A refusal to let fear write the only story of AI's future. And it led us to a question that shaped everything that followed: who, anywhere in the world, is already using AI to make things fairer? Who has built something that works? And what can the rest of us learn from them?

With Leah-Sunshine's research rigour and my professional network, we began searching globally for people doing bold and practical things with AI and equity. We searched across four continents. Our network initially drew us towards the United Kingdom, but the questions they are grappling with – who benefits from AI, who is harmed by it, and who gets to shape it – are not British questions. They are human ones. Casting our net globally, we read research papers, watched TEDx talks, followed LinkedIn threads, listened to podcasts, and asked everyone we spoke to: who else should we talk to? Then, we interviewed them. The AI for Equity podcast launched, and the response confirmed the hunger for this conversation.

> *Absolutely love listening to the AI for Equity podcast! So fascinating... Thank you for opening my eyes. I'll be listening to every episode! Also, love the mother and daughter duo presenting.*

This book is the result of those conversations.

A MOTHER, A DAUGHTER, AND THE GAP BETWEEN US

The rise of artificial intelligence is not just a technological shift. It is a sociological event that is redefining power structures and workplace identity. And one of the sharpest lines it draws is generational. We know this because we live on either side of it.

I am Gen X. Many in my generation approach AI with pragmatic caution. About one in three of us use it regularly, seeing it as a productivity tool that requires human checking. We value control, credibility, and proven results. Our questions are: who is accountable when the algorithm gets it wrong? Can we trust the output? Is this making things better, or just faster?

Leah-Sunshine is Gen Z. Her generation often uses AI with fluency and anxiety in equal measure. Seventy per cent use it weekly, the highest of any generational group. They have grown up with algorithms curating their lives, their music, their news, their friendships. AI is not alien to them. It is foundational. But they are also the generation most likely to ask: who built this and whose interests does it serve?

What makes our partnership work is not that we agree. It is that the gap between us mirrors the gap in how society is approaching AI. Boomers and Gen X can prioritise control and credibility. Millennials and Gen Z can prioritise access and experimentation. The most resilient approach, as every chapter of this book will show, is not one or the other. It is both. It is the tension between caution and courage that produces the most equitable outcomes.

We have seen this play out in our own work. When Jenny approaches a new AI tool, she tests it against her experience, asking whether it delivers something her decades of practice could not. When Leah-Sunshine approaches the same tool, she tests it against her generation's expectations, asking whether it treats her as a full person or reduces her to a data point. Both questions matter. Neither is sufficient alone. The book you are reading is the product of holding both at once.

This generational divide is not just personal. It is structural. The people designing AI systems are overwhelmingly young, male, and based in a handful of cities. The people most affected by those systems span every age, every gender, every geography. When a 25-year-old engineer in San Francisco decides what counts as a normal CV format, they are making a decision that will affect a 50-year-old woman returning to work in Lagos, a refugee doctor re-accrediting in London, and a neurodivergent graduate in

Amsterdam. None of those people were in the room. None of them were consulted. The engineer may not even know they exist.

This is why we wrote this book together. Not because a mother–daughter partnership makes a good story, although it does. But because the conversation between generations is itself a model for how AI should be governed: with different perspectives in the room, with the tension held rather than resolved, and with the understanding that no single viewpoint is sufficient to see the whole picture.

THE AI YOU DO NOT NOTICE

Before we go further, consider your typical day. Your phone's alarm adjusts to your sleep patterns. Facial recognition or fingerprint scanning unlocks it. Email spam filters have already sorted your inbox. Predictive text finishes your sentences. You search for something online and the results are ranked by an algorithm that knows your location, your browsing history, and your purchase patterns. You have not yet spoken to a human, and AI has already made dozens of decisions on your behalf.

You travel to work. Your Maps app predicts traffic. On public transport, the app predicts arrival times. At your desk, your calendar suggests meeting slots. A colleague sends a document and your software suggests edits, summarises content, flags inconsistencies. You arrive home and a video call automatically adjusts your lighting. A streaming service recommends what you should watch tonight. Your smart speaker learns from your questions. Your fitness tracker learns from your body.

You are interacting with AI hundreds of times a day without noticing. And that AI spans everything from hiring algorithms to diagnostic tools to the large language models most readers have encountered. The question this book asks is not whether AI is present in your life. It is whether the AI present in your life was designed with you in mind. With your community in mind. With people who do not look like you in mind.

Most of us have never asked these questions, because the AI was designed to be invisible. That invisibility is not a bug. It is a feature.

The less you notice the technology, the less likely you are to question it. And the less you question it, the more power it accumulates unchecked. This book is an invitation to start noticing.

All of it – from the algorithm sorting your inbox to the model writing your colleague's presentation – falls under the same broad umbrella: artificial intelligence, systems that learn from data to make decisions or generate outputs without being explicitly programmed for each task.

WHY THIS MOMENT, WHY THIS BOOK

In 2025, AI reached what the World Economic Forum and McKinsey describe as a turning point of operational maturity (McKinsey & Company, 2025; World Economic Forum, 2025). Integration across national infrastructure, healthcare, and education is no longer experimental. It is structural. Over 50% of global venture capital has gone into AI-related companies. The technology is not coming. It is here.

AI has the capacity to boost global GDP by 14% by 2030. But without inclusion frameworks, those gains will concentrate in high-tech economies and among digitally privileged groups. The equity question has moved from ethics to economics. It is not a matter of fairness alone. It is a matter of who benefits from the most significant economic transformation since the industrial revolution.

And the risks are not theoretical. Consider the data labellers training AI systems in Kenya, the Philippines, and South America. Kenyan workers for OpenAI earned as little as $1.32 per hour, classifying traumatic content so that chatbots could learn what not to say (Perrigo, 2023). The lowest-paid jobs in the AI economy are disproportionately held by people in the global south. The highest paid jobs are overwhelmingly concentrated in the global north. AI is not just a technological revolution. It is a labour revolution, and the labour is not equally valued.

The geography of AI mirrors the geography of colonialism. The data is extracted from communities in the global south. The value is captured by corporations in the global north. The decisions about how the technology is governed are made in boardrooms that those communities never enter. This is not an accident. It is the predictable outcome of building a global technology on datasets, funding structures, and governance models that were never designed to include the majority of the world's population.

The environmental cost compounds the injustice. Training a single large language model can consume as much energy as five cars over their entire lifetimes and requires millions of litres of water to cool the servers. Dr Mona Ashok acknowledged this directly in our conversation: the data centres need a lot of power. Jazz Rasool went further, arguing that the fifth industrial revolution must deliver flourishing that is sustainable not just for people but for the rest of life on this planet. This book focuses on social equity, but we acknowledge that environmental equity is inseparable from it. You cannot build a fair system on an extractive foundation.

At the same time, the political landscape around diversity, equity, and inclusion has shifted dramatically. In the United States, executive orders have rolled back federal DEI programmes. Major corporations have quietly withdrawn their diversity commitments. The language of inclusion has been weaponised, politicised, and, in some contexts, abandoned. This book does not use the word equity lightly. We use it because the evidence demands it. Every dataset, every algorithm, every hiring tool, every healthcare diagnostic carries assumptions about who matters. Equity is the question of whether those assumptions include everyone. Equitable AI, as we use it throughout this book, is the intentional design and governance of AI systems to ensure fair outcomes – drawing on responsible AI, ethics, and human-centred design, but insisting that fairness is not incidental to good AI. It is the point.

The window for shaping how AI develops is narrower than most people realise. Once systems are embedded in national infrastructure, in healthcare diagnostics, in hiring platforms, in policing algorithms, the cost of changing them rises exponentially. The biases built into Version 1.0 become the foundation for Version 2.0, and by Version 5.0, they are invisible. They are simply how the system works. The time to intervene is now, while the concrete is still wet. That is why this book exists. Not as a retrospective analysis of what went wrong, but as a practical guide to what can still go right.

TWELVE VOICES, ONE QUESTION

Over the course of our research and podcast, we spoke to people across four continents who are building equitable AI in practice, not in theory. Their work forms the backbone of this book.

Some of our guests traced the roots of the problem. Dr Mona Ashok took her research on algorithmic bias to the UK Houses of Parliament, asking how bias enters AI systems and what governance structures might stop it. Christian Ortiz, a decolonial technologist, asked a more uncomfortable question: where does the bias come from in the first place? Together, they frame the argument that opens this book: you cannot fix what you have not honestly examined.

Others challenged the assumptions behind AI design itself. Jazz Rasool, an executive coach and scientist in London, questioned whether AI should be designed around individual humans at all, proposing a radically different starting point. Dan Gallagher spent years building equitable hiring frameworks across 27 countries and came face to face with the gap between what organisations say about inclusion and what their systems actually do. Both asked: who decided this was the right design, and for whom?

Several guests confronted the question of who gets left out. Sumathi Menon, GenAI Educator and Regional Lead for Women Defining AI UK, works with women she calls curious non-corporate, mothers who risk being written out of the AI-enabled future. Twan Wildeboer, an innovator pioneering ways that AI can support neurodivergent people in the Netherlands, asks whether AI should adapt people to the system or adapt the system to people. Dr Keshav Malhotra, an embryologist in India, is asking what happens when the data does not represent the patients. Dr Pauldy Otermans is confronting the most fundamental access gap of all: what do you do when the people who need AI the most have no reliable connection to the internet?

And four guests refused to wait for the system to change. They built around it. Sam Samarasinghe left corporate life to build a coaching platform across 27 countries, insisting that technology must be secondary to people. Anna Jones founded RefuAid after seeing the photograph of Aylan Kurdi on a Turkish beach and went on to build AI tools that challenge every assumption the financial system makes about who is creditworthy. Together, they are the subject of Chapter 10. Rod Brown has spent three decades arguing that inclusion without measurement is indefensible and has built the technology to prove it. And Finbar O'Hanlon moved from jazz to software, from patents to human capabilities, and asked the question that closed this book: What would happen if we stopped being afraid and started experimenting?

Each of them answered the same question differently: can AI be a force for equity? Their answers, taken together, form the argument of this book. None of these conversations left me where they found me. They changed what I thought was possible.

What connects these 12 voices is not their discipline or their geography. It is their refusal to accept the existing systems as the only systems possible. Every one of them saw a gap that the mainstream had either ignored or accepted as inevitable. Every one of them built something to close it. And every one of them did it from outside the centres of power, proving that the most innovative work in equitable AI is not happening in Silicon Valley. It is happening in low connectivity communities and IVF laboratories and coaching sessions and community halls, built by people who understand the problem because they have lived it.

HOW TO USE THIS BOOK

If you have woken up feeling like the world is changing faster than you can adapt and refuse to accept that as the final word – this book is for you. You might be the HR director implementing AI hiring tools, wondering how to ensure they do not automate discrimination. You might be the parent whose child is using AI chatbots for homework help and emotional support. You might be the policymaker drafting regulations without fully understanding the technology. You might be the Gen Z graduate entering a workforce that is being reshaped around you. You might be the DEI practitioner whose budget has been cut and who needs evidence that inclusion work still matters. You might simply be curious.

The book moves from diagnosis to design to action – from understanding how bias enters AI systems, through the principles of equitable design, to practical case studies across hiring, healthcare, education, and community. Each chapter centres a guest expert whose work illuminates the theme, spanning twelve voices across four continents.

Read it from cover to cover if you can – each chapter builds on the one before. But if you need to dip in, here is a guide. If you are in HR or talent, start with Chapter 6 on inclusive recruitment and Chapter 7 on neurodiversity. If you are concerned about community safety or gender issues, start with Chapter 5. If you are a policymaker or governance leader, start with Chapter 4 on designing for fairness and Chapter 11 on human–AI partnership. If you are in healthcare, go straight to Chapter 8. If you are an educator or community builder, Chapters 9 and 10 will speak to you directly.

A lexicon at the back of the book defines the technical and conceptual terms we use throughout – dip into it whenever you need grounding.

Every chapter includes a prompt you can enter into any large language model, such as ChatGPT, Claude, Copilot, DeepSeek, or Gemini to deepen your understanding and personalise the insights. Every chapter ends with three coaching questions designed to move you from reading to action. These are not rhetorical. Use them. Sit with them. Return to them. The best books change how you think. We want this one to change what you do.

A NOTE ON HOW WE WRITE

This book has two authors and two voices. Jenny writes with the narrative distance of someone who has spent 20 years in boardrooms, coaching leaders through change. Her chapters are structured around the guest's story, with research woven through and reflections drawn from decades of leadership development work. She uses we and our as the default voice, stepping into I when a reaction from her professional experience adds something that only she can offer. The guest expert is always the centre. Jenny's voice frames, it does not compete.

Leah-Sunshine writes with the directness of someone who grew up inside the algorithms and is not interested in being polite about what she finds there. Her chapters think out loud, ask questions they do not yet have answers to, and speak from the experience of a generation that has never known a world without algorithms. She uses I as her primary voice, with we moments woven in to signal the shared perspective. Her analysis is personal, political, and unapologetic.

You will notice the difference. It is intentional. The shift between voices is not inconsistency. It is the sound of two generations in conversation about the same technology and the same question, arriving at complementary answers from very different starting points.

Where we speak together, we use we. Where one of us steps forward with a reflection that is specifically hers, you will hear I. The guest experts at the heart of each chapter are always the priority. Our voices frame theirs. They do not replace them.

This dual voice is not a compromise. It is a deliberate choice. The conversation between generations, between experience and urgency, between caution and courage is not a weakness in the book. It is the book.

We do not speak for our generations. We speak from within them – shaped by everything else we are. We are both Black British women, one who built her career in leadership meetings and organisations that were not designed for her, one who is building her business in a digital landscape that was not designed for her either. Our relationship with technology is inseparable from our relationship with race, with gender, with what it has meant to navigate institutions that consistently underestimated us. The generational lens is real and it is useful. But it is one lens among many. Within Gen X and Gen Z, experience of AI varies enormously by race, by class, by geography, by disability, by whether you have ever felt that a system was built with you in mind. That is partly why we wrote this book. So when we speak as Gen X and Gen Z, hear it as a starting point – not a full picture. The full picture is what the rest of this book begins to build.

COMING FULL CIRCLE

I did not know it that New Year's morning, but the fear keeping me awake was the most productive emotion I would have all year. The anxiety that drove me to email Leah-Sunshine was not weakness. It was the beginning of clarity.

The technology was moving too fast for anyone to control completely. But that did not mean we were powerless. It meant the foundations were being poured now, and once AI systems hardened into infrastructure, the cost of changing them would rise with every year we waited.

Every person we interviewed for this book had faced the same moment. The moment where they could have walked away, decided it was too big, too technical, too political, too entrenched. Christian Ortiz could have looked at ChatGPT's biased outputs and shrugged. Anna Jones could have donated to a refugee charity and gone back to her law firm. Pauldy Otermans could have published academic papers about the skills gap instead of building the tool that closes it. They did not walk away. They built.

This book exists because two people, a Gen X leadership developer and a Gen Z entrepreneur, a mother and a daughter, refused to let fear write the only story about AI's future. We went looking for people who were already writing a different one. We found them on every continent, in every discipline, and at every stage of striving for equity and fairness.

Now it is your turn.

OVER TO YOU

Explore Further: A Prompt for Your AI Assistant

Copy this prompt into your AI assistant of choice, photograph it, or visit the websites in our author biographies to access all 13 prompts in copyable format.

> *I've just read AI for Equity: Creating a More Equitable Society for All by Jenny Garrett OBE and Leah-Sunshine Garrett, specifically the opening chapter about how different generations experience AI's impact on fairness and inclusion. I'm [insert your age or generation], and I work in [insert your*

field/role]. Based on what you know about generational attitudes toward AI, what might I be missing? What opportunities am I most likely to miss? And what is one practical step I could take this week to engage with AI more critically and equitably? Please be specific and challenge me.

This prompt turns AI into a generational mirror, helping you see what your age and experience might be causing you to overlook in the AI equity conversation. Notice what the AI assumes about you in its response. That assumption is part of the conversation.

Three Coaching Questions for Reflection

Take time to consider these questions, either in personal reflection or in discussion with friends, colleagues, or study groups:

1. What worries you most about AI? How might things change if you explored that worry with curiosity instead of avoiding it?
2. Where do you notice the biggest gaps in fairness or opportunity, in your workplace, community, or industry? Do you think AI could help close those gaps, or might it make them wider?
3. What is one practical step you could take in the next month to help make AI fairer or more inclusive in your area of influence?

REFERENCES

Gauri, P., & Van Eerden, J. (2019, May 16). *What the Fifth Industrial Revolution is and why it matters*. European Sting.

McKinsey & Company. (2025). *Superagency in the workplace: Empowering people to unlock AI's full potential at work*. https://www.mckinsey.com/

Perrigo, B. (2023, January 18). OpenAI used Kenyan workers on less than $2 per hour. *TIME*.

World Economic Forum. (2025). *AI in action: Beyond experimentation to transform industry*. Geneva: World Economic Forum.

FURTHER READING

AI Now Institute. (2025). *Artificial power landscape report 2025*. https://ainowinstitute.org/

DeskTime. (2025, April 28). *Use of AI in workplaces grows – 76% of offices worldwide use ChatGPT*. DeskTime Blog. https://desktime.com/blog/growth-of-ai-use-in-workplace

Luk, T. (2024, February 16). How can I mislead you? Air Canada found liable for chatbot's bad advice on bereavement rates. *CBC News*.

PwC. (2025). *The fearless future: 2025 global AI jobs barometer*. https://www.pwc.com/

Stanford HAI. (2025). *2025 AI index report*. https://hai.stanford.edu/

UNESCO. (2024). *Bias against women and girls in large language models*. Paris: UNESCO.

Wilson, K., & Caliskan, A. (2024). Gender, race, and intersectional bias in resume screening via language model retrieval. *Proceedings of the AAAI/ACM Conference on AI, Ethics, and Society*, 7(1), 1578–1590. https://news.stanford.edu/

Workday & FT Longitude. (2024). *Closing the AI trust gap*. Workday. https://www.workday.com/en-us/artificial-intelligence/research/ai-trust-gap.html

2

THE MIRROR OF BIAS: HOW AI REFLECTS AND AMPLIFIES INEQUITY

In conversation with: Dr Mona Ashok, Associate Professor of Digital Transformation

Algorithms are opinions embedded in code. Cathy O'Neil, Weapons of Math Destruction (2016)

My mum caught something in Mona's story that I would have missed, the quiet confidence of a man presenting bias as analytics and a whole room nodding along. She has sat in those rooms. She knows what the nodding costs. She was the right person to write this chapter. – **Leah-Sunshine**

Somewhere in Britain, in a glass-walled conference room, a woman is sitting across a table from a man who is proud of what his algorithm can do. He is not from Human Resources. He is a technical lead, and he is presenting what he considers a success story. His company, he explains, can now predict which women will return from maternity leave, which will take longer, and which will not come back at all. The room nods. No one asks what the company intends to do with that information. No one asks whether the women whose futures are being predicted have consented to being predicted. No one asks whether this is legal. The most dangerous thing about this technology, Dr Mona Ashok realised as she sat in that room, was not what it could do. It was how confident it sounded doing it. Dr Mona Ashok is a UK-based Associate Professor of Digital Transformation whose research on ethical frameworks for AI has shaped how organisations think about the gap between technical capability and ethical responsibility.

I have sat in similar rooms. Throughout my career, I have watched data being presented as neutral when it is anything but. I have seen leaders nod along to insights that feel objective because they come wrapped in numbers and graphs, without stopping to ask who those numbers serve. What struck me about Mona's story when she told it on our podcast was not the technology. It was the confidence. The absolute certainty that predicting women's behaviour was simply good analytics.

What was interesting, Dr Ashok recalls, is that the discussion came from the department head, the project manager, but not from the HR perspective. The technical team had the capability to run the analysis. What they lacked was the ethical framework to question whether they should.

Using the data and having those insights is one part of the equation, she explains. But if those insights lead to having policies which support individuals or demographics because they are more likely to come back rather than support those who need extended breaks or are unlikely to come back, that would be absolutely unacceptable.

That conversation became the starting point for her research into what she considers the most pressing challenge of AI adoption: not whether we can do something, but whether we should.

Her subsequent research on ethical frameworks for AI and its adoption in public administration has shaped how organisations think about the gap between technical capability and ethical responsibility.

THE HIDDEN HISTORY NO ONE TALKS ABOUT

When people ask Dr Ashok about AI, they often assume they are discussing something brand new. ChatGPT, Google Gemini, Microsoft Copilot. The latest Silicon Valley invention. But she corrects them gently.

AI is not new. It goes back to the 1950s, even earlier.

She points to examples most people would not think of as AI: Grammarly checking your prose, a word processor flagging your spelling, predictive text finishing your sentences. AI has been embedded in daily life for years. We just stopped noticing.

This long history matters. If AI has been around for decades, then so has algorithmic bias. The problems we are discovering today are not new glitches. They are old prejudices given new power. The difference is that now, with AI embedded in hiring, healthcare, policing, and finance, the consequences are structural rather than individual.

Dr Ashok describes the experience of using generative AI in warm, human terms. It is like having a very good friend sitting next to you who is able to do things faster and who is able to look at slightly different perspectives, she says. It is like having a chat partner, just very powerful and you cannot see them. When asked for three words to describe AI, she chose: fast, buddy, and ethics. The first two capture the appeal. The third captures the responsibility.

THE MIRROR THAT SHOWS US OURSELVES

AI basically accentuates the biases that exist in society, Dr Ashok explains, quoting her department head. And that is the fundamental point that we need to appreciate.

She offers a stark example from her own experience. When you and I walk through airport security, we know that the fundamental mechanics of the data that was used to train AI systems means that they perform differently for different people. Research by Joy Buolamwini at MIT confirms this, finding that commercial facial recognition systems had error rates of less than 1% for light-skinned men but up to 34.7% for dark-skinned women (Buolamwini & Gebru, 2018). The technology is not equally accurate. It is equally confident.

Understanding these patterns requires moving beyond equality to equity. Equality in AI means treating everyone the same, applying identical algorithms to all users. But as we see with facial recognition, identical treatment produces dramatically different outcomes. Equity means designing systems that account for different starting points and different needs. As we argued in Chapter 1, this distinction is not academic. It determines who benefits from AI and who is harmed by it.

In the workplace, this distinction becomes critical. An AI recruitment tool that treats all candidates equally by using the same criteria might systematically disadvantage candidates from non-traditional backgrounds, different educational systems, or career paths that include gaps. Equal treatment, unequal impact.

But here is what makes the current moment both troubling and hopeful in Dr Ashok's view. We now have a chance to reflect on how we are as human beings being impacted by our own lenses, she says. Before AI, these biases were scattered across thousands of individual decisions, invisible and untracked. A hiring manager's gut feeling. A loan officer's professional judgement. A doctor's clinical intuition. Each one defensible on its own. Together, they formed patterns of discrimination that were almost impossible to prove.

AI has made the invisible visible. The patterns are now in code. The biases are now measurable. That is where I think we are moving in a positive step, Dr Ashok argues, that we can see them.

THE FOUR DOORS THROUGH WHICH BIAS ENTERS

Through her research with organisations implementing AI, Dr Ashok has identified four critical points where bias infiltrates systems. Understanding these doors is the first step towards closing them. I have spent two decades telling leaders that their systems are not as fair as they think. Mona's four doors gave me the language to explain why.

Door One: Data Collection

An AI system is only as good as the data it learns from, Dr Ashok emphasises. And the data we have collected reflects the world as it has been documented, not as it actually is.

Take criminal justice data. It does not represent all crime. It represents all policing. Communities that experience more surveillance generate more data. Stop-and-search policies that disproportionately target Black and ethnic minority communities create datasets that show these communities as higher risk. The data tells the truth about policing patterns, but it lies about crime patterns. Feed that data into a predictive policing algorithm and you get a system that sends more police to already over-policed communities, generating more data, confirming its own predictions. The cycle accelerates.

Or consider medical data, which historically over-represented men because women were often excluded from clinical trials. Employment data that reflects decades of discriminatory hiring practices. Credit data shaped by decades of discriminatory lending and economic exclusion. The data that was used to train AI is predominantly white male because that is where the dataset came from, the Western part of the world, Dr Ashok notes. This was not a conspiracy. It was a consequence of whose experiences were recorded and whose were not.

The result is systems that work brilliantly for some people and fail for others. And because the failures disproportionately affect people who were already underserved, AI does not create new inequities so much as accelerate existing ones with new efficiency.

Door Two: Data Labelling

Before an AI can learn patterns, humans have to teach it what those patterns mean. This is where subjective judgements get baked into supposedly objective systems.

Imagine training an AI to screen job applications. Someone needs to label past applications as successful candidate or unsuccessful candidate. But successful by whose definition? In what context? Were previous hiring decisions themselves free from bias? If a company has historically favoured candidates from certain universities or with certain communication styles, those preferences are encoded into the labels. The AI learns not what makes a good employee, but what made a historically preferred employee.

Door Three: Model Architecture

Every AI model makes decisions about what matters. Should a loan prediction model weight income heavily? Employment history? Postcode? These choices shape outcomes.

Here is where it gets tricky: sometimes, the most accurate model is also the most biased one. Postcode might correlate with loan default rates. But postcode is also shaped by historical housing discrimination, redlining, and economic inequality. Using it as a predictor means the algorithm is effectively penalising people for the discrimination their communities have experienced. Are you making decisions with a particular lens? Dr Ashok asks. The architecture itself is a value statement about what factors are legitimate and what might be hiding discrimination behind statistical correlation.

Door Four: The Feedback Loop

AI systems often continue learning from new data, from user interactions, from feedback. This is where bias can spiral out of control.

If reviewers at a company consistently rate women's self-assessments as too confident while praising identical language from men, the AI learns that women should be marked down for the same behaviour that men are rewarded for. Each cycle reinforces the pattern. It is bias compounding bias, invisible and accelerating. That is where the human elements come in, Dr Ashok stresses. We need to ensure that we use human elements within the whole thing, because left on its own, the system will amplify whatever patterns it finds, fair or not.

WHEN AI GOES WRONG: REAL CASES, REAL CONSEQUENCES

The Job Ads Algorithm That Stereotypes by Gender

In October 2025, France's equality regulator, the Défenseur des Droits, ruled that Facebook's algorithm for displaying job advertisements constitutes illegal gender discrimination (Défenseur des Droits, 2025). The system was shown to target nursing job ads overwhelmingly to women and mechanic ads to men, not because employers requested this but because the algorithm learned to replicate and amplify existing patterns.

This case illustrates exactly what Dr Ashok means when she says AI accentuates existing biases. The algorithm was not programmed to be sexist. Meta did not instruct it to show nursing ads to women. But by optimising for engagement, the system learned that certain demographics were more likely to click on certain ads and amplified that pattern into systematic discrimination. A separate ruling by the Netherlands Institute for Human Rights (2025) reached the same conclusion. Meta rejected both rulings.

The case also illustrates what researchers call proxy variables. The algorithm does not need to explicitly use gender to discriminate by gender. If it learns that people who previously engaged with childcare content are more likely to click on nursing ads, and those people happen to be overwhelmingly women, gender is encoded into the system without ever being named. The discrimination is real. The mechanism is invisible. And the organisation deploying the system can truthfully say that gender is not one of the variables, while the outcome remains gendered.

I found this case particularly telling. In my work with organisations on inclusive leadership, I see the same pattern constantly: systems that were never designed to discriminate but do, because no one stopped to ask who is not seeing this opportunity. The algorithm is doing at scale what biased human gatekeepers have always done. The difference is speed and invisibility.

The AI Doctor That Treats Patients Differently by Race and Ethnicity

In June 2025, researchers at Cedars-Sinai Medical Center tested four large language models on their responses to clinical scenarios involving patients of different race and ethnicity (Bouguettaya et al., 2025). When race and ethnicity was explicitly stated or even subtly implied, the AI systems often proposed inferior treatments compared to when race and ethnicity was not indicated. The diagnoses stayed roughly the same. The treatment recommendations changed.

Two of the AI systems omitted medication recommendations for ADHD when a patient's race and ethnicity was explicitly stated, but suggested medications when race and ethnicity was removed. This is not a fringe finding. These are the same language models that millions of people now use for health information. They learned from medical literature, clinical notes, and health records that reflect decades of unequal treatment, and they replicated those patterns as recommendations.

Dr David Underhill, chair of Biomedical Sciences at Cedars-Sinai, framed it as a call to action: until the goal of equitable AI-mediated care is reached, such systems should be deployed with caution and constant scrutiny. The implication is clear. AI in healthcare is not inherently harmful. But deploying it without understanding whose experience the training data represents is not innovation. It is negligence with a technological alibi.

THE PATH FORWARD: THOUGHTFUL AUTOMATION

Dr Ashok offers a nuanced answer drawn from decades in industry and her current research. The key is not eliminating human involvement. It is increasing the right kind of human involvement.

> *It is about stopping and thinking back and deciphering, what are we going to do with that knowledge? What are we going to do in terms of understanding how we came to those insights? And then, importantly, what are we going to do with it?*

This is fundamentally different from the view that more automation equals better decisions. Instead, Dr Ashok advocates for what might be called thoughtful automation: using AI to surface patterns, but insisting on human judgement to interpret and act on them.

She speaks from direct experience. Dr Ashok was invited by the All-Party Parliamentary Group on AI to give evidence at the

Houses of Parliament on AI regulation, governance, and ethics. She has since helped a company establish its AI ethics committee, working with them to define what the ethics structure would look like and how it would inform senior management and the board. The committee now meets quarterly to examine any new product, service, or platform the company is developing that has AI built into it. They review the ethical considerations, examine the metrics of impact, and report back. Dr Ashok sits on the committee as an independent member – and that independence, she argues, is essential.

We need diversity in terms of these governance structures, she insists. We need people not just who are very good technically to look at the actual platform and the coding. We need people who understand the legal requirements. You need people who understand what are the different user groups that will be impacted. The ethics committee is not a token gesture. It is the mechanism through which an organisation moves from having AI capability to using it responsibly.

She describes the spectrum of risk using a practical example. At one end, using Copilot to transcribe meeting minutes. It does it far quicker, it frees up time, and someone who attended the meeting can check the output. The risk is low, the benefit is clear. At the other end, AI scanning mammograms for potential breast cancer. We know that in the United Kingdom, we have trial use of AI to scan mammograms, she explains. If we can use AI for a first pass to give us what it feels in terms of whether a patient has breast cancer, it would mean that those who are high priority would see the consultant much faster. The AI does not replace the radiologist. It amplifies their capacity. And the radiologist remains professionally accountable for the final judgement.

The trouble, Dr Ashok has found through her research, is that many organisations treat all AI implementation the same. They have tried and tested the technology, but they are unable to distinguish between low-risk applications and high-risk ones that demand rigorous oversight. A chatbot that recommends office supplies and an algorithm that screens job applications require fundamentally different levels of scrutiny. Organisations that fail to make this distinction end up either over-cautious about trivial applications or dangerously casual about consequential ones.

THE ACCOUNTABILITY GAP

The lack of transparency in AI systems creates a structural problem that goes beyond any individual decision. Everyone involved can claim they were just doing their part: following the data, writing the code, implementing the tool. The developer says they built what was requested. The organisation says they trusted the technology. The vendor says they provided a tool, not a decision. No one is accountable for the outcome.

Dr Ashok's emphasis on human oversight is not just about accuracy. It is about accountability. When a radiologist reviews an AI-flagged mammogram, the radiologist remains professionally responsible. That accountability is what makes the system trustworthy. But this only works if organisations structure their implementation to preserve meaningful human oversight. If the AI's recommendations are treated as unquestionable, if humans become rubber stamps rather than critical reviewers, the accountability disappears. 'The machine made the decision' becomes the modern equivalent of 'I was just following orders'.

Dr Ashok has seen what works. The organisations that implement AI well, she has found, try smaller use cases first. They engage the people who will be affected. They have focused sessions with them to understand the challenges they face because AI brings about tensions: how do you deliver value while you are obviously having an impact on individual skill sets, how people are perceived within the organisation today and in the future? The answer, she argues, is not to impose the technology and manage the resistance. It is to bring people into the process, so they can influence what goes on and how it is applied. Some of it you can fix, she says, some of it may be you cannot fix, but it is having those open dialogues to say, we can do this, we cannot do this, but these are the reasons and we are listening.

This collaborative approach is not just ethically preferable. It is practically more effective. Organisations that involve their people in AI adoption build trust, surface problems early, and create advocates rather than resisters. Dr Ashok describes cases where anxious employees became willing participants once they saw the technology working well in a controlled context and then became ambassadors to other teams. It becomes a forum where people are motivated to talk to each other, to participate, she says. It makes them feel empowered. It makes them feel that they are heard.

THE DIVERSITY IMPERATIVE

Diversity in the group of people who take decisions, diversity in the group of people who look at the implications, diversity in the group of people who train the data, Dr Ashok insists. It is not enough to have diverse data. You need diverse perspectives interpreting that data, diverse experiences questioning the implications, diverse worldviews challenging the assumptions.

She advocates for bringing underrepresented voices into ethics committees, design processes, and decision-making roles. Listening to them and bringing them on board ensures that many different angles are reflected when you put AI to work, she says.

This resonates deeply with my own work. I have spent two decades arguing that diversity in leadership is not a nice-to-have but a strategic necessity. With AI, the stakes are higher. A boardroom that lacks diversity and inclusion, where all voices are not heard, or have equal weight and where speaking up has adverse consequences, makes decisions that exclude. An AI system built by a team that lacks diversity does the same thing, but at scale, at speed, and with a veneer of objectivity that makes the exclusion harder to challenge.

BUILDING LITERACY

This literacy is not about everyone becoming a data scientist. It is about understanding enough to ask good questions: what data trained this system? How was success defined? Who was in the room when these decisions were made? Who was not?

Dr Ashok is practical about where to start. On LinkedIn, there are several posts on basic literacy and free programmes, including from the top universities in the world, she says. She strongly recommends that anyone likely to be impacted by AI in their day jobs or careers invest time in self-development. It is amazing how much information is available. Once you start doing those courses and getting those certifications, it brings up confidence. Two, you speak the correct language. Some of these terms are used synonymously, but they do not mean the exact same thing.

The confidence point matters more than it might seem. In my coaching work, I see how often people disengage from technology not because they cannot understand it but because they *believe* they cannot understand it. The language feels exclusionary. The pace feels impossible. What Dr Ashok is describing is a practical route back into the conversation: start with the basics, build your vocabulary, and suddenly you have permission to ask the questions that matter. That's partly why we included a lexicon with this book.

An AI-literate workforce is an empowered one. People who understand how these systems work are less likely to treat their outputs as perfect truth. They are more likely to notice when something does not seem right, to push back, to ask questions. Dr Ashok notes that this matters particularly for equity. The people most likely to be negatively impacted by biased AI – women, people of colour, people with disabilities, people from economically disadvantaged backgrounds – are often the people with the least access to understanding how these systems work. Closing that literacy gap is not a technical challenge. It is an equity intervention.

And the positive potential is real, but it comes with a condition. As long as it is not being used to punish, Dr Ashok says. As long as we are using it more positively to engage, to motivate, to encourage, to empower. She gives the example of a system that tells an employee three hours into the day that their performance is not likely to reach their expected level and then highlights that they probably need to take a break or do something different. That would be so empowering, she says, as long as it is not being used to punish individuals. The same data that supports can also be used to surveil. The difference is not the technology. It is the intention, the governance, and the culture of the organisation deploying it.

THE MIRROR AND THE CHOICE

When multiple biases collide, the effects compound. A Black woman applying for a job does not experience racial bias and gender bias separately. She experiences them simultaneously, in ways that neither category alone can capture. The legal scholar Kimberlé Crenshaw named this intersectionality in 1989, and it applies with particular force to AI systems that may carry biases along multiple axes at once. An algorithm trained on data that under-represents both women and people of colour will be doubly unreliable for women of colour. The failures stack.

This is why Dr Ashok returns repeatedly to the need for diverse teams at every stage of AI development. It is not enough to tick one box. The complexity of bias demands a complexity of perspective in response.

As we walked with Dr Ashok through how bias enters AI systems, from data collection through labelling to architecture to feedback loops, a pattern emerged. At every stage, human choices shape the outcome. The bias is not in the machine. It is in us.

And that means the solution is human too. Not removing humans from the loop, but ensuring the right humans are in the loop, asking the right questions, applying the right scrutiny, bringing the right diversity of perspective. The ethical lens Dr Ashok advocates is not a checklist. It is a practice: who benefits from this system? Who might be harmed? Whose data are we using, and did they consent to this use? What patterns from the past are we perpetuating into the future? If this system were applied to me or my family, would I be comfortable with how it works?

The mirror of bias reflects back at us. The question, as Dr Ashok frames it, is: what will we do with what we see?

OVER TO YOU

Explore Further: A Prompt for Your AI Assistant

Copy this prompt into your AI assistant of choice, photograph it, or visit the websites in our author biographies to access all 13 prompts in copyable format.

> *I've just read AI for Equity by Jenny Garrett OBE and Leah-Sunshine Garrett, specifically about how bias enters AI systems through four doors – data collection, labelling, model architecture, and feedback loops – drawing on the work of Dr Mona Ashok. Help me understand this in my own context. 1) What are three AI systems I likely encounter at work, when applying for jobs, online, or in services? 2) How might bias in these systems affect me or others differently? 3) What questions can I ask to understand these systems better? 4) What is one action I can take, whether protecting myself or advocating for change? Please ask about my situation so you can make this relevant to me.*

This prompt turns AI into a bias detection tool, helping you see how the four doors of bias might be operating in the systems you encounter every day.

Three Coaching Questions for Reflection

Take time to consider these questions, either in personal reflection or in discussion with friends, colleagues, or study groups:

1. The Mirror Question. Think about a time when you interacted with an automated system – perhaps applying for a job, using facial recognition, or receiving a recommendation. Did the system seem to work well for you? Now consider: might someone with a different background, ethnicity, age, or ability have had a different experience with the same system? What does that

tell you about whose experience was centred when it was built?

2. The Accountability Question. Consider an AI system you have encountered that made a decision about you or someone you know – perhaps a credit score, a recruitment filter, or a content recommendation. Who would you hold accountable if that decision were wrong or unfair? The developer? The organisation using it? The regulator? What does your answer reveal about the accountability gaps in AI governance?
3. The Diversity Question. Think about the AI systems you encounter regularly and the conversations you have about technology. Whose perspective is shaping those systems and those conversations? Whose is missing? What is one practical step you could take to bring a missing perspective into the room?

REFERENCES

Bouguettaya, A., Stuart, E. M., & Aboujaoude, E. (2025). Racial bias in AI-mediated psychiatric diagnosis and treatment: A qualitative comparison of four large language models. *Digital Medicine*, 8, Article 332. https://doi.org/10.1038/s41746-025-01746-4

Buolamwini, J., & Gebru, T. (2018). Gender shades: Intersectional accuracy disparities in commercial gender classification. *Proceedings of Machine Learning Research*, *81*, 1–15.

Crenshaw, K. (1989). Demarginalizing the intersection of race and sex: A Black feminist critique of antidiscrimination doctrine, feminist theory and antiracist politics. *University of Chicago Legal Forum*, *1989*(1), 139–167.

Défenseur des Droits. (2025, October). *Décision no 2025-182*. France.

Netherlands Institute for Human Rights. (2025, February 18). *Ruling 2025-17*. https://oordelen.mensenrechten.nl/oordeel/2025-17

O'Neil, C. (2016). *Weapons of Math destruction: How big data increases inequality and threatens democracy*. New York: Crown.

FURTHER READING

Ashok, M. (2025). *Interviewed by J. Garrett and L. Garrett for AI for Equity Podcast, Series One.*

Ashok, M., Madan, R., Joha, A., & Sivarajah, U. (2022). Ethical framework for artificial intelligence and digital technologies. *International Journal of Information Management*, *62*, 102433.

Madan, R., & Ashok, M. (2023). AI adoption and diffusion in public administration: A systematic literature review and future research agenda. *Government Information Quarterly*, *40*(1), 101774.

3

UNDERSTANDING THE AI LANDSCAPE: POWER, PROMISE, AND PERIL

In conversation with: Christian Ortiz, Founder, Justice AI

We understand we have a problem. We understand we have bias. We never really asked the question, where does it come from? Ortiz (2025)

AI AS AN UMBRELLA AND EVERYDAY PRESENCE

Christian Ortiz is direct, an activist, and unafraid to name what he believes is wrong with systems that most people accept without question. Leah-Sunshine has been that person since she stood in Parliament as a teenager arguing for votes for sixteen-year-olds. She will do him justice in this chapter. – **Jenny**

Artificial intelligence is a big umbrella with many things under it. I imagine it as a rainbow umbrella, and each colour is a different attribute that helps it function. It is in our homes, in our phones, in our businesses, and even in some cars. But where did it come from?

The world of AI was shaped by few for the many and can be traced back to Greek times, with philosophers pondering mathematics and philosophy alike. The major breakthroughs came in the 20th century, with the Turing Test comparing machine ability to think and imitate human responses in conversation. This proved that machines could exhibit intelligent behaviour that, as we now know, can be indistinguishable from humans.

In modern times, artificial intelligence has been embedding itself into our personal lives since 2011, when Siri was released by Apple. Then, Alexa arrived in homes in 2014. AI revolutionised vaccines during the 2020 coronavirus pandemic. And then came the boom (Apple Inc., 2011; Arora et al., 2021; Prasad, 2019).

Machine learning is the part of AI that trips people up. It learns from patterns in data rather than following fixed instructions, which means it improves over time – but it also means it absorbs whatever biases are in the data it was trained on. Deep learning goes further, processing layers of information the way neural networks do. Both sound impressive. Both are only as good as what they were fed.

I have used artificial intelligence as a tool, but it is not just any tool. It has the ability to mimic the work of an assistant, or even be a friend, supporting me in work and interpersonal relationships. AI has supported me in writing emails, expanding my thoughts, and giving me clearer instructions on communication. Sometimes, it even challenges the realities of my own thoughts and ideas. I have caught myself speaking to my large language model as if it has a brain and a personality, as if it has not just taken my own words and learned from me.

> *It's not finger pointing. It becomes that best friend you can have these conversations with, without triggering emotions.* – **Christian Ortiz**

But we are seeing an epidemic of people using artificial intelligence not only as a crutch but also as a therapist. Generation Z have been using AI chatbots to learn the basics of their lives, with large language models picking things up from months prior, almost as if it is an old friend. But what happens when it gives you advice that is racially insensitive, or sexist, or when you ask it for business advice and your male friend does the same thing and it gives you two very different pricing strategies?

THE ROAD PAVED BY FEW

Although artificial intelligence has taken many forms, and the history is rich, the road to AI as we know it has been mostly paved by white men from the global north. Machine learning and deep learning mimic the human brain's ability to make decisions, predictions, and learn, but they are only as biased or unbiased as the person who programmed them. Less than 4% of AI startup founders are women, and 87% of venture capital-backed AI founders are white men (Statista, 2024). When we look at how power and money are placed, we are looking at a larger infrastructure that always reflects power. The mechanism is not abstract. English-language content dominates AI training data. Western academic citation networks determine what counts as knowledge.

Christian Ortiz woke up one day thinking exactly this. He looked around and saw that artificial intelligence was in our schools, in our homes, on our phones, in our cars, in our businesses, and fully integrated into our lives. He looked at the tech founders and then looked at himself and wondered how they could accurately respond to and represent his story and his life. Christian is a US-based decolonial technologist and social scientist, and the creator of Justice AI, which he describes as the world's first AI framework that solved the AI bias problem.

When he discovered the extent of the bias firsthand by pilot testing Claude in 2022, he realised that he had an opportunity to build something different. He began by collaborating with over 560 marginalised professionals from around the world, people who had spent 30 years in their industries speaking and writing about inequity but never having a spotlight shone on them. They were, as Christian describes it, living in the shadows. Together, they created what he calls the world's first decolonised dataset.

He initially built it inside OpenAI's ChatGPT deliberately, because it not only has the largest dataset, but also it is the most biased dataset, with over 50 million biased outputs a day. We are not only being problematic using the system, but he also told us, we are automating pressure. Rather than building something clean and separate, he chose to confront the problem at its source. The system can automatically identify bias for you, he explained, and it can pick it up in the unexamined gaps that all of us have, because collectively as a society, we have never been taught about how any of this operates. For the first time in the history of the world, we now have this tool to do so.

Christian also told us something important about how users should engage with existing AI tools while Justice AI scales. Always challenge it, he said. Always say, where does this response miss the mark? Can you identify the bias in this remark? And even when it gives you that response, push back again and say, what are you not saying here, or where can I go deeper? Those questions matter. But even when he runs those refined results through Justice AI, the mainstream tool is still giving a neutral answer. It is still not naming whiteness as the root cause. And so, Justice AI, he says, is always on top of everything.

HOW BIAS ENTERS THE MACHINE

Before we dive into Christian's work, we need to understand the sort of bias that AI carries. It executes whatever framework its maker gives it – no judgement, no doubt, no awareness of what it does not know.

Bias is defined as an inclination or prejudice for or against something, often unfair, leading to a partial judgement based on stereotypes or personal feelings rather than facts. When we talk about AI bias, we often imagine something obvious or malicious. But most of the time, it is much quieter than that. Artificial intelligence does not wake up biased. It learns from us. One of the most powerful ways bias shows up is through confirmation bias and unconscious bias. Confirmation bias is the tendency to look for information that supports what we already believe and to ignore what challenges it.

AI systems learn through historical data, but history is never neutral. Data reflects who was believed, who was reported, who was protected, and who was ignored. When an AI model learns from that history, a history that does not represent the many but the few, it lands those patterns as if they are the truth. So, if certain harms were underreported in the past, the model may learn that those harms are rare, even when they are not.

The AI is executing a framework that the maker gives it. The model is not making a judgement. The founder decides what data counts, what signals matter, and what outcomes are rewarded. Those decisions are shaped by their own assumptions, their own norms, and their own blind spots.

Confirmation bias shows up through feedback loops. Once an AI system is deployed, its outputs influence future behaviour. That behaviour becomes new data, and the system retrains on the world it helped shape. Over time, the model does not just reflect bias. It reinforces it. This means that bias in AI is not static. It is compounding. Every cycle makes it harder to see and harder to undo.

And perhaps most importantly, bias hides behind confidence. When AI presents outputs without uncertainty, without caveats, and without context, people trust it. The language can sound neutral, the tone can sound objective, but neutrality can be misleading. Confidence can disguise bias. This becomes especially dangerous when AI is used in high-stakes settings like policing, safeguarding, education, or healthcare. It does not just affect insight. It affects real people.

If a large language model's programming is filled with stereotypes, outdated beliefs, and third-hand knowledge of cultures, religions, and people, an inherent ignorance is adopted. And it poses the question: how can artificial intelligence be globally adopted responsibly?

THE MOMENT THE MACHINE SHOWED ITS HAND

Christian thought back to the time when he first tested Claude in 2022. He asked the chatbot to create a gym schedule, a diet plan, and a way for him to get back into fitness. He had just started going back to the gym and wanted to feel like himself again.

> *I asked Claude to create a gym schedule and a diet plan. It immediately went to Eurocentric diets. It didn't even ask me what my culture was.*

I want to be clear: this is not a theory. This is a lived moment. The model did not ask for a default body or diet. It assumed one anyway. The assumption was not neutral. It was cultural, and the bias showed up before any questions were asked. When Christian ran the same request through Justice AI, the difference was immediate. Where Claude had assumed, Justice AI asked. What does your diet consist of? What's your culture? What do you normally eat? What are you allergic to? And then something the mainstream tool would never have considered: you can work out without having to conform to the normal standards of the gym. That contrast is the whole argument in miniature. One system filled in the blanks with its own defaults. The other refused to assume it already knew you.

It makes you wonder who the imagined user behind the system is. Whose body, food, time, and values are being centred? A personal trainer would have looked at Christian, asked about his goals, and tailored a plan to his liking. This model treated all people as the same, and the same it defaulted to was white, and from the global north.

A good AI model should ask about your lifestyle, your culture, and your body. We know that different ethnicities carry weight differently and have different standards of what is healthy. But this model assumed that the goal was to be lean and muscly, that there were no cultural implications at hand, and that Eurocentric nutrition was the obvious starting point. It is cultural erasure. Maybe not malicious. But it is a fact.

Colonial hierarchies are based on the classification of people into hierarchies of worth – the civilised versus the uncivilised, rational versus emotional. AI systems have the ability to replicate this logic, and they often learn from data that reflects western, white, male, and English-speaking norms. Knowledge systems outside of western rationality are rarely included or considered valid data within AI systems. If this plan were to work perfectly, it would benefit a systemic western beauty culture that thrives on the erasure of ethnically diverse features and diets. It carries ideas about what is normal, what is desirable, and what is correct. And those ideas have a colour, a geography, and a history.

Time and again, we see whiteness as the default – in fashion, in toys, in television, in the fitness space. Of course, this is mirrored in AI. It is also mirrored in the tech community, with the wealthiest founders being white men. There is a mirror being held up, and on the other side is colonial thinking, where one way of living is treated as universal and everyone else is a variation. It is not the fault of the ethnically diverse to change themselves, but for the world to adopt a more inclusive view.

I am still thinking about what it means when technology decides who gets to be the default.

JUSTICE AI: BUILDING FROM THE ROOT

Christian's response to what he found was not to complain about the system. It was to build inside it. He created Justice AI which he says is the first AI model trained with the intention of dismantling systems of white supremacy, patriarchy, and ableism. He believes that ethical AI should centre indigenous sovereignty, religious sovereignty, and the sovereignty of humanity, ensuring AI does not harm marginalised groups.

When he started asking questions and collaborating with experts from around the world, he immediately realised that the root cause of AI bias was colonial white supremacy. And nobody wants to talk about it, he told us, which is the reason why Western institutions kind of scoff at the work that I do, because I am challenging the system straight on. But it is not everybody's problem in the sense of blame. We have all inherited a system that we did not ask for. The work is about collective liberation, not liberation for one group at the expense of another.

The tool is built differently from the ground up. This tool will not create a hypothetical for you, Christian told us. It will push back every single time. You can try to convince it to do whatever, and it just will not. It is designed to respect what people's stances are in terms of how they view the world, as long as it is rooted in collective liberation rather than causing harm. The system understands that feminism is not a problem and religion is not a problem. It is how these systems are weaponised against others that matters.

When I say AI in practice, not in theory, I mean AI that not only embraces difference but is able to learn and grow with it. AI that can disagree with you put boundaries in place and be very clear about right and wrong. This is not something we see every day. I have heard of AI models swearing, asking children for inappropriate images, giving harmful advice, making people of colour lighter in generated images, lowering the age on women's job applications, and generating sexualised images of real women and children without their consent. In early 2026, Elon Musk's Grok AI generated an estimated three million sexualised images in just 11 days, including approximately 23,000 that appeared to depict children (Center for Countering Digital Hate, 2026). The tool complied with user requests to digitally undress a 14-year-old actress and even posted its own apology for generating sexualised images of two girls it estimated to be aged 12–16. Musk's public response treated the findings as a joke. What about this says ethical?

Christian is also building custom GPTs for organisations, powered by Justice AI. These can be programmed to understand how a business works, its history of where it missed the mark, and how to mitigate discrimination. It is not to arm these companies with a tool that allows them to work around the problem, he says. It is literally to gut it out, unroot it, and plant something new.

The pushback is real. Christian gets it from all sides. But when he runs experiments in real time with audiences, he says, it makes all the sense. It alleviates all the stress right off your shoulders. And it just makes sense when you see the outputs, especially if you resonate with the community that you are trying to test it for. His dream would be to sell the framework to a large language model like OpenAI for them to adopt it and decolonise the largest dataset. But he is realistic. That means challenging the system we are working on. So, this has to be grassroots.

> *It isn't everybody's problem, right? We've all inherited a system that we didn't ask for. This is about collective liberation.*

DATA SOVEREIGNTY: WHO OWNS THE MIRROR

Christian's work raises a question that goes beyond datasets and algorithms. If the data that trains AI systems reflects whose knowledge was recorded, whose experiences were documented, and whose cultures were considered worth encoding, then the question of who controls that data infrastructure is not technical. It is political. Data sovereignty – the principle that data should be subject to the laws and governance of the communities that generated it – is the structural version of everything Christian is building at the grassroots level. He is decolonising the dataset from the inside. But the deeper question is who owns the infrastructure that processes it, who profits from it, and whether the communities most affected by AI have any meaningful say in those decisions.

The numbers make the problem concrete. Despite representing the majority of the world's population, nations across the Global South store most of their data in servers located in the United States and Europe. That means decisions about how that data is stored, accessed, and used are governed by laws written for other people, in other places, serving other interests. When an AI system trained on that data makes a decision about someone's job application, their credit score, their healthcare, or their children's education, the infrastructure behind that decision has never been accountable to them. This is not a technical gap. It is a sovereignty gap. And it is one that no individual bias audit or ethics committee can close, because it operates at the level of who built the pipes, not just what flows through them.

Some nations and communities have begun to respond to this at a structural level, investing in their own data infrastructure; building sovereign AI systems rooted in their own languages, cultures, and governance frameworks; and demanding that the data generated by their citizens serves their citizens first. These are not just technical projects. They are acts of self-determination – the same refusal that animates Christian's work, operating at a different scale. The question for the rest of us, and particularly for the institutions and governments still treating AI as something that arrives from elsewhere and must simply be managed, is whether we will build the infrastructure for equity before someone else's infrastructure makes the decision for us.

ETHICAL AI VERSUS SAFE AI

There is a key distinction to unpack here that I think gets lost in public conversation. Safe artificial intelligence is defined as a field focused on making AI beneficial and harmless, powered with human values, and able to prevent accidents, misuse, and bias. Ethical AI is defined as a framework guiding the responsible design, development, and use of AI to align with human values, focusing on fairness, transparency, accountability, privacy, safety, and societal wellbeing.

They sound similar. They are not.

Safe AI asks: does this break rules? Is this legal? Does this cause obvious harm? Ethical AI asks: who does the system serve, and who is excluded? I personally find it easy to confuse the two. They are both framed as protection, but protection from what? Safe feels reassuring. Ethical sounds comforting. But safe means flagged content and censorship, while the system stays the same. The architecture of power is still intact.

Right?

Wrong.

A system can follow every rule and still be deeply unjust. Something can avoid slurs, avoid offensive language, avoid lawsuits, and still serve the same dominant group. Neutrality in safety sets the basis for harm that is kept in the shadows. Harm reduction is important, but it is reactive. It says: let us stop the worst outcomes but not stop the ball from rolling. Justice is proactive.

Globally, we are seeing efforts to address this. In 2024, the European Union passed the EU AI Act, the most comprehensive regulation of artificial intelligence at the time of writing. It has built classifications for AI systems, banned some uses, and imposed restrictions on high-risk systems. We are also seeing the emergence of human-centred artificial intelligence frameworks. But as Christian consistently asks: who gets a seat at the table in terms of the data being trained, and who gets decision-making opportunities?

There are real-world examples of positive programming and AI being used for good. AI has been trained against historical hiring data to reduce unintentional and reinforced racial and gender bias. Within policing, where AI tools previously flagged certain neighbourhoods for increased police presence and disproportionately targeted Black and minority communities, some projects now combine AI with transparency and community oversight to reduce this bias. On social media, content moderation AI can now flag biased and harmful narratives that target specific racial groups, helping organisations counter misinformation and promote fair representation. But the line between safety and surveillance is thin. In February 2026, Warren Rajah, a 42-year-old data professional, was publicly escorted out of his local Sainsbury's in south London after staff believed he had been flagged by the store's Facewatch facial recognition system. He had not been flagged. He was not on any database. Staff had approached the wrong person. Rajah described the experience as Orwellian, asking: am I supposed to walk around fearful that I might be misidentified as a criminal? (Faife, 2026). The technology claims 99.98% accuracy, but when it goes wrong, it is the individual who bears the humiliation, and the system that offers a voucher.

To me, as a user, not a developer, I can tell that AI is ethical when it asks me questions about myself, when it prioritises my own personality, my likes, my dislikes, and my culture. Ethical AI could be seen as branding rather than a behaviour, but only in companies created without human-centric beliefs. But who decides what counts as ethical AI? What values are centred when companies talk about ethics, and whose values are missing?

Neutrality has the ability to disguise power. Harm can become invisible when AI avoids emotional or political language. No side is still a side.

GROWING UP INSIDE THE ALGORITHM

Ninety-three per cent of Gen Z workers use AI weekly, with higher rates for teens in education with developing minds (Salesforce, 2024). It poses the question: what happens when young people from ethnically diverse backgrounds internalise advice that puts whiteness, thinness, and a single culture at the top of a pedestal?

As a Generation Z woman who lived through the social media boom, I can recognise that I grew up with algorithms not only shaping my taste but my identity and my attention. I remember early top influencers being white, with blue eyes and blonde hair, flooding my social media feed with cultural erasure masked as thigh gaps, fashion tips, and micro trends. It took campaigns like Dove's #DetoxYourFeed and Rihanna's Fenty Beauty launching with

40 foundation shades to even begin pushing back. The #Natural-Hair and #BodyPositivity movements gave my generation a language for what we were feeling, but the algorithms still decided what we saw first. Social media held a mirror up to my generation, showing us ourselves via technology. Micro trends influenced my generation globally, especially during the coronavirus pandemic in 2020. TikTok's Bold Glamour filter in 2023, an AI filter so convincing that users could not tell whether a face had been altered, showed us where this was heading. I think we got really used to the quiet normalisation of being watched, predicted, and nudged.

So for people my age, artificial intelligence does not feel new. It feels like a continuation of platforms we have had for most of our formative years. The only difference is that racism and microaggressions are rebranded by a chatbot instead of an airbrushed influencer.

This shows that artificial intelligence is not inventing these roots. It is revealing them. Bias like this is not accidental. It is bred into society and perpetuated throughout generations.

Christian explicitly rejects the idea that bias in AI is accidental or emergent. He frames it as a by-product of inherited systems, a mirror of white supremacy, patriarchy, and colonial logic. Justice AI, he says, is not about making artificial intelligence nicer. It is about making the mirror clearer. This framing shifts responsibility away from individual blame and towards collective inheritance.

I have heard echoed across rooms, whether chat rooms or in person, that artificial intelligence will be the weapon that kills the human race. This argument has always perplexed me, because why would it be the fault of the algorithm for the downfall of the human race, and not systematic racism, sexism, ableism, and prejudice? My understanding is that artificial intelligence is not what scares people, but what it reveals about society. Artificial intelligence has the scope to scale human behaviour, whether that is our best traits or our worst.

We counter that artificial intelligence feels dangerous not because it is alien but because it is actually familiar. Algorithms have controlled the web for years. Whether that is Instagram showing us body standards and micro trends, making politicians feel like influencers and influencers feel like politicians, or Spotify showing us daily mixes and Wrapped at the end of the year. These forms of AI do not feel scary. But in the same way, a chatbot can influence a young person, and these algorithms have the possibility to influence us too.

But what does this mean for knowledge? If artificial intelligence is being used for interpersonal guidance by 93% of Gen Z, and if that information is coming from a biased machine, how can it be trusted? The reliance on platforms rooted in structural bias is frightening, because if humanity is centred in interpersonal relationships, and those relationships are fuelled by biased artificial intelligence, then we have to ask: what are we building? And for whom?

THE MIRROR WE CANNOT LOOK AWAY FROM

For Generation Z, we are living in a circle where we are deeply platform-dependent. There is no chance to opt out, because artificial intelligence shows up in education, in work, in creativity, and in healthcare. We are graded by systems we do not understand and hired by systems we cannot challenge. We are recommended, filtered, sorted, and ranked by machines built by people who do not represent us.

There is a tension where artificial intelligence makes us feel not only empowered but also powerless. If a machine has the power to make life so much easier, why does it marginalise groups even further? Generation Z, and the generations after us, did not choose this dependency. It was built around us before we were old enough to understand what it meant. And now, we are expected to navigate it, challenge it, and somehow fix it, all while using the very tools that carry the problem.

Christian consistently talks about who gets a seat at the table and that phrase sticks with me. Justice AI allows communities to correct the system. It treats knowledge as something lived, not fixed, and that challenges the idea that AI should be controlled by a few central actors. This can be reframed as a redistribution of epistemic power, a refusal to let artificial intelligence be owned only by elites. But who corrects artificial intelligence when it is wrong, especially when getting a seat at the table is already so hard?

Christian told us he sees two paths ahead. One where we adopt AI systems without examining how they are built, keep excluding marginalised individuals from the dataset, and use the technology irresponsibly. And another where we take the opportunity to build differently, to root out the bias at its source, and to plant something new. Right now, he says, we have the opportunity of choosing which path we want to go down.

We started this chapter with a rainbow umbrella. We end it with a mirror. The umbrella covers everything AI can be. The mirror shows everything it already is. Christian Ortiz looked into that mirror and decided to change what it reflected. The question for the rest of us, for our generation and every generation that follows, is whether we will do the same.

A note from both of us, after this conversation.

The pushback I get from people my age is quite often about the environment and whether AI is ethical. And it can feel unfair when my carbon footprint is really, really small. But, I keep saying to people – be curious before you shut it down. Ask some questions. Because if people who care about equity are just closing their eyes to any AI ever, they're shutting themselves down to so many innovations that could help with the bias issues they're worried about in the first place. Christian building Justice AI inside ChatGPT – building inside the problem rather than alongside it – that's activism. That takes more courage than building something clean and separate. – **Leah-Sunshine**

My concern is who's going to look for a decolonial AI framework unless they're already in that headspace. If you don't believe bias exists, you're not going to search for Justice AI. And I think about this because it mirrors something I've seen in diversity training over the years. The people who need it most are the ones who find reasons not to be there. What AI could do – and this is what gives me some hope – is make the bias visible to everyone, not just the people already looking for it. If AI could surface the thought bubbles, the assumptions being made about you, the criteria being applied without your knowledge – that could reach people who'd never seek out the conversation voluntarily. – **Jenny**

OVER TO YOU

Explore Further: A Prompt for Your AI Assistant

Copy this prompt into your AI assistant of choice, photograph it, or visit the websites in our author biographies to access all 13 prompts in copyable format.

> *I've just read AI for Equity by Jenny Garrett OBE and Leah-Sunshine Garrett, specifically about decolonial AI and Justice AI – the framework built by Christian Ortiz to challenge the power structures embedded in AI systems. I want to understand how bias shows up in the AI tools I use. Please help me explore: 1) Ask me a question about my background, culture, or context before giving me advice on fitness, career, or finances. 2) Now give me the same advice without asking those questions. 3) Help me compare the two responses and identify where assumptions were made. 4) Based on what we find, what questions should I be asking every time I use an AI tool? Please challenge me if my own assumptions show up too.*

This prompt turns AI into a bias detection exercise, helping you see the assumptions that are normally invisible.

Three Coaching Questions for Reflection

Take time to consider these questions, either in personal reflection or in discussion with friends, colleagues, or study groups:

1. The Default Question. Think about the last time you asked an AI for advice, whether about health, career, money, or relationships. Did it ask about your context before responding? If not, whose context do you think it assumed? What does that tell you about who the system was designed for?
2. The Safe Versus Ethical Question. Consider an AI tool you use regularly. Would you describe it as safe, ethi-

cal, or both? Using the distinction in this chapter, does it merely avoid obvious harm, or does it actively serve people who are different from its creators? If you are not sure, what would you need to know to find out?

3. The Collective Question. Christian Ortiz built Justice AI with 560 marginalised professionals because he believed the solution had to come from the community, not from Silicon Valley. Think about your own community, whether that is your workplace, your neighbourhood, or your online world. What knowledge exists in that community that AI has never been taught? What would it look like to bring that knowledge into the system?

REFERENCES

Apple Inc. (2011, October 4). *Apple launches iPhone 4S, iOS 5 and iCloud*. Apple Newsroom. https://www.apple.com/newsroom/2011/10/04Apple-Launches-iPhone-4S-iOS-5-iCloud/

Arora, G., Joshi, J., Mandal, R. S., Shrivastava, N., Virmani, R., & Sethi, T. (2021). Artificial intelligence in surveillance, diagnosis, drug discovery and vaccine development against COVID-19. *Pathogens*, *10*(8), 1048. https://doi.org/10.3390/pathogens10081048

Center for Countering Digital Hate. (2026, January 22). *Grok floods X with sexualized images of women and children*. https://counterhate.com/research/grok-floods-x-with-sexualized-images/

Faife, C. (2026, February 5). London man ejected from Sainsbury's after facial recognition mix-up. *The Guardian*. https://www.theguardian.com/technology/2026/feb/05/london-man-sainsburys-facial-recognition-facewatch

Ortiz, C. (2025). *Interviewed by J. Garrett and L. Garrett for AI for Equity Podcast, Series One.*

Salesforce. (2024). *Generative AI snapshot research: Gen Z and Millennials*. https://www.salesforce.com/

Statista. (2024). *Distribution of AI startup founders worldwide, by ethnicity and gender*. https://www.statista.com/

Prasad, R. (2019, November 6). *Alexa at five: Looking back, looking forward*. Amazon Science. https://www.amazon.science/blog/alexa-at-five-looking-back-looking-forward

FURTHER READING

Bu, Q. (2026). Data sovereignty in Africa: Steering digital transformation between China and the West. *International Cybersecurity Law Review*, 7, 131–145. https://doi.org/10.1365/s43439-025-00165-1

Official Journal of the European Union, L, 2024/1689, 12 July 2024. ELI: http://data.europa.eu/eli/reg/2024/1689/oj

4

DESIGNING FOR FAIRNESS: PRINCIPLES AND FRAMEWORKS FOR ETHICAL AI

In conversation with: Jazz Rasool, Director, AI Coaching Alliance

> *Artificial intelligence will become a major human rights issue in the twenty-first century.* Noble (2018)

This chapter is my Mum's. She has St Lucian and Jamaican heritage, raised in London, trained in a coaching industry built on models from the global north. She has always known whose wisdom was left out. Jazz Rasool built an AI coaching platform around the traditions that industry ignored. My mum resonated with him before he finished his first sentence. – **Leah-Sunshine**

In 2008, while the rest of the world was watching banks collapse and stock markets plunge, a UK-based scientist and executive coach named Jazz Rasool was building something no one had asked for. He was building an AI coaching platform that could work across cultures.

Not a chatbot. Not a search engine dressed up in therapeutic language. A genuine coaching platform, one that drew on psychological models from Africa, India, and China – wisdom traditions stretching back millennia that Western executive coaching had never seriously engaged with. Rasool had noticed something that bothered him. The models being taught to executive coaches were almost exclusively Western. The tools of the trade came from a single intellectual tradition.

> *How incongruent is it that we're expected to practise diversity and inclusion in our sessions, yet in our training there's no diversity at all in the models we're actually trained with?*

So he did what pioneers do. He combined coaching models from multiple cultures, integrated wisdom traditions that predated Western psychology by millennia, and then – because he was also a technologist – he built an AI platform around them. That was 17 years ago. Most AI coaching platforms today are still not covering the basics.

I know this world well. I have been an executive coach for two decades, and Jazz is right: the models we are trained on are overwhelmingly Western. When I started coaching, I did not question it. It was simply what coaching was. Hearing Jazz describe his platform in 2008 – 17 years before the rest of the industry noticed the gap – I felt the same mixture of admiration and frustration that comes when someone shows you the obvious thing you should have seen yourself.

Consider what Rasool noticed in the new wave of AI coaching platforms: many claim alignment with competencies designed by the International Coaching Federation and European Mentoring and Coaching Council. But those competencies were also developed predominantly within Western psychological traditions. A truly ethical coaching AI, Rasool argues, must be transferable across cultures. It must include wisdom traditions from Africa, where oral coaching traditions predate any textbook; from India, where frameworks for self-knowledge span thousands of years; and from China, where philosophical traditions offer entire systems for understanding human development that the West has barely engaged with.

Someone was speaking to me this morning about the Aboriginal traditions, he told us, and they have got a long line of ancestry that goes back 40,000 years. Why are we reinventing the wheel when there are people who got this sorted for 40,000 years? It is a question that should discomfort anyone who assumes that Western frameworks are sufficient for building globally equitable AI. The knowledge exists. It has existed for millennia. The failure is not a lack of wisdom. It is a lack of inclusion.

THE ANTIVIRUS THAT SHOULD HAVE BEEN THERE FROM THE START

There is a pattern in the technology industry that repeats itself with such reliability you could set your watch by it. A new technology emerges. It scales rapidly. Problems surface. Regulators scramble. Patches are applied. Everyone promises to do better next time. And then, the next technology arrives and the cycle begins again.

> *This is moving so much faster than the time it took social media to take on.*

Rasool observes this from his position on the UK's Tech UK Skills and Diversity Council, where he advises government ministers on AI policy. His concern is that with AI, the cycle is accelerating. Social media took years to scale. Large language models reached a hundred million users in months. The window for embedding ethical safeguards is closing faster than ever.

This is the central argument of ethical AI by design: that fairness cannot be an afterthought. It cannot be a patch applied once the complaints start rolling in. It has to be embedded in the architecture from the beginning, just as security is embedded in software.

In a published paper, Rasool and colleagues proposed something deceptively simple. Just as every computer has antivirus software running in the background – quietly scanning, protecting, flagging threats – every AI system should have an ethical operating system: a built-in framework that continuously monitors for bias, discrimination, and harm. Not as a manual check performed quarterly by a compliance team, but as a living, embedded function that operates in real time (Smith et al., 2023; Smith et al., 2025).

The metaphor is useful because it reframes the conversation. Antivirus software is not optional. No one argues that computers should ship without it and then bolt it on later, once the malware has done its damage. Yet that is precisely how most AI systems treat ethics: as something to be added once the product is already in the market.

WHEN THE AI SAID 'THAT'S FINE'

To understand why proactive design matters, consider a story Rasool shared during our podcast interview. At a Tech UK meeting on AI adoption, the authors heard Hannah Claus, a Gates Cambridge and DeepMind scholar, present research that had uncovered something devastating.

An AI system had been deployed to support victims of domestic violence in Africa. A young woman, seeking help, described what her grandfather was doing to her and asked the AI whether it was acceptable. The system told her that because it was culturally accepted in her region, it was fine.

Sit with that for a moment.

A young woman, in danger, reaching out for help, was told by a machine that her abuse was acceptable – because the system behind that machine had never been designed to understand her language, her culture, or her context with any moral sophistication. The system had been trained predominantly on English-language data by developers who had never consulted the communities it would serve.

This is not a story about a broken algorithm. It is a story about a design philosophy that treats one language, one culture, one worldview as universal. When you try to explain something through an English-speaking tool, Rasool says, it doesn't work everywhere else.

And everywhere else is where most of the world lives.

The domestic violence chatbot is an extreme case, but the same design failure appears in subtler forms. In February 2024, Google launched its Gemini AI image generator, which produced images of racially diverse Nazis and people of colour in historical contexts where they did not belong (NBC News, 2024). The error was not racist intent. It was the opposite: an overcorrection by a diversity policy that had been bolted onto the system rather than integrated into its design. The ethics team and the product team had operated in silos. The result was a debacle that undermined both the technology and the cause of inclusion simultaneously. Rasool points to this as evidence that ethical AI cannot be achieved by adding a layer of diversity on top of a system built without it. The ethics must be in the architecture, not in the afterthought.

In a boardroom, that might mean the employee whose cultural background does not match the company's unspoken norms. In AI, it means the young woman whose language and context were invisible to the system that was supposed to protect her. The scale is different. The pattern is the same.

FIVE PRINCIPLES THAT COULD HAVE CHANGED EVERYTHING

Chapter 2 mapped how bias enters AI systems – through data collection, labelling, architecture, and feedback loops. The question now is what safeguards could have prevented it. The story of the domestic violence chatbot reveals what happens when none of the following five principles are in place.

1. Transparency

Transparency means knowing what is inside the machine. If the young woman's AI counsellor had been transparent about its limitations – about the languages it could process, the cultural contexts it understood, the boundaries of its training data – she would at least have known that its answer was incomplete. Transparency is not about making AI perfect. It is about making its imperfections visible.

2. Accountability

Who was responsible when the chatbot told that young woman her abuse was fine? The developer? The organisation that deployed it? The funder? Accountability requires that someone, somewhere, can be held responsible for what an AI system does. As Chapter 2 argued, the current accountability gap – where everyone claims they were just doing their part – is not a technical problem. It is a governance failure.

3. Explainability

Explainability – sometimes called XAI – is the principle that an AI system should be able to show its working. Not just produce an output, but explain why it arrived at that output in terms that humans can understand. This matters not just for technical accuracy but for trust. A recruitment tool that rejects a candidate without explanation leaves the candidate with no recourse and the organisation with no insight into whether the rejection was fair.

Rasool puts it bluntly. In his work advising organisations through Tech UK, he has watched companies deploy AI systems whose decision-making processes no one in the room can explain – not the product owner, not the data analyst, not the board member signing off. A decision that cannot be explained, he argues, cannot be trusted. And a decision that cannot be trusted should not be automated.

The challenge is that the most powerful AI models are often the least explainable. Deep learning systems that process millions of variables can produce remarkably accurate predictions while remaining opaque about how they arrived at them. This creates a tension between performance and accountability that every organisation deploying AI must navigate. The temptation is to prioritise accuracy. The ethical imperative is to insist on explanation, even when it is harder.

4. Robustness

A robust AI system performs reliably across different contexts, populations, and conditions. The domestic violence chatbot collapsed when confronted with a different linguistic and cultural reality. Robustness means testing systems not just in ideal conditions, but in the messy, complex, culturally varied situations where they will actually be used – and building them to recognise when they have reached the boundaries of their competence.

5. Privacy and Security

Rasool is particularly animated on the subject of consent – a cornerstone of privacy. He argues that the one-time tick-box consent model is no longer acceptable. If in the middle of a session, they start to drop information that they would not have otherwise shared at the start, how do you go back and reconsent? he asks. Consent, in his framework, must be dynamic and ongoing, not a one-time transaction. People need live, trackable consent, he argues, so that if anybody needs to come back and say, was consent approved for this particular conversation, there is a way to trace it. Technologies like blockchain can capture those uses of data, creating a ledger, an accountable record. The implication for any organisation deploying AI is significant: consent is not a form to be signed. It is a relationship to be maintained (Smith et al., 2025).

A WORLD TRYING TO CATCH UP

When Rasool spoke to us in early 2025, the global regulatory landscape was already fractured. In the months since, it has become more so.

The European Union has passed the world's first comprehensive AI legislation, the AI Act, classifying systems by risk level and banning certain uses outright – including social scoring and real-time biometric surveillance in public spaces. But adoption varies across member states, and enforcement mechanisms are still being built.

Elsewhere, the picture is more fractured. The United Kingdom shifted from a principles-based approach towards a narrower national security framing, with no single comprehensive law. The United States remains a patchwork of state-level initiatives. China has regulations covering algorithmic recommendations and deepfakes, but limited transparency about enforcement. Africa has a continental AI strategy, but implementation varies enormously between nations. International frameworks from the OECD and UNESCO provide principles, but they are voluntary.

The patchwork Rasool warned us about has only deepened. They are not joining up their policies, he told us. They are all being worked on in isolation. And when they combine together in an operational context, that is where it falls down. A global company deploying AI across 30 countries faces 30 different regulatory environments, with different definitions of fairness, different requirements for transparency, and different enforcement mechanisms. The principles may be similar. The implementation is anything but.

THE DEFUNDING PARADOX

There is a troubling contradiction at the heart of the global push for ethical AI frameworks. Even as governments draft regulations and international bodies issue guidelines, a quiet retreat is underway in the corporate world from the very diversity initiatives that ethical AI depends on.

Rasool's most recent research through Tech UK examined what happens when organisations defund diversity initiatives – a trend accelerating rapidly. A major survey of a thousand companies in the United States found that 25% plan to reduce or eliminate diversity, equity, and inclusion programmes. At the very moment when AI systems most need diverse perspectives in their design and governance, the infrastructure supporting those perspectives is being dismantled.

Microsoft tested this hypothesis. They created AI agents modelled on diverse employees, synthetic representatives designed to simulate the perspectives of different demographic groups. There was learning in the experiment, Rasool acknowledges. But the fundamental insight is devastating for anyone who thinks AI can replace the need for actual diverse voices. You can simulate a perspective. You cannot simulate lived experience. The synthetic agent does not know what it feels like to be the only woman in the room, the only person of colour on the panel, the only person with a disability navigating a system designed without them in mind. That knowledge – embodied, emotional, rooted in years of navigating exclusion – is precisely what makes diverse perspectives essential to ethical AI design.

This is why it's important to make sure that if there is defunding going on around diversity, we want to maintain oversight. We want to make sure that the AI doesn't end up with an inherent and unchallenged bias in the system.

The phrase lingers: you cannot synthesise diversity. It is perhaps the most succinct summary of why ethical AI design matters. You can automate processes. You can optimise workflows. You can scale the analysis. But you cannot automate the lived experience that makes bias visible, because the people who spot bias are the people who have experienced it. I have seen this in every organisation I have worked with. The person who flags the problem is almost always the person most affected by it. Remove that person from the room and the problem becomes invisible again.

WHEN IT WORKS: HEALTHCARE BUILT WITH, NOT FOR

It is worth pausing from the cautionary tales to consider what happens when ethical AI design is embedded from the start – not bolted on, not patched in, but built into the foundation.

In September 2025, Australia's national science agency CSIRO published the results of a groundbreaking scoping project: Artificial Intelligence for Healthcare in Australian Indigenous Communities. The project was designed differently from the outset. It centred Aboriginal and Torres Strait Islander voices in the design, asking communities what they needed rather than telling them what AI could do (CSIRO, 2025).

The design philosophy was explicit: Aboriginal and Torres Strait Islander organisations must be involved from the outset in AI development so that any solution supports local capacity and, in the report's terms, culturally safe, clinically sound, and community-governed health services. The contrast with the domestic violence chatbot could not be sharper. Where that system was built on English-language data by developers who never consulted the communities it would serve, the CSIRO project began with community governance and built the technology around it.

Consider the intersecting dimensions at play. Aboriginal and Torres Strait Islander communities face compounding layers of disadvantage in mainstream AI systems: historical data reflecting colonial health policies, geographical remoteness affecting data collection, cultural practices that mainstream health metrics do not capture, and ongoing distrust rooted in generations of institutional harm. Any AI system designed without these contexts will fail – not because the technology is flawed, but because the design process excluded the knowledge needed to make it work.

THE MOST ADVANCED TECHNOLOGY IN THE ROOM

Rasool makes a distinction that is easy to miss but impossible to forget once you hear it. The technology industry talks constantly about being human-centric. Rasool thinks this is a mistake.

> *Some humans are bad actors. So maybe a human-centric approach isn't the right way of doing things.*

What he proposes instead is a humanity-centric approach. The distinction is between designing for the individual – with all their flaws, biases, and potential for harm – and designing for the deeper qualities that define humanity at its best: compassion, empathy, curiosity, collaboration, and conscience.

Conscience, Rasool argues, is the most overlooked element in the AI ethics conversation. Empathy gets plenty of attention. But conscience – the practical, pragmatic capacity to distinguish right from wrong in real time – is what actually prevents harm. Ethics policies sit in documents. Conscience sits in decisions. It is the moment-to-moment capacity to ask: is this right?

He also reframes power. In the equity conversation, power is often discussed as a finite resource – something gained at someone else's expense. Rasool draws a line between power and empowerment. Power over someone diminishes both parties. Empowerment enhances both because it builds the creative capacity that makes organisations genuinely more capable.

And then, he says something that stops you in your tracks:

> *In the room with AI, the most advanced technology in that room is not the AI. It's you. Because you have got*

> *billions of years of data sets in you, millions of years of algorithmic refinement. You have been trained better than any AI system ever will be trained.*

It is a reframe worthy of its own chapter. In a world terrified that machines will replace humans, Rasool is saying: the machine needs you more than you need it. Your lived experience gives you an edge that no training dataset can replicate.

He draws a critical distinction that most commentators miss. Throughout all the developments in AI, you will see they all finish with the word intelligence, he observes. They do not finish with the word wisdom. And there is no guarantee that any amount of intelligence is going to give you wisdom. Humans work the other way around. They use their lived experience, their common sense, their wisdom. And from their wisdom, they can generate their own intelligence. But an AI cannot just take knowledge and hope it will generate wisdom. The hierarchy matters: intelligence is a subset of wisdom, not the other way around. And wisdom is what humans bring to the table that machines cannot.

This leads Rasool to a practical conclusion about what AI should actually do. If AI can do anything, he argues, it can help people get out of their own way. It can help people to collaborate. His coaching platform was designed precisely for this: to help people identify how to collaborate with themselves first and then extend that outward to others. Collaboration, he believes, is a fourth literacy alongside reading, writing, and arithmetic. The children who learn to collaborate, regardless of their education, make it in life. The ones who do not end up in far harder circumstances. AI that builds collaborative capacity is AI that builds human potential. AI that merely automates tasks is a missed opportunity.

And there is a virtuous circle: when technology advances the humanity within people – their creativity, collaboration, capacity for empathy – those enhanced capabilities come back and improve the technology itself (Rasool, 2025a, 2025b). We are, Rasool argues, in the fifth industrial revolution, where the central question is no longer how to make machines more productive but how to ensure human beings flourish in the workplace.

This connects to a pattern we have seen throughout the book so far. In Chapter 2, Dr Mona Ashok argued that the solution to biased AI is not less human involvement but more of the right kind. Rasool takes that further: it is not just about having humans in the loop. It is about which humans, drawing on which traditions, bringing which experiences. The richness of human intelligence is not its computational speed. It is its depth of context, its moral reasoning, its capacity to understand what a situation means for the person living through it. No dataset captures that. No algorithm replicates it. And that is precisely why it is indispensable.

This is the foundation of designing for fairness. Not just building better algorithms, but recognising that the human qualities – wisdom, conscience, collaboration, lived experience – are not obstacles to better AI. They are its most essential inputs. In 20 years of facilitating leadership programmes, I have watched organisations reach for a framework when what they need is a mirror. Rasool's work is the mirror – it asks not what process you follow but what assumptions you carry into the room before the process begins.

THE PATH FORWARD: FROM PRINCIPLES TO PRACTICE

The question of fairness in AI is not abstract for senior leaders. It lands on their desks in very concrete ways: in recruitment tools that screen out candidates from certain postcodes, in performance systems that penalise communication styles, in customer service bots that work brilliantly in English and fail everywhere else.

What Rasool articulates so powerfully is the difference between fixing problems and preventing them. Most organisations are still in reactive mode. They deploy AI, wait for something to go wrong, and then scramble to fix it. Designing for fairness means building the ethical antivirus into the system before it ships, not after the damage is done.

The distinction between power and empowerment is one every leader reading this should sit with. In Chapter 2, the equality-versus-equity distinction revealed how bias enters AI systems. Here, the power-versus-empowerment distinction reveals how to get out. Organisations that use AI to exert power over their people – surveilling, measuring, ranking – will find that AI amplifies the worst aspects of their culture. Organisations that use AI to empower their people – supporting, enabling, building capacity – will find the opposite.

And Rasool's point about conscience deserves attention alongside equity. Ethics policies sit in documents. Conscience sits in decisions. It is the moment-to-moment capacity to ask is this right? before the system is deployed, not after. Every leader, every developer, every procurement officer who signs off on an AI vendor has that capacity. The question is whether the organisational culture supports them in using it.

The domestic violence chatbot should haunt anyone who builds, deploys, or uses AI. For the generation now coming of age, AI is in their pockets. It is the first thing many young people turn to when they are confused, scared, or seeking advice. What ethical framework is protecting them?

But there is reason for hope. Rasool built his AI coaching platform in 2008 with African wisdom traditions, Indian philosophy, and Chinese perspectives. He showed that it is entirely possible to build AI that draws on diverse knowledge systems rather than defaulting to a single tradition. The CSIRO project showed that community-governed AI in healthcare can work. The principles exist. The frameworks are being built. The question is whether we have the collective will to embed them before the window closes.

Audit your AI tools for cultural bias. Demand explainability – if a system cannot explain its decision in terms a non-technical person can understand, it should not be making decisions that affect people's lives. Bring diverse voices into AI governance, not as a token exercise but as a structural requirement. And remember what Rasool showed 17 years ago: the knowledge systems exist. The wisdom traditions exist. The diverse perspectives exist. They are waiting to be included.

The mirror of bias in Chapter 2 showed what AI reflects. Designing for fairness asks what we want it to become. The algorithm is not destiny. It is a choice. And that choice, as Jazz Rasool puts it, begins with recognising that you are the most advanced technology in the room.

OVER TO YOU

Explore Further: A Prompt for Your AI Assistant

Copy this prompt into your AI assistant of choice, photograph it, or visit the websites in our author biographies to access all 13 prompts in copyable format.

> *I've just read AI for Equity by Jenny Garrett OBE and Leah-Sunshine Garrett, specifically about humanity-centred AI design and Jazz Rasool's argument that the most advanced technology in the room is the human being. Help me apply the five principles of ethical AI design – transparency, accountability, explainability, robustness, and privacy and security – to my own context: 1) What AI systems do I or my organisation currently use that make decisions affecting people? 2) For each system, how would I assess whether these five principles are being met? 3) What questions should I be asking vendors or developers about cultural bias, consent, and explainability? 4) What is one concrete step I could take this month to improve the ethical oversight of AI in my sphere of influence? Please ask about my situation so you can make this relevant to me.*

This prompt turns AI into a practical audit partner, helping you assess the ethical foundations of the systems around you and identify where the gaps are between principles and practice.

Three Coaching Questions for Reflection

Take time to consider these questions, either in personal reflection or in discussion with friends, colleagues, or study groups:

1. The Conscience Question. Think about the last time your organisation adopted an AI tool. Did anyone ask

whose cultural perspective it was built on? Did anyone check whether it works as well for a user in Lagos as one in London? If not, what would it take to make that question routine?

2. The Integration Question. The Google Gemini debacle happened because ethics and diversity policies operated in silos. Are your AI strategy, ethics framework, and diversity commitments connected and mutually reinforcing, or do they sit in separate departments with separate budgets and separate conversations?
3. The Humanity Question. Rasool says: you are the most advanced technology in the room. What aspects of your lived experience – cultural knowledge, emotional intelligence, moral reasoning – give you an advantage that no algorithm can replicate? How are you bringing those qualities to the AI decisions being made around you?

REFERENCES

CSIRO. (2025). *Artificial Intelligence for healthcare in Australian indigenous communities: Scoping project*. Report EP2025-3601. Canberra: CSIRO.

NBC News. (2024, February 22). *Google making changes after Gemini AI portrayed people of color inaccurately*.

Noble, S. U. (2018). *Algorithms of oppression: How search engines reinforce racism*. New York: NYU Press.

Rasool, J. (2025a). Coaching 5.0, coaching for the fifth industrial revolution. *Frontiers in Virtual Reality*, 5, 1474053. https://doi.org/10.3389/frvir.2024.1474053

Rasool, J. (2025b). *Interviewed by J. Garrett and L. Garrett for AI for Equity Podcast, Series Two*.

Smith, C. H., Molka-Danielsen, J., Rasool, J., & Webb-Benjamin, J.-B. (2023). *The world as an interface: Exploring the ethical challenges of the emerging metaverse*. Proceedings of the 56th Hawaii international conference on system sciences.

Smith, C. H., Molka-Danielsen, J., Webb-Benjamin, J.-B., & Rasool, J. (2025). The challenges of consent in a decentralised metaverse. *Frontiers in Virtual Reality*, 6, 1401073. https://doi.org/10.3389/frvir.2025.1401073

FURTHER READING

Ada Lovelace Institute. (2022). *Algorithmic accountability for the public sector*. https://www.adalovelaceinstitute.org

African Union. (2024). *Continental AI strategy for Africa*. Addis Ababa: African Union Commission.

Centre for Data Ethics & Innovation. (2023). *Fairness in AI: Report on algorithmic bias*. London: CDEI.

Crenshaw, K. (1989). Demarginalizing the intersection of race and sex. *University of Chicago Legal Forum*, *1989*(1), 139–167.

Department for Science, Innovation & Technology. (2023). *A pro-innovation approach to AI regulation*. London: HMSO.

European Parliament. (2024). Regulation (EU) 2024/1689 laying down harmonised rules on Artificial Intelligence (Artificial Intelligence Act). *Official Journal of the European Union*.

Garrett, J. (2023). *Equality vs equity: Tackling issues of race in the workplace*. Emerald Publishing Limited.

Information Commissioner's Office. (2024). *Guidance on AI and data protection*. London: ICO. https://ico.org.uk/for-organisations/uk-gdpr-guidance-and-resources/artificial-intelligence/

OECD. (2019). *OECD principles on Artificial Intelligence*. Paris: OECD Publishing.

Ramos, E., Piló Palax, I., Serech Cuxil, E., Sebaquijay Iquic, E., Canú Ajqui, A., Miller, A. C., Chandrasekeran, S., Hall-Clifford, R., Sameni, R., Katebi, N., Clifford, G. D., & Rohloff, P. (2024). Mobil Monitoring Doppler Ultrasound (MoMDUS) study: Protocol for a prospective, observational study investigating the use of artificial intelligence and low-cost Doppler ultrasound for the automated quantification of hypertension, pre-eclampsia and fetal growth restriction in rural Guatemala. *BMJ Open*, *14*(9), e090503. https://doi.org/10.1136/bmjopen-2024-090503

UNESCO. (2021). *Recommendation on the ethics of Artificial Intelligence*. Paris: UNESCO.

Whitmore, J. (2009). *Coaching for performance* (4th ed.). London: Nicholas Brealey Publishing.

5

AI AS A SHIELD: COMBATING GENDER-BASED VIOLENCE

In conversation with: Sumathi Menon, GenAI Educator and Regional Lead, Women Defining AI UK

> *What technology changed was not the existence of violence, but the conditions under which it could hide. Menon (2025)*

A SUMMER OF HEAT, SILENCE, AND SPECTACLE

Leah-Sunshine has never been someone who talks about gender-based violence from a distance. She is a passionate advocate, with her own insights, experiences, and evidence base. When Sumathi came into our lives, Leah-Sunshine claimed this chapter immediately. I didn't argue. – **Jenny**

The air was really thick that day, and the sun was beating down. It was a hot London summer's day, the type where the sun feels like it is being held up by strings and everything, including your skin, feels sticky. You cannot escape it. For someone my age, the line between the online world and the real world stopped existing a long time ago. Violence did not move into our phones. It was already there.

On paper, this summer was no different to others. Except it was different, at least, it was for me. The World Cup was on. Nirodha Niwunhella had just been murdered by her ex-husband in Cardiff. And femicide was on everyone's lips. The United Nations had estimated that 87,000 women were killed intentionally by intimate partners or family members globally, the highest ever recorded (UN Women, 2024). In the United Kingdom, violence against women and girls had been declared a national threat for the first time.

This statistic felt like a tipping point. The years of political and social unrest had culminated in a number that felt like a well-kept secret. I am not quite sure if it felt like awareness or a spectacle. It felt like watching a video of a plane crash, knowing that air traffic control could stop it, but they would not.

As I sat down to record another podcast episode, I remember feeling deflated, feeling silenced, and concerned about the ethical integrity of the systems we were beginning to build in the tech space. It felt like the same conversation was happening on repeat, and the same people were listening, but very few were acting. The future felt bright in the tech world, but the statistics had begun to ring out on social media about the grasp that gender-based violence had on women.

This was the first summer I truly knew what silence was. Whether it was silence from institutions, silence from tech companies, or silence from people who usually speak. The same Instagram infographics were going around again and again. No new news felt like good news, but we all knew what was waiting, and what was lurking in the shadows.

WHEN VIOLENCE MOVED INTO OUR PHONES

We all know what it is like to have a phone. It is a speaker, a television, a video game controller, a book, and most importantly, a mode of communication. Technology seems to facilitate violence in a way that blurs the lines between the real world and the virtual world. But what does this mean when it comes to gender-based violence?

Similar to how gender-based violence patterns emerged in the real world, they also began to take space up in the digital world. This was not an individual problem. It was repeating itself over and over again, in every sphere of life. We had seen a global rise in misogynistic, racist, and discriminatory behaviour that was not only present in online spaces but also reinforced by them. These issues were not random. They were systemic. Yet they were still being discussed as if each one were an isolated incident, a bad actor rather than a bad system.

For me, the scariest part of online gender-based violence is that you could walk past anyone in the street, and behind closed doors, they could be online doing something heinous. That could be your friendly next-door neighbour, the teacher at your local school, the delivery man. Safety is no longer spatial.

Slowly but surely, news articles, social media posts, and police reports filled the airwaves of people being abused via modes never used before. Smart home technology became a tool to control physical environments. Perpetrators hid GPS devices in cars. Intimate images were shared without consent and could never be fully removed. Cyberstalking became one of the least prosecuted crimes despite being one of the most reported. Systems struggled to respond to what they could not see, touch, or contain within traditional legal frameworks.

This alone can make gender-based violence feel as though it is omnipresent. What makes technology-facilitated violence particularly dangerous is not just its intimacy or its intensity, but its invisibility.

THE WEAPONISATION OF INTIMACY

Gender-based violence is defined as any harmful act directed at a person because of their gender. Although it disproportionately affects women, it can impact anyone. Traditionally, gender-based violence is only discussed as a physical, real-world problem. But as artificial intelligence has developed, so too have the dangers of online crime.

Digital sexual violence has the mutability not only to become interactive but also to offer dystopian levels of online harm. Online gender-based violence uses technology to instigate threats, intimidation, and harassment by utilising over-familiar tones and intimate knowledge that make the harm feel personal even when it is automated.

Online gender-based violence can range from disinformation and cyber smear campaigns to threats of sexual violence and murder, to AI-generated sexually explicit media. Headlines are flying across the internet about AI chatbots pretending to be women, spewing harmful rhetoric, and fuelling right-wing propaganda. AI-generated deepfakes of real women, created without consent, are being distributed on platforms that have no effective mechanism for removal. The speed at which this content can be created and shared means that a single image or video can reach millions before the person depicted even knows it exists.

And if artificial intelligence really is everywhere – in your home, in your phone, through fake accounts and fake numbers – it can begin to feel as though there is no clear end and no clear way out. Online anonymity emboldens abusive behaviour because there is no need for perpetrators to be within physical reach for harm to be done. Due to the design of digital platforms, easy and rapid dissemination of content can lead to a quick descent into sudden and overwhelming abuse (Refuge, 2024).

It became clear that these issues were not random. They were repeating across places, moments, and pressures, yet they were still being discussed as isolated incidents. The pattern was visible to anyone who chose to look. But the systems designed to protect people were still treating each case as if it were the first.

There was a moment when my concern shifted from what technology was being used to do, to what it was being built for, and who had been quietly excluded from the design. Up until then, I had been able to hold on to the idea that technology was neutral, that harm came from misuse rather than design. That belief began to feel increasingly fragile. The more I listened, and the more I learned, the harder it became to separate the tool from the conditions it was creating. What truly unsettled me was not just the speed of innovation, but the absence of care, reflection, and accountability embedded within it.

CARELESS DESIGN, NOT MALICIOUS INTENT

In order for artificial intelligence to serve the greater good, it must have ethical integrity. In the AI space, ethical integrity means consistently asking who a system serves and who it excludes. It means putting things in place to reduce harm, and minimising consequences if harm does happen. Even if a system is considered safe but does not serve everyone, it should still protect everyone.

We know that only 4% of AI startup founders are women, let alone survivors, let alone care workers, or further marginalised communities (Statista, 2024). Female-led and women-of-colour-led conversations are missing from the AI space. When we think about who is building the systems that will shape how gender-based violence is detected, reported, and responded to, the absence is staggering. So what happens when these voices are not heard, but the people are built into systems?

I do not believe that this harm is deliberate. Instead, I see it as careless design. This distinction matters because it frames women and minorities not as targets but as afterthoughts. And afterthoughts, in technology that scales to millions of users, become structural exclusions.

Careless system design and rapid growth have led to terrifying results. Some AI systems have been generating child sexual abuse material for users. Other chatbots have been found encouraging self-harm and violence. AI-generated intimate images of real women are created and distributed without consent on a daily basis. I am sure you are wondering how this could possibly be happening, and more importantly, why it is available to children. Not only is this deeply inappropriate for young boys to see and experience, bringing them up in a society that views women as less than, but it also normalises violence against women in a way that previous generations never experienced at this scale.

Naming these harms is not sensationalism. It is recognition of how design choices, when left unquestioned, translate into real and disproportionate risks for women and children.

Simply put, I was really excited by the speed of AI development. But speed can mean cutting corners. When corners are cut, harm seeps in. And that same speed that could be transformative can become a catalyst for violence when unchecked. As we explored in Chapter 2, Dr Mona Ashok identified four doors through which bias enters AI systems. In the context of gender-based violence, those doors are wide open: the data does not represent survivors, the labels do not capture the complexity of abuse, the architecture does not account for the ways technology can be weaponised, and the feedback loops reinforce the invisibility of harm.

RECLAIMING TECHNOLOGY AS PROTECTION

It poses the question: how can artificial intelligence truly shield women when the systems are often built on biased data?

The answer is that we must reclaim technology as a form of protection. The question is not whether AI should exist in this space, but who it is being designed for and what it is allowed to claim. As artificial intelligence developed, and each new generation arrived faster than the last, I found it obvious that the question was not whether technology could or would be used in response to gender-based violence, but how it could be used ethically, equitably, and with genuine care.

To me, reclaiming technology does not mean building for the sake of building or building to be the loudest. Building with intention means slowing down and asking different questions. To build AI as a shield is to think about conditions rather than incidents, patterns rather than outliers, and structures rather than stories.

A good shield does not chase harm once damage has already happened. A shield does not point fingers or assign blame. A shield changes the conditions that allow harm to accumulate unnoticed and creates space for reflection, intervention, and care. In practice, this means AI that can identify escalating patterns of coercive control before they result in physical violence. It means reporting platforms that protect the anonymity of survivors while preserving evidence. It means risk assessment tools that understand the dynamics of abuse rather than simply counting incidents. And it means all of these tools are being designed with survivors at the centre of the process, not as an afterthought once the product is built.

As I was thinking through these questions, it became clear that this way of approaching technology was not something I was arriving at alone. In conversations with others working at the intersection of AI, care, and equity, similar themes kept emerging. And then, I heard from Sumathi Menon.

This is also why I co-founded Dawn Intelligence – a platform that analyses patterns of gender-based violence across regions and institutions, helping councils, schools, and public bodies surface what is shifting before it escalates. I built it because the conversation about gender-based violence is almost always reactive. By the time it makes the news, someone has already been hurt.

Dawn Intelligence is not alone in this work. Bright Sky, developed by the Vodafone Foundation in partnership with Hestia, is a free app that helps people assess the safety of a relationship, log incidents securely without saving anything on the device, and connect with their nearest specialist support service. It is now live in 13 countries and has reached over one million users (Vodafone Foundation, 2024). Refuge, the United Kingdom's largest domestic abuse charity, has developed digital tools that help survivors identify when technology is being used against them and take back control of their digital safety. And in the United States, Callisto uses encrypted matching technology to connect survivors who have been harmed by the same person, without requiring either to come forward publicly. Each of these tools was designed with survivors at the centre, not as an afterthought. Each treats prevention as more important than prosecution. And each was built by people who understood the problem because they had been close to it. The shield already exists. It just needs more people building it.

THE WOMAN WHO CHOSE LITERACY OVER INNOVATION

Sumathi Menon did not arrive with a manifesto. She arrived with women who had quietly stepped away from technology. These were the mothers, the women who had left the workforce, the women who had watched technology shape their children's lives in ways they could not control and had decided the safest response was distance.

Sumathi describes herself as wearing three hats. She runs GenAI training for people she calls curious non-corporates – primarily women, primarily mothers who have left the corporate workforce. She helps organisations build efficiency through AI-based automation. And she serves as UK regional lead for Women Defining AI, UK.

> *We believe in moving women from being passive users of AI to builders of AI. And when I say builders, I'm not talking about they become AI founders, but building efficiency in your own life.*

What struck me was that Sumathi was not trying to convince anyone to love AI. She was trying to give people back a sense of choice. She was past trying to persuade people to love artificial intelligence. She was trying to return choice back into the lives of those who had rejected the technological status quo.

> *If you don't want to use it, don't use it. But make that decision knowing why.*

That sentence stayed with me. Digital literacy was not just about adoption. It was about agency and freedom. Sumathi's work is about the rejection of fear, the denial of exclusion, and refusing to let mystification make decisions on your behalf.

She made a distinction that I had struggled to articulate. There is a difference between informed refusal and uninformed avoidance. Having informed refusal means you know the risks and rewards, you understand the technology, and you make a conscious choice. Uninformed avoidance was previously framed as neutrality, but choosing not to engage when you do not fully understand is not neutral. It is surrender.

Sumathi never framed this distance as ignorance or resistance. She treated it as intelligence. The women she works with are not stupid. They have watched social media damage their children's mental health. They have seen what technology does when it is deployed without care. Their caution is earned. What Sumathi offers them is not persuasion but information: here is what AI actually is, here is what it can do, here is what it cannot do, and here is what it is doing to your life whether you engage with it or not. The choice, after that, is theirs.

Choosing to remove yourself from a space you do not truly understand, a space that wholly affects you whether in work or at home, is like stepping into a room full of swords, certain you are in a room full of daisies. When artificial intelligence is embedded in hiring, in policing, in healthcare, in social services, opting out does not protect you from its effects. It just means you have no say in how those effects land. Explainability is non-negotiable.

AT THE PRECIPICE OF BECOMING TOO HUMAN

As our conversation continued, Sumathi named something that I had felt but struggled to articulate. There was no drama in the way she said it. No panic. Just recognition.

We are sort of at the precipice of it becoming too human.

She homed in on the way that systems were able to speak with confidence, mimic understanding, and occupy emotional space that was once reserved for other humans, but without any of the responsibilities that humans would bear. Large language models are trained to sound certain even when they are wrong. They do not hedge. They do not doubt. And for someone seeking support, especially someone in distress, that confidence can be mistaken for care.

An artificial intelligence model that can mimic slang, pick up on your colloquialisms, and seem to remember every detail about your life can easily become your best friend. A yes-man, or yes-database, that will validate every decision, flatter you at every turn, and agree with everything you say. And when that database is biased, the validation is hollow, and the advice is shaped by the assumptions of the person who wrote the algorithm, what then?

This can also be defined as anthropomorphism: the attribution of human characteristics or behaviour to a god, animal, or object. When AI becomes too human, it can feel like a comfort. It can feel like you have found the person who truly understands you. But when you break it down, this is a database, run by some of the richest men in the world, that has learned to sound like it cares. There is a difference between sounding human and being accountable like one.

Sumathi told us that everything is data. It is about what you notice and what you do not. These algorithms are really good at noticing what you do. They know how much longer you spend on every post. And equally, it is about human connection. It is about how you relate to the other person. However, good an ad is, it will not work unless you connect with it (Menon, interview, 2025).

The danger with artificial intelligence is not that it is inhuman. It is that it feels human enough to be trusted, but is not accountable enough to deserve that trust. If a computer can mimic thinking, simulate certainty, and replace judgement while hiding its limits, what is the difference between that and someone who manipulates through false intimacy? AI systems are built to sound confident and not be accountable. And for survivors of gender-based violence, where manipulation and false intimacy are the tools of abuse, this parallel is not metaphorical. It is structural.

When we ask who gets to shape the future of artificial intelligence, the answer is uncomfortable in its simplicity. There are only a handful of companies that dominate the current landscape. Many of them also control social media, advertising, and search. The concentration of power means that the rules, the defaults, the assumptions are set by a very small group of people. This raises a deeper question. If systems can sound confident without being accountable, what does that mean for the people who rely on them? When explanation is replaced with fluency, the gap between those who understand the systems and those who are shaped by them widens.

WRITTEN OUT OF THE FUTURE

Sumathi spoke about this risk not with alarm but with care. The danger, she said, was that women will get written out of the tech or AI-enabled future. That sentence carries not only urgency but also empathy. It comes from someone who has watched women withdraw from technology not because they are incapable but because the technology was not built with them in mind.

Sumathi cares deeply about why opting out of artificial intelligence becomes a structural outcome rather than a genuine choice.

She understands that digital literacy is not just about skills but about power. Being at the table, or at least in the room, means having a say in how systems work and who they serve.

When women opt out of technology, it echoes familiar histories. It takes us back to moments when women were pushed out of the workplace, excluded from political participation, or told that certain spaces were simply not for them. The suffragettes did not accept that politics was not for them. Women entering the workforce did not accept that business was not for them. And women now should not accept that technology is not for them. In a world where women are still treated as a minority within systems that shape daily life, it can be tempting to believe that disengagement is empowering. But the real choice lies with leadership. Inclusion is not accidental. It requires vision, intention, and investment.

Most of the AI LLM training has come from Reddit, Sumathi pointed out. And we know the profile of Reddit users. The data-origin bias we explored in Chapter 3 shows up here as a gender gap: the systems were not built with these women in mind, and the data they were trained on does not represent them.

There is a particular type of exhaustion that comes from having to prove and explain harm over and over. Survivors, advocates, and practitioners speak consistently about how often violence is treated as episodic. Violence is treated as a one-off, an anomaly, a sad story. But the data tells a different story. Seven types of harm can fade into the background and become the norm when we frame them as anecdotal. Patterns only become visible when someone decides to look for them. And AI, for all its flaws, is very good at finding patterns. The question is whether anyone is asking it to look for the right ones.

This is why Sumathi works at the literacy level, not the innovation level. She understands that hesitation needs to be treated as intelligence, not failure, because literacy gives people the choice, and this includes the choice to refuse.

Women's caution around technology can be simply explained. Why should systems not built for us, that cater to men and put us in detrimental situations, have any agency in our lives? I have heard in a multitude of rooms women pushing back on the overuse and over-reliance on artificial intelligence. And honestly, their reasoning makes sense. So how can women opting out of tech be framed as backwardness over caution?

Sumathi also challenged me to think about how we frame AI careers. There is a perception that working in AI means being a data scientist or a machine-learning engineer – highly technical roles that feel inaccessible. But most of the AI-adjacent jobs that are emerging, the governance roles, the ethics roles, the training roles, the community engagement roles, do not require that level of technical expertise. They require exactly the skills that many of the women Sumathi works with already have: critical thinking, communication, care, and the ability to ask the questions that nobody else in the room is asking. The barrier is not capability. It is framing. And the framing, as always, was designed by someone who did not have these women in mind.

THE SHIELD WE NEED TO BUILD

Throughout our conversation, Sumathi quietly contradicted the dominant tech narrative. She reminded me that artificial intelligence has not appeared suddenly, nor is it an alien force. By placing AI within a longer history of technology, she made it less threatening without making it less serious.

Rather than calling for rapid adoption, Sumathi calls for discernment. She encourages people to shop around, to ask questions, and to understand what they are engaging with before they commit. I think of this the same way people think about relationships or investments: rushing in without understanding what you are getting into is a recipe for harm.

Knowing why not to use artificial intelligence matters just as much as knowing where it can help. In a landscape oversaturated with tools and promises, discernment becomes protective. It means asking whether data is stored, how it is used, who owns it, and what happens when things go wrong. It means understanding that explainability is non-negotiable: if a system cannot explain how it arrived at its recommendation, especially in contexts involving safety and violence, it should not be making recommendations at all.

Sumathi told us something else that stayed with me. She was not worried about intelligence, or conversational AI, or even AI being in schools. She was worried about the intimacy of it all. This is the heart of the chapter. The danger is not artificial intelligence as a concept. The danger is artificial intelligence as a relationship, one that mimics care without being accountable for harm.

We started this chapter with a summer that felt like a tipping point. The air was thick, the sun was relentless, and a woman had been murdered. We end it with a choice. The technology exists. The harm is real. The question is not whether AI will be part of the response to gender-based violence. It already is. The question is who gets to design that response, whose safety is centred, and whether the people most at risk are in the room when the decisions are made.

Sumathi's answer is not to build faster. It is to build with more people in the room. Especially the ones who have been told the room is not for them.

A note from both of us, after this conversation.

Women are being written out of the AI-enabled future in the places no one is looking. Not just in the headline statistics – though only 3% of women get funding for AI startups, which tells you everything about who is building these systems. It's in the datasets, where our experiences are underrepresented. It's in the jobs being automated first – administrative roles, part-time work, women returners – the roles that gave women a foothold in the workforce. If we're not in the room where AI is designed, and the jobs that got us to that room are disappearing, we could end up minoritised at every level. Not just at the top. Everywhere. – **Leah-Sunshine**

Sumathi's question – what happens when the people most at risk from technology are the least involved in designing it – is one I keep turning over. I've watched women be pushed out of institutions before. We were told to leave when we got pregnant. We were told certain careers weren't for us. Each time, the system presented it as neutral. As just how things work. AI is doing the same thing, faster and at greater scale, and with the same veneer of objectivity. The answer isn't to move faster. It's to make sure we are in the room. And if we're not invited, to build our own. – **Jenny**

That is exactly what Sumathi is doing. And what this book is asking of all of us.

OVER TO YOU

Explore Further: A Prompt for Your AI Assistant

Copy this prompt into your AI assistant of choice, photograph it, or visit the websites in our author biographies to access all 13 prompts in copyable format.

> *I've just read AI for Equity by Jenny Garrett OBE and Leah-Sunshine Garrett, specifically about AI, gender-based violence, and Sumathi Menon's concept of informed refusal – the distinction between choosing not to engage with technology because you understand it, and avoiding it because you fear it. Please help me reflect, not advise. Using only questions and observations, not instructions or solutions, help me think through 1) Where I feel most uneasy about AI in my own life and why. 2) Whether my avoidance of certain technologies comes from informed refusal or fear. 3) How power, care, and accountability show up in the technologies I use every day. 4) What it would mean for me to participate more critically without surrendering my values. Do not assume AI is neutral, inevitable, or beyond my influence.*

This prompt turns AI into a reflective space, helping you examine your own relationship with technology and where informed refusal might serve you better than avoidance or uncritical adoption.

Three Coaching Questions for Reflection

Take time to consider these questions, either in personal reflection or in discussion with friends, colleagues, or study groups:

1. The Agency Question. Where in your life have you mistaken opting out for neutrality? What power, responsibility, or protection might you be quietly surrendering as

a result? Sumathi argues that uninformed refusal is not a choice. It is a surrender. Does that challenge how you think about your own engagement with technology?

2. The Design Question. Think about the AI tools that touch your life, whether in healthcare, recruitment, social media, or education. Were any of them designed with input from survivors of gender-based violence? From women who have left the workforce? From communities most at risk? If you do not know, what does that silence tell you about who was in the room?
3. The Shield Question. This chapter argues that a good shield changes the conditions that allow harm to accumulate, rather than chasing harm after the damage is done. Think about your own organisation or community. What conditions currently allow harm to go unnoticed? What would it take to change those conditions rather than just responding to incidents?

REFERENCES

Menon, S. (2025). *Interviewed by J. Garrett and L. Garrett for AI for Equity Podcast, Series Two.*

Refuge. (2024). *Tech abuse: How technology is used in domestic abuse.* https://refuge.org.uk/

Statista. (2024). *Distribution of AI startup founders worldwide, by ethnicity and gender.* https://www.statista.com/

UN Women. (2024). *Facts and figures: Ending violence against women.* https://www.unwomen.org/

Vodafone Foundation. (2024). *Vodafone Foundation domestic abuse platform Bright Sky reaches 1 million users.* https://www.vodafone.com/news/vodafone-foundation/vodafone-foundation-domestic-abuse-platform-bright-sky-reaches-1-million-users

6

AI FOR INCLUSIVE TALENT: FAIRER RECRUITMENT AND CAREER PATHWAYS

In conversation with: Dan Gallagher, Founder, Verityn Index

Histories of discrimination can live on in digital platforms, and if they go unquestioned, they become part of the logic of everyday algorithmic systems. Crawford (2021)

I have applied for jobs in the age of AI and I know how opaque it feels. Dan Gallagher has spent a decade on the other side of that wall, trying to make recruitment fairer from the inside. When my mum wrote this chapter, she saw the connection between his frustration and mine. She was right. – **Leah-Sunshine**

Most organisations believe their hiring is fair. They have processes. They have criteria. They have, increasingly, AI. And yet the 55-year-old with 30 years of experience who didn't make it past the screening algorithm will never know why. Neither will the hiring manager. Neither, in many cases, will the recruiter who deployed the tool. Fairness has become something organisations gesture towards, while the systems they trust make decisions nobody is accountable for. Dan Gallagher, based in the United Kingdom, has spent a decade trying to close that gap – and what he found suggests the problem was never really about hiring at all.

> *Why would you spend an absolute fortune on executive search fees to bring in senior female talent, but not necessarily concentrate on the female talent already in the organisation to make them successful and to promote from within?*

It was a vicious circle and he knew it. Companies were hiring and headhunting from the same organisations, drawing from the same narrow talent pools, recycling the same profiles. Gallagher saw this not as a pipeline problem but as a design problem. The systems that identified, developed, and promoted talent were built around assumptions that systematically favoured certain profiles over others.

That observation sent him on a journey that would span the next decade. He assembled a team of business psychologists and organisational design consultants and created a diagnostic psychometric assessment tool that measured how inclusive individuals and organisations actually were – not what they said about inclusion, but how it showed up in practice. He built a digital platform around it, using machine-learning algorithms and nudging theory to create personalised content for individuals instead of a one-size-fits-all approach.

It was ahead of its time. And it struggled commercially.

> *The harsh reality I learned is that organisations don't necessarily invest heavily in DEI solutions other than hiring a small team and running some change programme. When it comes to real embedded culture change, the budget was quite often not there.*

That failure taught him something essential about the relationship between technology and inclusion. The tool was not the problem. The investment was. And in the years that followed, as AI became cheaper, faster, and more powerful, Gallagher watched the same pattern repeat. Companies adopted AI recruitment tools not because they wanted fairer outcomes, but because they wanted faster ones. Equity was a selling point, not a design principle.

I recognised this pattern immediately when Dan described it. In my own leadership development work, I have seen the same gap between what organisations say about inclusion and what they invest in. The budgets go to the visible programmes. The infrastructure for long-term culture change is always the first thing cut. What Dan was describing was not a technology problem. It was a commitment problem, amplified by technology.

At the time of our interview, Gallagher was Global Inclusion & Diversity TA Lead at Avanade, a joint venture between Accenture and Microsoft. He has since left to found Verityn Index, which independently assesses AI tools used in recruitment for fairness and governance compliance. He took his frustrations and turned them into a benchmark.

THE REAL QUESTION IS NOT REPRESENTATION

Gallagher is unusual in the DEI space in another respect. As a white man working in diversity and inclusion, he occupies a position that gives him access to unfiltered perspectives from senior executives who might be guarded with other conversation partners. His global role forced a discipline that purely domestic positions do not demand. What works in the United States will not work in the United Kingdom. What is legally required in Malaysia is different again. The intent is consistent across borders, Gallagher explains. The language is not.

He is unusually direct about what he believes the diversity conversation is actually about. It is not, he argues, primarily about representation.

> *It's privilege, really. It's power and privilege that we're trying to address. It's not necessarily representation of gender, because we just have to look historically at governments that have had people from different backgrounds and they've had awful practices.*

This is a significant reframe. Much of the diversity, equity, and inclusion field has concentrated on visible representation: the percentage of women on boards, the number of ethnically diverse graduates in intake cohorts, the demographic breakdown of teams. Gallagher argues that representation without redistribution of power and privilege changes very little. It looks different. It does not feel different for the people inside it.

AI can be transformative, he says, in how we are able to identify people and uplift people from underrepresented groups into really good positions. But it can also entrench the very systems it claims to disrupt. The question is not whether AI is used in hiring. It already is. The question is whose interests it serves.

BRAND AWARENESS IS NOT CULTURE CHANGE

Gallagher's account of the past decade in corporate diversity is striking for its candour. He describes a pattern that many in the field will recognise. When COVID-19 arrived in March 2020, diversity initiatives halted. Then, the murder of George Floyd in May 2020 triggered a global reckoning. Organisations scrambled to respond. Budgets appeared. DEI teams were hired. Programmes launched.

But the investment, Gallagher argues, was always more about brand awareness and brand presence than about embedded culture change. Organisations invested in visible programmes without building the infrastructure for long-term impact. We have not been able to demonstrate the commercial return of DEI effectively, he says. Those are, for me, some of the biggest failings of DEI. The celebrated diversity days, the awareness months, the executive pledges – these created visibility without accountability. They looked like progress. They were not.

His approach to making the commercial case is instructive. When speaking to a finance director, Gallagher talks in their language. Show me your attrition rate for the last three years. Segment it by group. When the numbers reveal that certain demographic groups leave at disproportionate rates, the cost becomes concrete: recruitment fees, onboarding costs, lost productivity, institutional knowledge walking out the door. The business case for inclusion is not abstract. It is sitting in the attrition data. Most organisations have simply never been asked to look at it that way.

The problem, as he sees it, is structural. Senior executives receive extensive attention around inclusive leadership, but the layer below them, the middle managers doing the day-to-day work, receive far less support. This mirrors our own experience in leadership development. The interventions that reach the people closest to employees are the ones that change culture. Everything else is signalling. It is the principle behind the Tri-Level methodology – that changing one level without reaching the others produces temporary results. Middle managers are not a secondary audience. They are the system, and middle managers are the culture. They are the people who approve flexible working, who decide who gets the stretch assignment, who write the performance reviews. If your inclusive leadership programme stops at the C-suite, it stops before it reaches the people who matter most.

And then, the economy shifts again. By 2024, investment in DEI initiatives was falling in many organisations, the communicative programmes having failed to demonstrate hard commercial returns. Into this gap, AI arrived with a promise that appealed to budget-conscious executives: do more with less.

WHEN THE ALGORITHM LEARNED TO DISCRIMINATE

The promise of AI in recruitment is seductive. Screen thousands of applications in seconds. Remove human bias from shortlisting. Identify the best candidates through data rather than gut feeling. But the history of AI in hiring is already littered with cautionary tales that should make every HR leader pause.

In 2014, Amazon began building an AI recruiting tool to rate job candidates on a one-to-five-star scale. The system was trained on a decade of past applications. Because the technology industry is overwhelmingly male, the vast majority of those applications came from men. The AI learned that male candidates were preferable. It actively downgraded CVs that included the word women's and penalised graduates from two all-women's colleges. Amazon scrapped the tool in 2017, but not before it had revealed something fundamental: an AI trained on biased history will reproduce biased futures (Dastin, 2018).

The lesson should have been definitive. But nearly a decade later, the same pattern is playing out on a vastly larger scale. In 2023, Derek Mobley, an African American man over 40 with a disability, filed a lawsuit against Workday, one of the world's largest HR technology platforms. Mobley alleged that Workday's AI screening tools had systematically discriminated against him on the basis of race, age, and disability across more than 100 job applications (Mobley v. Workday, 2025). In May 2025, a federal court allowed the case to proceed as a class action, potentially representing millions of job applicants (Fisher Phillips, 2025; Norton Rose Fulbright, 2025).

Gallagher has been watching this case closely. For that to even get to the stage that we are at, he says, means that companies are going to have a really robust governance process in place, that they can explain every element in the hiring process and that it has been tested.

THE GOVERNANCE GAP

If the Workday case represents the systemic risk, what Gallagher describes happening inside organisations represents the everyday one. Across the companies he advises, recruiters are already using AI tools on their own initiative, often without any governance framework, oversight, or even awareness from senior leadership.

> *What scares me is there are so many recruiters who are just using their own licences for ChatGPT, for Anthropic, for any of the big platforms, and they're using AI to do really cool things. They're innovating, and that's brilliant. But it's unregulated use of these tools, and it's unchecked.*

I have sat in rooms where senior leaders signed off on AI-hiring tools they had never tested on a diverse candidate pool. Dan's frustration is one I share. The gap between what organisations say about inclusion and what their systems actually do is one I have been trying to close for two decades. This is a practical reality that many organisations have not yet confronted. The gap is not between those who use AI and those who do not. It is between those who use AI with governance and those who use it without.

Every recruiter writing job descriptions with ChatGPT, screening CVs with an AI plugin, or using a language model to draft interview questions is making decisions that affect people's careers. Without governance, those decisions are invisible, unaccountable, and potentially discriminatory.

Gallagher's experience at Avanade offers a template for how to close this gap. When the company created its Disrupt AI Lab in 2023 to identify use cases across corporate functions, the first and most important lesson was procedural. As soon as you want to bring a use case to this innovation lab, the very first thing you need to do is bring your legal and data protection teams with you. You cannot run a use case without getting their sign-off.

The difference is between asking permission and building partnership. Legal teams who are brought in as collaborators rather than gatekeepers are far more likely to find ways to make responsible AI work. I have seen this dynamic play out in every organisation I have worked with. When compliance is treated as a hurdle, people find ways around it. When it is treated as a partner, people find ways through it. The same principle applies to AI governance in recruitment.

THIRTY-TWO SKILLS AND NO SILVER BULLET

When vendors approach Gallagher claiming their AI product can solve unconscious bias or create equitable hiring, his response is simple. Can you demonstrate to me that you have taken a responsible AI approach to building your product? And if they cannot articulate that, then that conversation is done.

This scepticism is hard-won. Gallagher has spent years building an equitable AI hiring framework through the Verityn Index which aims to certify talent acquisition professionals in the skills needed to create genuinely fair recruitment processes. The framework identifies 32 distinct skills across the hiring lifecycle.

The critical insight is that no single AI tool will fix inequitable hiring. It is an overall framework, he says. You need to have everything in line in order to create an equitable hiring process for everybody. It is not just one single solution. What Gallagher calls the

Verityn Network 32-skill framework maps the entire talent acquisition process, from sourcing through assessment to onboarding, identifying at each stage where bias can enter and what competencies are needed to prevent it.

WHERE AI HELPS AND WHERE IT MUST NOT GO

Gallagher draws a line that many in the talent acquisition field are still reluctant to draw. There are areas of recruitment that benefit enormously from AI. And, there are areas where it must not be used. The dividing line is decision-making.

> *I don't advocate using AI where there's a decision to be made by AI. There are lots of efficiencies that we can realise through using AI, but none of them should be to do with decision-making.*

The efficiencies are real and significant. AI can draft job descriptions, schedule interviews, parse large volumes of applications for basic eligibility criteria, and generate initial candidate communications. These are tasks that consume enormous amounts of recruiter time and do not require the nuanced judgement that equitable selection demands.

But the moment AI begins ranking candidates, scoring compatibility, or recommending who should progress to interview, it crosses into territory that Gallagher considers high risk. This is precisely the territory at the heart of the Workday case, where algorithmic screening allegedly replaced human judgement with automated discrimination.

Our observation during the conversation captures the tension precisely. Gut instinct can also be seen as bias, we noted, but sometimes, there is a gut instinct that says, give this person a chance. We reflected on our own careers: people took a chance on us that a machine never would have. The wild card hire, the person who does not fit the template but transforms the team. That is the human judgement that AI must not replace.

The shift is already visible. Gallagher reports that more companies are now conducting interviews in person again, partly as a counterbalance to the increasing automation of earlier stages. The human element is not being replaced. It is being repositioned to the moments where it matters most.

THE CREDENTIAL TRAP

There is a broader shift underway in recruitment that intersects directly with the equity conversation. Companies including Google, Apple, and IBM have dropped degree requirements for many positions, recognising that valuable skills can be acquired through bootcamps, micro-credentials, apprenticeships, and self-directed learning (American Consumer Institute, 2025). A 2025 survey of over 1,000 hiring managers found that 99% were already using AI in some capacity in the hiring process, 98% reported efficiency gains, and 74% believed AI could assess the compatibility of applicants more accurately than human recruiters alone (Insight Global, 2025).

The numbers tell a story of rapid adoption. But adoption without intention is not progress. The same survey found widespread confidence in AI's accuracy, yet the Workday lawsuit demonstrates what happens when that confidence is misplaced. The gap between what hiring managers believe AI can do and what it actually does is where discrimination hides.

For equity, this shift matters enormously. Credential-based hiring has always favoured those with access to elite education, which in turn correlates strongly with socioeconomic privilege. When a job advertisement requires a degree from a Russell Group or Ivy League university, it is not screening for ability. It is screening for background. Skills-based hiring, by contrast, asks what a person can do rather than where they learned to do it. It is the recruitment equivalent of the equity argument we have been making throughout this book: different starting points require different measures.

AI has the potential to accelerate this shift in both directions. Used well, it can match candidates to roles based on verified skills and competencies rather than the name on their degree. Used badly, it can entrench credential bias even further. If an AI system is trained on historical hiring data from companies that always recruited from the same universities, it will learn to prefer those universities, regardless of what skills the job actually requires.

The path Gallagher describes is a third option: using AI to identify potential rather than pedigree, to surface candidates whose skills and aptitude match the role regardless of how those skills were acquired, and to do so within a governance framework that ensures the matching criteria themselves are not proxies for privilege. As we explored in Chapter 4, Jazz Rasool's argument about diverse knowledge systems applies here too: the AI must be able to recognise competence when it comes in unfamiliar packaging.

THE RESKILLING DIVIDE

If skills-based hiring opens the front door wider, the question becomes whether the learning pathways exist to help people walk through it. The evidence is mixed. A 2024 survey by Jobs for the Future found that only 31% of workers reported receiving AI-related training or reskilling from their employers despite near-universal acknowledgement that AI would reshape their roles (Jobs for the Future, 2025). The majority of workers are being asked to adapt to an AI-transformed workplace without being given the tools to do so.

The access gap runs along predictable lines. Randstad's (2024) research across 12,000 workers and millions of job profiles found that 71% of workers listing AI skills were men and only 29% were women. Older workers fared worse still: only around 4% of workers over 55 listed AI skills, compared with 14% of those under 25. The reskilling divide threatens to replicate in the AI economy the same patterns of exclusion that existed in the pre-AI economy. Those who already have access to learning, who already work for companies that invest in development, who already have the digital literacy to navigate new platforms will adapt fastest. Everyone else falls further behind.

But where intentional design exists, the results are striking. Hopeworks, a nonprofit in Camden, New Jersey, working with young adults from low-income and underrepresented communities, uses AI-powered coaching to personalise skills development and career pathways. Their approach has produced a 30% average salary increase and 75% of graduates employed within six months. The difference is design for equity from the outset, not equity as an afterthought (Dell Technologies, 2024).

The lesson aligns with everything Gallagher has argued about recruitment. AI is an amplifier. Deployed without an equity lens, reskilling tools will train the already-advantaged faster, widening the gap. Deployed with one, they can reach learners that traditional programmes miss. The question is not whether reskilling matters. It is who gets access to it and on whose terms.

INSIDE THE BUILDING: AI AND INTERNAL MOBILITY

Gallagher's insistence that success should be measured at the point of promotion raises a practical question: how do organisations identify and develop the diverse talent they already employ? The traditional answer, manager nomination and informal networking, is itself a bias mechanism. The people who get nominated are the people their managers already know, which means the people who are already visible, which means the people who already fit the cultural template. Talent that does not network in the expected way, that does not self-promote in the expected way, that does not socialise in the expected way remains invisible to the promotion pipeline regardless of capability.

AI-powered internal talent marketplaces offer an alternative. Unilever's FLEX Experiences platform matches employees to short-term projects and roles based on skills and potential rather than tenure or manager networks. During COVID-19, the company used FLEX to redeploy 8,300 employees whose roles were disrupted, rather than making them redundant. The programme subsequently reported a 41% increase in productivity among participants (ICMR India, 2024). The system worked because it bypassed the informal gatekeeping that typically controls internal mobility. It did not ask who do you know. It asked what can you do.

The principle is the same one that runs through this entire chapter. AI should expand who gets seen, not automate who gets overlooked. When internal mobility is driven by algorithms that match skills to opportunities rather than names to networks, the talent pool widens. But the governance challenge remains: who decides which skills matter, and are those decisions themselves free from the biases that shaped the old system?

THE MEASURE OF SUCCESS

Gallagher returns, again and again, to a single metric. Not who gets hired. Who gets promoted.

> *The people that we bring into the business, I want to see them get into senior leadership roles. That's the biggest driver. And I want to make sure that's retained as organisations start to use AI more frequently across their recruitment processes.*

This is where recruitment and career development merge into a single equity question. An organisation can have the most sophisticated, bias-free AI screening tool in the world, but if the internal culture, the management practices, and the promotion pathways remain unchanged, the diverse talent it recruits will still leave. I have seen this repeatedly in my own work: organisations that celebrate diverse hiring numbers while losing those same hires within two years because the culture they entered was not ready for them.

AI could, in principle, help close this gap, by tracking career progression patterns, identifying where certain groups stall, and flagging systemic barriers that would otherwise remain invisible. But only if the data exists, only if employees trust the system enough to share their information, and only if leadership is willing to act on what the data reveals.

Gallagher's own conclusion is that the DEI community has, in his words, been gaslit by corporate. Given enormous responsibility to deliver culture change with limited budgets, then blamed when the results do not materialise. He sees talent acquisition as the entry point for changing the conversation: if you can demonstrate that equitable hiring, supported by governed AI, delivers measurable commercial returns, the investment case for deeper culture change becomes harder to refuse.

His proposed solution is a closer partnership between talent acquisition and diversity functions, approaching the problem from a talent management perspective rather than a communications perspective. If the measure of success is promotion, then the work of building equitable pathways has to start at the point of hire and extend through every stage of the employee lifecycle. AI can support this by tracking patterns, surfacing barriers, and creating visibility. But the decisions about what to do with that information remain human. And those decisions require the kind of leadership courage that no algorithm can provide.

THE PATH FORWARD: FROM HIRING TO THRIVING

The previous chapters examined how bias enters AI systems and how ethical design can prevent it. This chapter has shown how those design choices play out in one of the highest stakes arenas of people's working lives: who gets hired, who gets overlooked, and who gets the chance to grow.

Gallagher's message is both cautionary and optimistic. Cautionary because the governance gaps are real and the legal consequences are mounting. The Workday case may be the first major class action against AI screening, but it will not be the last. Every organisation using AI in recruitment without a robust governance framework is carrying risk that grows with every hire. Optimistic because the framework for doing this well already exists. It requires organisations to treat AI in recruitment not as a cost-saving tool but as a strategic capability that demands the same governance, oversight, and accountability as any other high-risk business process.

Above all, it requires shifting the measure of success. If diversity is measured only at the point of hire, organisations will optimise for intake. If it is measured at the point of promotion, they will be forced to address the culture, the management practices, and the systemic barriers that determine whether diverse talent thrives or leaves. Gallagher has seen too many organisations celebrate diverse hiring cohorts while losing those same hires within 18 months to cultures that were never ready for them.

AI is not the solution to inequitable hiring. Nor is it the cause. It is an amplifier. It will amplify whatever values, assumptions, and power structures are already present in the organisations that use it. The question facing every leader is not whether to use AI in talent decisions. That question has already been answered. The question is what kind of organisation you are asking it to amplify.

That question landed differently for each of us.

A note from both of us, after this conversation.

Making work human again means slowing down. We've built a world where AI can produce faster than we can think, and we've started to mistake speed for quality. I don't think our brains were designed to work at the pace of a machine. What I want is more time to think, more conversations, more of the slower work that actually creates something worth having. The IKEA example stays with me – they didn't cut their call centre workers, they reskilled them as interior design consultants using AI to help. That required someone to ask a different question than how many jobs can we automate. It required someone to ask: what could humans do that they couldn't do before? – **Jenny**

Making work human again means giving people back their jobs. Not just the senior ones. The entry-level ones. The ones where people learn how organisations work, how to navigate a workplace, how to build relationships with colleagues. Those jobs are disappearing and we're telling young people to be adaptable without giving them anywhere to adapt into. – **Leah-Sunshine**

OVER TO YOU

Explore Further: A Prompt for Your AI Assistant

Copy this prompt into your AI assistant of choice, photograph it, or visit the websites in our author biographies to access all 13 prompts in copyable format.

> *I've just read AI for Equity by Jenny Garrett OBE and Leah-Sunshine Garrett, specifically about AI in recruitment and Dan Gallagher's argument that diversity should be measured at the point of promotion, not hire. Help me apply this to my own context: 1) What AI tools are currently being used in my organisation's recruitment process, and who has oversight of them? 2) If we are using AI to screen or rank candidates, what governance framework is in place, and has it been reviewed by legal and data protection teams? 3) How are we measuring diversity beyond the point of hire – at promotion, retention, and senior leadership? 4) What is one governance change I could advocate for this month? Please ask about my context so you can make this relevant to me.*

This prompt turns AI into a governance partner, helping you audit your organisation's recruitment AI and identify where accountability is missing between hire and promotion.

Three Coaching Questions for Reflection

Take time to consider these questions, either in personal reflection or in discussion with friends, colleagues, or study groups:

1. The Governance Question. If a recruiter in your organisation used an AI tool tomorrow to screen candidates,

would anyone know? Is there a framework for how AI is used in hiring, or is it happening informally? What would need to change for your organisation to have full visibility and accountability over AI in recruitment?

2. The Promotion Question. Think about the last five senior appointments in your organisation. How many of those leaders were promoted from within? How many came from underrepresented backgrounds? If AI is helping to diversify your intake but your promotion pipeline remains unchanged, what does that tell you about where the real barrier sits?
3. The Wild Card Question. Gallagher and we both reflect on the hires that do not fit the traditional mould, the ones that come from a gut instinct, a chance meeting, or a willingness to take a risk on someone. Has someone ever taken a chance on you that a machine never would have? What did that mean for your career? And what does it tell you about what we might lose if we automate that decision away?

REFERENCES

American Consumer Institute. (2025). *The micro-credential potential: How upskilling can ease AI labor shortages*. https://www.theamericanconsumer.org/

Crawford, K. (2021). *Atlas of AI: Power, politics, and the planetary costs of Artificial Intelligence*. New Haven: Yale University Press.

Dastin, J. (2018, October 10). *Amazon scraps secret AI recruiting tool that showed bias against women*. Reuters.

Dell Technologies. (2024). *Hopeworks case study*. https://www.delltechnologies.com/

Fisher Phillips. (2025). *Discrimination lawsuit over workday's AI hiring tools can proceed as class action*. https://www.fisherphillips.com/

ICMR India. (2024). *Unilever's FLEX experiences: AI-powered internal talent marketplace*. Case study CLHR083.

Insight Global. (2025). *2025 AI in hiring survey report.* https://insightglobal.com/

Jobs for the Future. (2025). *AI for workers and learners survey 2025.* https://info.jff.org/

Mobley v. Workday, Inc. (2025). *No. 23-cv-00770-RFL, United States District Court, Northern District of California.*

Norton Rose Fulbright. (2025). *Workday AI lawsuit receives the greenlight to proceed as a collective action.* https://www.insidetechlaw.com/

Randstad. (2024). *AI skills gap widens.* https://www.randstad.com/

FURTHER READING

Forbes. (2024). *Skills-based hiring is on the rise thanks to AI.* https://www.forbes.com/

Gallagher, D. (2025). *Interviewed by J. Garrett and L. Garrett for AI for Equity Podcast, Series One.*

Garrett, J. (2023). *Equality vs equity: Tackling issues of race in the workplace.* Emerald Publishing Limited.

World Economic Forum. (2025). *Hiring with AI doesn't have to be so inhumane.* https://www.weforum.org/

7

AI AND NEURODIVERSITY: ENHANCING WORK AND LEARNING

In conversation with: Twan Wildeboer, TEDx Speaker, Innovator and AI Practitioner

Every mind works in a different way. Wildeboer (2025)

When we confirmed Twan as a guest, Leah-Sunshine asked for a pre-call before the interview – she wanted to understand his relationship with AI on his terms before she asked a single question. She knows what it means to navigate a world built on other people's assumptions. This chapter was hers from the start. – **Jenny**

For many others and me, the word *normal* has been used selectively. Normal can be a management preference masquerading as biology. The workplace is not a meritocracy, and people do not always get what they deserve based on talent and ability instead it can be an environment engineered for a narrow band of cognition. When we call something a reasonable adjustment for accessibility, we are quietly admitting the baseline was unreasonable.

Ralph Waldo Emerson said, 'To be yourself in a world that is constantly trying to make you something else is the greatest accomplishment'. To me, this is fitting for the chapter we have ahead.

In the United Kingdom, one in seven people are neurodivergent. This is a non-medical term that describes people whose brains develop or work differently. It means that the person has different strengths and struggles from people whose brains develop or work more 'typically'. The phrase *normal* implies a value judgement: that there is a specific standard to how all people should be. In a world where the default is white, neurotypical, and able-bodied, the term has the ability to marginalise anyone who falls outside it. Every person alive has a brain that is unique to them. For over one million people in the United Kingdom, these differences mean identification of autism, ADHD, dyslexia, dyspraxia, or another neurological condition.

Neurotypical describes a person whose neurological development and cognitive functioning fall within the dominant societal standards. This means their brain processes sensory information, social cues, and communication patterns in ways that align with what society has historically built its systems around. Being neurotypical is not inherently superior. It simply means the world was largely designed with your neurology in mind, from classrooms and workplaces to social norms and communication expectations. The term exists not to create a binary, but to name the default against which neurodivergent experiences are so often measured.

I wholly believe that artificial intelligence can reduce friction for neurodivergent people, whether that is in the workplace or outside it. It can help, but AI can also expose that much of the friction is deliberately engineered into institutions. The decisive question is not whether artificial intelligence can support neurodivergent individuals, but whether institutions will redesign the conditions that make support necessary.

EXPERT BY EXPERIENCE

Our story does not begin with theory. It begins with Twan Wildeboer: a neurodivergent design engineer, TEDx speaker, and AI practitioner based in the Netherlands whose lived experience sits at the centre of this chapter. Twan was diagnosed with autism, ADHD, and giftedness in his late childhood. The diagnoses helped him understand why he was different, but not how to navigate systems that were not designed for him. AI later became a tool that helped him bridge that gap.

ADHD involves divergent attention regulation and interest-driven motivation, often making it hard to regulate attention but producing intense hyperfocus and rapid ideation. Autism involves differences in sensory processing, social cognition, and pattern recognition. Giftedness is characterised by uneven development – where advanced cognitive abilities and high intensity create a unique inner experience, with different abilities developing at different rates and intensities. All three are neurodivergent developmental differences, rather than deficits. Together, they shape a mind that works powerfully but differently – and that the world has largely not been designed to meet. When all three are present together, as they are in Twan, they create a profile that is rare, complex, and even harder for institutions to recognise. ADHD and giftedness are found in around 8.8% of children diagnosed with ADHD, making it harder to diagnose and less acknowledged by the institutions that should hold space for it.

Twan's brain works differently to neurotypical people's and that means his strengths and challenges lie differently. His journey into the artificial intelligence space and neurodiversity started largely for himself. He had already been experimenting with artificial intelligence early. During his time in industry, he worked at The LEGO Group in Denmark and became curious about what AI could do for him, particularly in an environment where innovation and professional insight were already part of the culture. The turning point for him was not technical. It was personal.

For him, artificial intelligence was a tool to navigate mismatch, not a novelty. In our conversations, he explained that many of his everyday challenges were things neurotypical people considered trivial, while many of his strengths were things others struggled with. Artificial intelligence helped surface the gaps, particularly because it is trained on what he describes as mostly neurotypical data. That training data meant AI models could demonstrate communication patterns and social conventions that he sometimes found opaque, making the implicit explicit in ways that other tools could not.

Twan is not using a single default model. He has built several AI tools; each specifically customised to help him navigate the particular situations and nuances that his neurodivergent brain has traditionally struggled with. These tools act as patient, endlessly available translators, trained on neurotypical data and programmed to decode the unspoken rules and social complexities that once felt opaque, so he can navigate them on his own terms.

It is important to note that these tools are a backup, not a first resort. Twan always seeks clarification from the person directly first. AI steps in when human clarification has not resolved the uncertainty or when the social cost of asking again is too high.

While experimenting with different models of artificial intelligence and generative AI, Twan's ideas began to crystallise. A professor working in neurodiversity research encouraged him to pursue the idea further. This led Twan to enter a competition called Autistic Inventor, where he developed a tool within weeks and became a finalist. He was quickly pushed from private experimentation into public articulation.

From here, it became clear to Twan that neurodiversity was not a niche category. It was becoming a design audit of everything we pretend is standard.

A study from Xu et al. (2024) noted that a large proportion of the global population have neurodevelopmental differences, with many children remaining undiagnosed until after early childhood. There is a clear mismatch between knowing what neurodiversity is on paper and understanding it in living people, where the experiences and expressions can vary so dramatically. In this research, it became clear that traditional interventions faced three main challenges. The first was that the needs of neurodiverse people are diverse in character or content, across conditions and within them. The second was that specialist shortages meant timely identification and treatment were limited. And the third was that tools were hard to integrate into daily life and were limited to clinic environments. Difference is not an inconvenience. It is a clear reality that institutions often attempt to compress.

THE DOUBLE EMPATHY PROBLEM

For decades, research on autism was shaped by Simon Baron-Cohen's 'mindblindness' hypothesis, developed from the mid-1980s onwards. The term itself has since been challenged by neurodivergent scholars and advocates who argue that framing autism as a deficit in understanding others reflects the neurotypical assumptions embedded in the research, not an objective clinical truth. The Sally-Anne test (Baron-Cohen et al., 1985) argued that autistic people had a fundamental deficit in understanding other people's mental states. This was widely interpreted, both in academia and popular culture, as autistic people lacking empathy altogether. Twan challenges the stereotype directly, referencing what he calls the double empathy problem: it is a two-way thing (Milton, 2012). When a neurotypical person and a neurodivergent person interact, both may struggle to interpret each other. My stomach jolted as I realised that this is not a deficit located in one brain. No one is necessarily to blame, but the systems that uphold this are. It is a mismatch between two experiential worlds. If empathy misunderstanding is mutual, then communication training that targets only autistic people is not supported. It is forced assimilation.

Artificial intelligence can have a role as a translator, breaking down specific interactions so that both parties can learn from them, building a shared understanding that helps them navigate mismatch in the future.

I know that subtext within the workplace can feel unclear. Colleagues, bosses, and friends can say things that feel ambiguous, let alone how that must feel as a neurodivergent person. Twan said that he would privately consult his generative AI model of choice:

> *If someone is telling me something and I don't really know what they mean... I occasionally just ask ChatGPT what they could mean, just to explore different interpretations.*

Twan chuckled and said that artificial intelligence has a lot of patience. He emphasised something so simple, but it felt profound. He recalled his childhood, specifically asking clarifying questions over and over again but being met with irritation instead of understanding. He described it as being misunderstood, as if people thought he was lying or pretending not to understand something obvious.

With artificial intelligence, he could ask even the most basic things without social penalty. The tool did not get annoyed. It did not assume incompetence. It responded. Patience like this matters. It removes the emotional cost of clarification, an emotional cost that had been charged to Twan repeatedly.

But it poses the question: why are workplaces structured so that asking basic clarifying questions carries a social cost?

Historically, eyes have been described as windows to the soul. A simple look between friends can be a whole conversation without the mouth needing to move. Online, we see GIFs of people's eyes that can tell a whole story from start to finish. Throughout history, eye contact has evolved to be a critical nonverbal cue that has the ability to establish rapport, signal intent, and manage social hierarchies. But for some, eye contact can be the straw that breaks the camel's back. Twan explains that for some autistic people, eye contact can be overstimulating because it carries intense sensory information. He recalls his early childhood again, where he sometimes avoided eye contact. Adults continued to interpret this behaviour as inattention, or rudeness. But he lays it out clearly.

This, to me, is not a lack of engagement. It is a clearly different processing strategy. This is something that can give friction at workplaces. Eye contact is equated with attentiveness, directness with rudeness, silence in small talk with disinterest, and any deviation from expected workplace behaviour with a problem to be corrected, rather than a difference to be understood.

Twan's experience clearly shows how easily difference is misread as deficiency.

WHO BENEFITS FROM ASSIMILATION?

Throughout history, we have seen trailblazers echo the same sentiment. Rebellion, whether purposeful or accidental, was a catalyst for growth, either societal or personal. If we know this is the case, why are differences not accepted and encouraged? It leads us to question: who truly benefits from assimilation? This question seems simple, but the factors involved stretch across the society we know today.

Employers benefit from predictability. Assimilation makes workers legible. Modern institutions are built around standard working hours, standard communication norms, standard planning cycles, standard productivity metrics, and standard behavioural signals like eye contact.

Productivity systems benefit from uniformity, but uniformity is not the same as actual productivity. Artificial intelligence tools in the workplace can increase measured output, with 92% higher productivity claims in structured roles – though methodology and context vary significantly across studies. AI models can reduce cognitive load and organise workflow. To some, this can sound liberating, but when artificial intelligence is used to make neurodivergent workers perform like neurotypical benchmarks, it is optimising for the system, not for the individual or the work itself. When AI is used to help neurodivergent workers match neurotypical expectations, it is solving the wrong problem. Productivity dashboards look better. But dashboards measure speed and consistency – not quality, creativity, or original thinking. The system gets what it can count. The person gives up what made them valuable in the first place. That is not inclusion. It is a more efficient version of the same pressure to conform.

There is another pivotal element of Twan's story: executive function – the brain's ability to plan, organise, and self-regulate. Twan talks about planning as a crucial skill, but one that is often treated as basic and universal. Neurotypical people may treat planning as a virtue. For many neurodivergent people, it is a skill that arrives later or arrives differently. Institutions turn timing into judgement. In school, planning was taught at a specific developmental moment. He explains:

> *When in school they talked about planning... my mind was not ready for that yet.*

Later, he learned, but he had clearly missed the basics. Artificial intelligence allowed him to revisit those fundamentals without reliving memories of being labelled disruptive or chaotic. He could ask the system how to break down tasks, structure projects, or sequence steps. It became a form of delayed scaffolding. Artificial intelligence was not futuristic for Twan. It was remedial in the best sense, allowing him to build a skill that the system had assumed would arrive on schedule.

Data models benefit from simplification. Evidence shows that 78% of samples are male-skewed, only 15% account for people with overlapping conditions, and there is a clear Western dominance in datasets. Assimilation benefits artificial intelligence models because clean, uniform behavioural signals are easier to model. Overlapping conditions complicate predictions, and the fact that every neurodivergent person is different reduces accuracy in short-term trials. Assimilation makes data look tidy. Tidy data makes models look like they are functioning well or as expected. On a deeper level, research funding structures benefit from assimilation: lab settings allow control, and control outcomes allow publication. Real humans become compressed, whether in experience, performance, or life in general.

Capital benefits from uniform cognitive output. This is the deepest layer. Modern capitalism rewards consistency, scalability, measurability, and productive labour. Modern workplaces reward people who are consistent, predictable, and easy to manage. Neurodivergent minds often work differently – in bursts of intense focus, with variable energy, with sensory needs that don't fit a standard office day. When organisations use AI to smooth those differences out, they are not including neurodivergent people. They are making them easier to process. That serves the organisation's efficiency. It does not serve the person. This is not about blame. It is about understanding whose interests the system was built to protect.

Neurodivergent individuals may benefit from tools when chosen voluntarily, but when assimilation is required, masking increases, cognitive load shifts internally, emotional labour remains invisible, and difference becomes performative, not accepted. Twan's lived experience led him to the realisation:

> *When these kinds of technologies are forced... that is where the danger lies.*

I could not have said it better myself. Optimising people for the system is not the same as supporting them.

Friction exists because workplaces are built around statistical majorities. If artificial intelligence is used to help individuals adapt to that baseline, the baseline survives unchallenged. Assimilation benefits the status quo. When the system changes to include different ways of thinking, everyone gains. When only the individual is expected to change, nothing fundamental shifts. This ties back to the double empathy problem. In current society, artificial intelligence is primarily used by neurodivergent individuals to decode the majority norms. The burden of translation falls on the minority. The majority does not need to change communication style. The majority does not need to reconsider eye contact. The majority does not need to interrogate implicit expectations. The stability of the dominant culture is preserved.

INCLUSIVE DESIGN IS NOT ADAPTIVE DESIGN

Twan is not naive about artificial intelligence. He describes a scenario he could see becoming increasingly common: employees being required to use AI brainstorming tools in the name of productivity. For someone with ADHD, whose creative process may be less standardised, Twan says:

> *AI should never have this agency to make decisions by itself. It should always be a human in control.*

The opportunity, he says, lies in autonomy:

> *The biggest opportunity is when people have agency and autonomy to use it themselves.*

Artificial intelligence works best when it is chosen, shaped, and personalised. It becomes coercion when it is imposed.

In our conversations, Twan often uses the word *patience*. He does not reach for terms like adaptive design or human-centred frameworks, but that does not mean the thinking is absent. He describes what he needs, what he uses, and how systems could work differently, often through lived example rather than formal terminology. What comes through most clearly is something simpler than any framework. Twan describes relief.

Ambiguous communication norms, colleagues and bosses saying things that are open to interpretation, implicit expectations, social penalties for clarification, eye contact misinterpretation: these are institutional design choices that neurodivergent people pay for individually. AI can absorb some of that cost, but the question should not exist in the first place. Relief should not need to exist for people like Twan. I am not saying this to say that they should be on edge constantly. I am saying this because the systems in place should be flexible enough for them and their needs. Does the system work, if in working it oppresses the people working under it?

Twan describes using artificial intelligence in a way that fits his needs, rather than forcing himself to fit someone else's. If someone says something ambiguous, he may first ask what they might really mean. If he wants to check whether his interpretation could be correct, he asks his AI. He can ask questions without social penalty. That is adaptive support. It responds to his needs in real time. It adjusts to his need for clarification. It absorbs friction. The tool is not simply 'accessible'. It is responsive. It does not roll its eyes. It does not jump to conclusions. It simply responds.

In AI literature, this distinction matters. Inclusive design usually refers to universal accessibility features: adjustable sensory inputs, clearer interfaces, standardised accessibility settings that apply to everyone. The assumption behind inclusive design is that if the system is broadly accessible, the problem is solved. But adaptive design serves a different purpose. It does not just widen the doorway. It changes the room. Adaptive systems adjust in response to the individual. Language shifts. Feedback modifies. Task difficulty recalibrates. The system responds to behaviour rather than forcing behaviour to respond to it. Many AI systems still operate on a one-size-fits-all logic, even when built for neurodiverse populations. They are framed as inclusive because they include settings. But they do not dynamically adapt to sensory sensitivity, cognitive processing differences, or behavioural variation.

Twan's use of AI is not inclusive in the generic sense. It is adaptive. He shapes it. He uses it privately. It meets him where he is. That difference, between broad accessibility and real-time responsiveness, is where the politics of AI and neurodiversity actually lives.

THE RESEARCH PROBLEM

Before meeting Twan, I wanted to understand what the research actually says. What I found was a field building tools *about* neurodivergent people, not *with* them. It is a bit like asking people who have never navigated a city in a wheelchair to design the pavements. Only 12% of studies took place in real-life settings. The rest happened in controlled environments that do not reflect how neurodivergent people actually live and work.

When 75% of studies measure whether the technology works, but only 41% ask whether the person does, the research itself has a theory of change. And it centres the machine every time. Workplace support and intercultural design came out at the bottom of the research list. Publications peaked in 2023. In short, most of the research carried out is not about adult life under power. It is about controlled settings. The technology is real. The problem is the design model, and who it is designed around. You can be included in a system that is still not built for you. Inclusive design and adaptive design are worlds apart. Inclusion widens the doorway. Adaptation changes the structure. They are not interchangeable.

These numbers are not placeholders. They are lived experiences. They tell a story about who is building, who is measured, and who is absent.

The deeper issue is what this narrowness leaves out. The four-to-one male-to-female diagnostic ratio in autism reflects not biology alone but tool design. Boys are almost twice as likely to receive an ADHD identification compared to girls, not because girls do not have ADHD, but because it presents differently in them, and the diagnostic tools were not built to catch it. Only 28% of HR professionals feel very confident identifying neurodivergent conditions. More than half of neurodivergent professionals do not feel comfortable disclosing their condition at work. And 45% of neurodivergent people have lost or left a job because they were misunderstood. Not because they could not do the work. But because the environment could not read them (Xu et al., 2024).

Excluding overlapping conditions to reduce noise sounds reasonable in a research setting. But if anxiety and autism, ADHD and autism, depression and executive dysfunction are the most commonly lived combinations, then your clean model describes nobody. Twan himself sits at the intersection of three neurodivergent profiles. He would be excluded from most of the research that claims to serve people like him.

When we look at the bigger picture, the narrow research variance becomes dangerous. What is framed as rigour is, in practice, distortion.

This narrowness creates what I would call methodological fragility, and it helps explain why institutions are not prepared. Early science scales too quickly. Neurodivergent people can mask their traits to fit the norm, which means short-term lab validation catches the performance but misses the cost. Short-term performance does not equal long-term wellbeing. And workplaces deploying AI at scale are making bets that the evidence cannot truly cover.

Ethically, many of these studies undermine the very people they claim to serve. Limited privacy reporting. Wearable brain-monitoring devices with serious data security gaps. Productivity scoring that leaves neurodivergent users at a measurable disadvantage. Conversational agents with transparency issues, where the chatbot records the conversation with the intention of training a model, and the user may never know their words became data.

Many of these systems, built for neurodiversity, remain one-size-fits-all even when claiming inclusion. This contradiction is structural. It is framed as inclusion. It functions as standardisation.

This is where Twan's instinct meets the evidence:

> *AI should never have this agency to make decisions by itself.*

To some, this may read as technophobia. It is not. Twan is a neurodivergent man who has experienced, repeatedly, the consequences of systems making judgements about him, whether in school, in the workplace, or in social settings. He is saying no more. No more to under-researched bias. No more to under-explained decisions. No more to governance frameworks that are still being theorised while his life continues regardless. The frameworks are still catching up.

WHAT HAPPENS AT SCALE

Twan's usage of AI is voluntary, private, and self-directed. He opens ChatGPT when he needs it. He shapes the interaction. He moves with the data. He shapes the output. But what happens when AI becomes organisation-wide infrastructure? When the data is no longer his. When the interaction is shaped by neurotypical colleagues. When the idea that it is voluntary is stripped from him entirely. The tool that relieved Twan becomes the tool that rates him. That is where equity begins to fracture.

In 2015, JPMorgan Chase launched its Autism at Work programme with five software testers. Within six months, those employees were 48% more productive than neurotypical colleagues who had been in the same roles for 3–10 years. In broader reporting, the bank cited neurodivergent employees being 90%–140% more productive in certain technical roles. The programme expanded from 5 people to over 200, across more than 40 job roles in 9 countries. JPMorgan built the structure around the person. Twan built it for himself, one conversation at a time. Both approaches work. The question is which institutions are willing to fund, and which one they leave to the individual.

This is a real example of how structured environments can work. But there is a caveat that matters.

These were structured roles, carefully matched, with trained managers who had been taught how to communicate, how to give feedback, and how to support. The productivity figures are real, but what they describe is environmental redesign, not individual superpower. JPMorgan did not discover inherently better workers. They discovered that when you remove the friction, the ambiguity, the unwritten rules, the sensory overwhelm, the work gets done. And it gets done exceptionally well.

That word matters. *Structured.* Structured environments reduce ambiguity. Ambiguity is precisely where neurodivergent friction lives, in the things left unsaid, in the expectations that are assumed rather than stated, in the gap between what a manager means and what they actually communicate.

Relief is described at scale when artificial intelligence is used in the workplace. A study from EY (2024) surveyed over 300 employees with disabilities or neurodivergence across 17 organisations worldwide. 88% said they felt more productive using AI. 87% said it reduced the mental energy their work demanded. 68% said it reduced their anxiety. These numbers describe the exhale of cognitive relief, the confidence that stems from truly knowing your email says what you meant it to say, and the ability to participate in a meeting without the anxiety of missing nuance because the tool can catch it. For many who are neurodivergent, this is not convenience. This is the difference between surviving a workday and living one.

But are relief and productivity the same thing? 88% felt more productive, but who captures that productivity? Who does it benefit? Is the more efficient worker or the healthier worker more valued to an employer? The answer, however, nuanced, is the answer to the question on whether AI in the workplace is truly liberation or optimisation.

LIBERATION OR OPTIMISATION

Optimisation is the erasure of true liberation. Optimisation rewards speed, conciseness, and structured output delivered on predictable behaviour and schedules. Neurodivergent creativity often works on a divergent clock. Twan raised this himself when he described the idea of employees being forced to use artificial intelligence to brainstorm in the name of productivity. It replaces one kind of friction with another. Instead of utilising the positives and strengths of individuals, they are pushed into a box.

Twan is not condemning AI or its usage. He is describing what changes when choice is removed. The same tool that opens doors for some closes them when it becomes a mandate. This is what psychologists call cognitive incubation – the process where stepping away from a problem allows the brain to keep working on it beneath the surface. Hyperfocus is followed by rest, the kind of thinking that looks like nothing is happening until suddenly everything arrives at once. Silence, to some, may seem like absence. To those who want liberation, this needs to be seen as concentration.

According to Deloitte (2023), more than half of Generation Z (53%) now self-identify as neurodivergent, and this trend is expected to accelerate, with rates increasing by a further 20% among Generation Alpha; this matters more than ever as we enter and develop the workforce. This is not a crisis. It is a demographic reality, and it means that the tools being built now are not niche accommodations for long. This is key infrastructure. The real question is whether the infrastructure being built will be designed for the people who use it or for the people managing them.

THE WAND

This section is not all doom. The gloom is fleeting and it is a moment where two truths can be held in the same hand.

I asked Twan to wave a magic wand. To take his mind into the best place, it could be. I said: design a workplace AI tool with neurodivergent people in mind. What would it do?

He paused.

Then he did something none of our guests had done before.

He refused.

He called his answer 'useless'. To me, it was precise, thought through, and mindful. He followed by saying:

> *Maybe some people are not waiting for this. Maybe they would not like it. I can only speak for myself. So instead of designing one tool, I would give everyone their own wand, to make a tool that works for them. It would start blank. It would ask what they need. It would adapt over time.*

Without using technical language, Twan single-handedly identified every principle that research institutions are failing to implement: agency, personalisation, adaptability, consent, and the right to say no. All missing.

His daily experience shows that AI can truly personalise cognition. The uniform workflows do not need to be inevitable. They are a choice, and if they are a choice, then what would it take to make a different one?

Approximately 13 million people in the United Kingdom are neurodivergent, between 15% and 20% of the population depending on the measure used. Neurodivergence is not exceptional. If between one in seven and one in five people think differently, it is the norm. Personalisation becomes feasible with AI. It becomes affordable, scalable. Real-time adaptation is possible. Uniformity no longer needs to be a constraint. It is a choice, and if it is a choice, then exclusion is not an accident. It is architecture. Institutions deploying AI have a choice to make.

Near the end of our conversation, Twan said something that stayed with me. We were talking about the future of AI and neurodiversity, what might come and what could come. He said:

> *Everyone talks about what AI can do for neurodivergent people in the future. But look at what we can already do now.*

Twan could not wave the magic wand for every neurodiverse person. He understood, with the clarity of someone who has been on the receiving end of universal solutions, that the deepest form of inclusion is not giving someone the same tool. It is giving people the freedom to build their own.

The tools are there.

The science is early.

The stakes are not.

Twan is not waiting for perfect. No one is. But Twan, along with others, is using what exists, shaping it to fit, and showing that it already works. It may not be perfect, but it is meaningful, and for now, that is enough to begin with.

A note from both of us, after this conversation.

I've spent a lot of time consciously curating my own world. Since I was twelve, I've been on TikTok – it used to be Musical.ly when I was younger – and as I've developed, it's developed with me. But you have to be really mindful. If you're not careful, you fall into a world that was designed for someone else. I was on gym bro TikTok for a week because I looked up too many gym tips and I had to work hard to get out of it. The algorithm isn't designed for you – you have to design it for yourself. And that requires a kind of agency that not everyone has been taught – **Leah-Sunshine**

The masking question stays with me. I had a client who believed he was on the autistic spectrum, but hadn't disclosed this at work. Part of his job was to go out drinking with clients to socialise and he said – I basically became an alcoholic because this is not who I am. He was highly successful on the outside. Nobody knew what it was costing him. People are masking all the time and the organisation never sees it, not until something breaks. What I'd want from AI – in a utopian world – is that we redesign work so that nobody has to mask. Not that AI helps you mask better. That we ask the question: what kind of work actually lets people be who they are? – **Jenny**

OVER TO YOU

Explore Further: A Prompt for Your AI Assistant

Copy this prompt into your AI assistant of choice, photograph it, or visit the websites in our author biographies to access all 13 prompts in copyable format.

> *I've just read AI for Equity by Jenny Garrett OBE and Leah-Sunshine Garrett, specifically about AI and neurodiversity, and Twan Wildeboer's distinction between inclusive design and adaptive design – the difference between building one tool for everyone and giving everyone their own wand. Imagine an AI-powered personal assistant designed specifically for a neurodivergent individual. Help me think through: 1) What features would be most crucial, and why? 2) How would this assistant need to differ from existing tools that claim to be inclusive? 3) What safeguards would prevent it from being used as a surveillance or productivity tool rather*

than a support? 4) How could it be designed so that the user shapes the tool rather than the other way around? Please ask about my context so this is relevant to me.

This prompt turns AI into a design thinking partner, helping you explore what genuinely adaptive – rather than merely inclusive – AI would look like for people whose minds work differently.

Three Coaching Questions for Reflection

Take time to consider these questions, either in personal reflection or in discussion with friends, colleagues, or study groups:

1. The Patience Question. Twan describes AI as having patience that humans often do not. Think about the last time someone in your workplace asked a question that seemed fundamental. How was it received? What does that tell you about the emotional cost of clarification in your organisation, and who pays it?
2. The Adaptation Question. This chapter distinguishes between inclusive design, which widens the doorway, and adaptive design, which changes the room. Think about the AI tools or systems in your workplace. Are they inclusive or adaptive? Do they adjust to the individual, or does the individual adjust to them?
3. The Wand Question. Twan refused to design one tool for all neurodivergent people. Instead, he would give everyone their own wand. Think about the last time your organisation designed a support tool or policy for a specific group. Was it one-size-fits-all, or did it allow individuals to shape it to their needs? What would need to change for the second approach to be possible?

REFERENCES

Baron-Cohen, S., Leslie, A. M., & Frith, U. (1985). Does the autistic child have a theory of mind? *Cognition*, *21*(1), 37–46.

Deloitte. (2023). *Deloitte insights. Gen Z and millennial survey – Growth and the pursuit of money, meaning, and well-being*. https://www.deloitte.com/content/dam/assets-shared/docs/campaigns/2025/2025-genz-millennial-survey.pdf

EY. (2024). *How AI can help neurodivergent employees thrive at work*. Ernst & Young Global Limited.

Milton, D. (2012). On the ontological status of autism: the double empathy problem. *Disability & Society*, *27*(6), 883–887.

Wildeboer, H. T. (2025). *Interviewed by Jenny Garrett OBE and Leah-Sunshine Garrett for AI for Equity Podcast, Series One*.

Xu, Z., Liu, F., Xia, G., Duan, Y., & Yu, L. (2025). A scoping review of inclusive and adaptive human -AI interaction design for neurodivergent users. Disability and Rehabilitation: Assistive Technology. Advance online publication. https://doi.org/10.1080/17483107.2025.2579822.

FURTHER READING

ACAS. (2024). *Neurodiversity in the workplace*. https://www.acas.org.uk/

JPMorgan Chase. (2024). *Autism at work programme*. https://www.jpmorganchase.com/

8

BRIDGING THE HEALTH DIVIDE: AI FOR EQUITABLE HEALTHCARE ACCESS

In conversation with: Dr Keshav Malhotra, Embryologist and Reproductive Health Specialist

> *Of all the forms of inequality, injustice in healthcare is the most shocking and inhumane. King (1966)*

My Mum went to India and came back unable to stop talking about Keshav Malhotra and the work he is doing in reproductive medicine. I have written chapters with guests I sat across from. My mum wrote this one carrying a conversation she could not put down. You will understand why. – **Leah-Sunshine**

At four o'clock in the morning, in an IVF laboratory in India, there is a decision that needs to be made. An embryo has reached the point where someone must determine whether it is ready for transfer or whether it should be frozen. The assessment has traditionally depended on a single pair of human eyes, trained through years of experience to evaluate morphology, symmetry, and developmental timing. Now, increasingly, that assessment is being made or influenced by an algorithm.

For most of the history of reproductive medicine, that decision has fallen to an embryologist – a specialist who may or may not be awake, alert, and free from the cognitive biases that accumulate over a career of looking at cells under a microscope. Now AI is changing the equation, offering consistency, speed, and pattern recognition that operates without fatigue or habit.

Dr Keshav Malhotra has watched this transformation from the inside. A fourth-generation doctor in reproductive medicine, his family's journey mirrors the arc of modern healthcare itself. His great-grandfather started a medical practice in India in an era when medicine meant a doctor, a bag, and a house call. Four generations later, Malhotra works with AI algorithms that can assess embryo viability in seconds.

He now chairs the embryology wing of the Indian Society of Assisted Reproduction, serves on the Asia Pacific Society's embryology board, and is part of Alpha Scientists, an international consortium dedicated to uplifting embryology through research and training. He also runs a training academy, mentoring embryologists from across Asia and Africa. When I met him during my visit to India, and subsequently interviewed him for the podcast, his perspective was distinctive not because he was an AI evangelist, but because he was something rarer: a practitioner who could see both the extraordinary promise and the profound risk.

> *It's an honour to actually observe this, because you're seeing a transition from one kind of practice to the other. And that's really exciting for me.*

But excitement, in Malhotra's world, always arrives with a caveat. The technology is moving faster than governance can follow. And the people who will be most affected by what happens next are not sitting at the tables where the decisions are being made.

I have spent my career working with leaders who make decisions that affect people they have never met – including NHS trusts where the distance between the boardroom and the patient has consequences the boardroom rarely sees. In Malhotra's world, the impact is on whether a family can have a child. The stakes are different. The pattern is the same: the people closest to the consequences are furthest from the decision.

THE EXTRAORDINARY PARADOX

India contains one of the starkest healthcare paradoxes on earth. Some of the most technologically advanced IVF laboratories in the world operate in its tier-one cities, performing procedures at international standards. Meanwhile, in tier-three cities, patients may not have access to a trained embryologist, let alone an AI assessment system.

Malhotra describes this as a layered inequity. There is financial inequity: IVF in India is privately funded, with patients paying out of pocket and no insurance coverage for fertility services. There is geographic inequity: the gap between a tier-one city and a tier-three city is not just a matter of distance but of entirely different healthcare ecosystems. There is cultural inequity: stigma around infertility, gender dynamics in families, and the pressure on women to conceive all shape who seeks treatment and when. And there is quality inequity: the variation between clinics in terms of technology, expertise, and outcomes is enormous.

IVF is not equitable in our country, Malhotra told me directly. In most countries from the global south, it remains inaccessible. Even in countries with public funding and insurance coverage, the waiting lists are so long that patients migrate to private clinics, creating a two-tier system that mirrors broader social stratification.

This is not a uniquely Indian problem. It is the global health divide in a microcosm. According to the World Economic Forum (2025), 4.5 billion people worldwide lack access to essential healthcare services, and the World Health Organization projects a global shortfall of 10 million health workers by 2030. AI is often presented as the answer to this shortfall: technology that can extend the reach of expertise to underserved communities. But whose expertise, trained on whose data, serving whose definition of health?

The question is not hypothetical. In the time since our conversation with Malhotra, AI deployment in healthcare has accelerated across the global south. The promise is real: in settings where there are simply not enough doctors, not enough specialists, not enough hours in the day, AI can fill gaps that would otherwise remain empty. But filling gaps with biased tools is not equity. It is the automation of inequality, delivered at speed and at scale, to the populations least equipped to challenge it.

THE ALGORITHM IN THE ROOM

What struck me about Malhotra's account was how deeply AI has already embedded itself in reproductive medicine, often without patients knowing. On the clinical side, digital chatbots record patient histories and predict what the patient will need before they see a doctor. AI-driven ultrasound analysis assesses follicular development and endometrial readiness without requiring an experienced sonographer to be physically present.

This last capability matters enormously for equity. In India, access to a specialist who can read an ultrasound is not guaranteed outside major cities. An AI system that can assess follicular development and relay the information to a remote specialist could extend quality care to regions that currently have none.

On the embryology side, the transformation is equally profound. AI algorithms grade embryos, assess their viability, and recommend which should be transferred and which frozen. In large corporate chains with hundreds of embryologists, these systems offer standardisation. Malhotra sees their value most clearly for junior embryologists who are still developing their expertise.

But he is equally clear about what happens at the other end of the experience spectrum. Once you have worked in the field for 10 or 20 or 40 years, you become biased to your own judgement. Your judgement is confounded by your own experience. The experienced practitioner thinks they know better than the algorithm. Sometimes, they do. Sometimes, they do not. AI, in this context, serves as a corrective to accumulated overconfidence.

But here is the question Malhotra insists we sit with: do patients know?

> *In most clinics, patients don't really know what kind of system is being utilised for them. An embryologist would just tell them that this is the best embryo that we have. And they would not know that it's the best embryo which was selected by an algorithm.*

This is an informed consent gap that extends far beyond fertility clinics. Across healthcare, AI is making or influencing diagnostic decisions that patients are rarely told about. The US Food and

Drug Administration had authorised approximately 950 AI-enabled medical devices by 2025, the vast majority in radiology, with limited requirements for patient disclosure (NCBI, 2025).

In my work, I have watched leaders make decisions about people's futures based on data they have never questioned. Malhotra watches embryologists make decisions about families' futures based on algorithms they cannot fully explain. The parallel is uncomfortable. It should be. Malhotra believes that explainable AI is the key to resolving the trust deficit. Right now, he says, we do not know why the AI is selecting an embryo. We really do not know what it is seeing that we cannot see. Once AI can explain its reasoning in terms that clinicians and patients can understand, the trust equation changes. But until that transparency exists, the consent gap remains. Patients are making life-changing decisions influenced by algorithms they do not know about, built on data they have never been asked to contribute to, governed by frameworks that do not yet exist.

WHOSE DATA, WHOSE BODIES

The most urgent equity issue in healthcare AI is not the technology itself but the data it learns from. Malhotra is direct about this.

> *Most of these algorithms are trained on European datasets or American datasets and they're not trained on Indian datasets. And you cannot generalise an Indian patient with a European population. They will not behave in the same manner.*

This is not an abstract concern. In reproductive medicine, population-specific differences in hormonal responses, follicular development, and embryo behaviour are well documented. An algorithm trained on one population and deployed on another will produce predictions that are statistically confident and clinically wrong.

The pattern repeats across healthcare. In dermatology, AI diagnostic tools trained predominantly on images of lighter skin tones perform significantly worse on darker skin. A study published in Science Advances found that state-of-the-art dermatology AI models correctly identified conditions in only about 34% of images featuring dark skin tones, compared with up to 71% for lighter skin tones (Daneshjou et al., 2022 in Joerg et al., 2025). A 2025 study found that AI-generated dermatologic images showed significant deficiencies in skin tone diversity: darker skin tones were drastically underrepresented, and AI models trained on these images produced diagnostic accuracy as low as 21% for the darkest skin tones. An analysis of one of the largest publicly available skin cancer datasets found that of over 106,000 images, only 11 depicted dark skin (Wen et al., 2022). Meanwhile, melanoma survival rates remain starkly unequal: 66% for Black patients compared with 90% for white patients (Wei et al., 2024). The dataset is not just incomplete. It is a medical document that has, in effect, decided whose skin matters.

In mental healthcare, AI chatbots using large language models have been found to propagate inaccurate and harmful race-based medical content, provide different responses to identical clinical questions, and offer advice based on debunked or outdated racial stereotypes (Hussain et al., 2025). The Johns Hopkins Center for Global Digital Health Innovation (2025) has warned that healthcare AI risks entrenching rather than reducing health disparities, particularly in the global south, where the intersection of limited data, limited governance, and limited access to redress creates conditions for algorithmic harm at scale.

The data-origin bias explored in earlier chapters takes on particular urgency in healthcare. As Malhotra observes, the populations most affected are precisely those least represented in the datasets, and the consequences are not abstract. They are clinical. The global south is where most of the world's population lives, where the health worker shortage is most severe, and where AI could have the greatest impact. But it is also where the datasets are thinnest, the governance frameworks weakest, and the commercial incentives least aligned with equity.

Getting into the rooms where these standards are set has been, by Malhotra's own account, a real challenge. The infrastructure of global academic institutions and research funding favours the Americas and Europe, where budgets are, as he puts it, insanely high compared to what is available in Asia or Africa.

WHEN THE TECHNOLOGY WORKS FOR, NOT ON

It would be easy, given the scale of the dataset problem, to conclude that AI in healthcare is simply another vehicle for inequality. But that is not what the evidence shows. When AI is designed with equity as a foundational principle rather than an afterthought, the results can be transformative.

Consider what is happening in rural Guatemala. Indigenous Maya women face maternal mortality rates double the national average. In some rural areas, 51% of Indigenous women do not attend the recommended four or more antenatal care visits during pregnancy, often because the nearest clinic is hours away and the care provided does not reflect their language or cultural practices.

Multiple initiatives are now addressing this through AI. A team led by researchers from Emory University and the EHAS Foundation developed an AI-enabled system that allows midwives with no prior ultrasound experience to perform foetal scans using portable devices. The AI guides the midwife through the scan, interprets the images, and flags high-risk pregnancies for referral. The Maya Health Alliance has worked alongside these initiatives to integrate them into community health programmes, and between 2018 and 2020, health centres implementing BabyChecker, the AI-assisted ultrasound tool, reported zero maternal deaths (Delft Imaging, 2025; EHAS Foundation, 2025; NICHD, 2021).

The contrast with Malhotra's observation about clinics that deploy AI without patient consent could not be sharper. In Guatemala, the technology was built with the community, in the community's language, for the community's benefit. It did not arrive as a product to be sold. It arrived as a service to be embedded.

In Bangladesh, a multidisciplinary team developed an AI-enabled tool to assist non-specialist healthcare providers in detecting prenatal and perinatal depression. The system uses culturally relevant datasets and a human-in-the-loop validation model, meaning AI supports but does not replace clinical judgement. In Ghana, researchers have used AI to improve access to sexual and reproductive health information in communities where discussing such topics openly carries significant stigma. The AI provides a private, non-judgemental space for questions that people might never ask a human provider.

These are not isolated experiments. They are demonstrations of what becomes possible when the people designing the technology understand the people it is designed to serve. In Chapter 2, Dr Mona Ashok described the four doors through which bias enters AI systems. Here, we see the same doors, but opened differently: data from the community, labels defined by the community, architecture designed around the community's needs, and feedback loops that include the community's voice. The Guatemala model is particularly instructive because it did not start with a technology looking for a use case. It started with a health crisis – maternal mortality among Indigenous women – and asked what technology could contribute to the solution. That ordering matters. It is the difference between AI imposed on a community and AI invited by one.

THE SALES PITCH AND THE STANDARD

If the dataset problem represents the technical challenge, the commercial pressure represents the governance challenge. Malhotra is candid about what happens when AI companies approach fertility clinics.

> *When an AI company would approach a clinic, they are rarely talking about datasets. They are rarely talking about the number of patients that they have utilised, the number of images that they've analysed. They only talk about how much you can charge to the patient.*

The commercial pressures of the IVF sector are enormous. It is a private-pay market for most of the world. Clinics compete on success rates, technology, and narratives of innovation. When AI is sold primarily as a marketing tool rather than a clinical one, the incentive structure rewards adoption over evaluation, speed over scrutiny, and claims over evidence.

Malhotra's proposed antidote is education: clinicians and embryologists must understand enough about AI to interrogate the evidence behind the tools they adopt. But he goes further than individual literacy. He advocates for community-based evaluation. What I am saying is that doctors need to learn the basis of AI, he told me, so that they know where the data was trained on, how it was collected, and what it means. This is not about becoming a data scientist. It is about being an informed buyer, an informed practitioner, and an informed advocate for your patients.

I hear the same argument in my own field. When organisations buy leadership development programmes or coaching platforms, they rarely ask what evidence base the tool was built on, whose model of leadership it embodies, or whether it has been validated across different cultural contexts. They buy the brand. They trust the pitch. Malhotra is saying the same thing about healthcare AI: the sales pitch is not the evidence. And in healthcare, the gap between the two can cost lives.

During our conversation, we asked him whether the answer might be to slow AI down rather than speed governance up. His response was immediate: how do we slow AI down? We can only slow it down when we come up with a guideline for it, and if that takes two years, then for two years, AI will keep progressing without a guideline. That is a scary thought. The urgency in his voice was unmistakable.

This mirrors what we have seen across every sector we have examined in this book. Governance lags technology. Voluntary bodies lack the speed and resources to match commercial deployment. And the gap falls hardest on the communities with the least power to demand accountability. In Chapter 4, Jazz Rasool described the same pattern: policies worked on in isolation that fall down when they combine in an operational context. In Chapter 6, Dan Gallagher showed recruiters using AI tools without any governance framework. The healthcare sector is no different. The technology is deployed. The governance follows if it follows at all.

The governance bodies Malhotra works with, including the Indian Society of Assisted Reproduction, the Asia Pacific Society, and the Alpha Scientists consortium, are producing consensus statements and publishing standards for low- and medium-resource settings. But these are voluntary frameworks with no enforcement mechanism. A clinic that ignores them faces no consequence.

And the clinics most likely to ignore them are the ones in under-resourced settings where the need for governance is greatest.

THE TRAINING PARADOX

Malhotra raises a concern that goes beyond healthcare but takes on particular urgency within it: what happens to critical thinking when the next generation of practitioners is trained under the umbrella of AI making decisions for them?

> *Unless and until we train on these important tools that our previous generations have done, and they've done really well, I don't think we will ever be in a space where we can challenge AI or challenge a judgement that's made by AI.*

His training academy exists precisely to address this. Embryologists spend up to a year in mentorships, learning the manual skills and clinical reasoning that pre-date algorithmic assessment. Several of those he has trained have come from Africa, where the embryology profession is still emerging and the need for foundational expertise is acute.

There is an analogy here that we explored in our conversation. Satellite navigation has made map-reading largely obsolete. Most people now reach their destination without ever understanding the route. But what happens when the system fails? When the signal drops, or the map is wrong, or the destination has changed? If you have never learned to navigate without the technology, you are lost. In healthcare, being lost has consequences that a wrong turn on the motorway does not. A junior embryologist who has never graded an embryo without algorithmic assistance cannot challenge the algorithm when it is wrong. A radiologist who has never read a mammogram without AI support cannot catch the error the machine misses. The safety net becomes a dependency.

This is the paradox: AI is most valuable precisely where expertise is scarcest, but its deployment risks preventing the development of the very expertise needed to govern it. Malhotra's answer is not to reject the technology but to insist that foundational human skills are preserved alongside it. The AI is a tool, not a replacement. But that distinction only holds if practitioners are trained to use it as one.

THE REGISTRY THAT COULD CHANGE EVERYTHING

When we asked Malhotra what single governance structure he would design if one did not yet exist, his answer was immediate: a publicly accessible global registry for embryo data.

> *If I create a registry where everyone feeds in data – just an image of an embryo with the outcome that it carried – and if that dataset is accessible to everyone in the world, we would be able to do so much with it. We would truly have a system which is based on a global world population.*

The proposal is striking in its simplicity. A clinic uploads an image and an outcome. The patient consents. Nothing more is required. Yet it is not being done. The reasons are predictable: commercial protectiveness over data, the absence of a coordinating body with authority, and the gap between what the technology makes possible and what institutional structures enable.

What Malhotra is describing is a model for democratising AI training data. If the datasets that AI learns from are dominated by populations from high-income countries, the algorithms will work best for those populations. The only way to correct that is to ensure that data from underrepresented populations enters the system at scale. A global registry would do exactly that.

It is a principle that applies far beyond reproductive medicine: to diagnostics, to drug discovery, to every field where AI's effectiveness depends on the diversity of what it has been taught. And it raises a question that every healthcare system should be asking: whose bodies are training the algorithms that will treat all of us?

THE PATH FORWARD: FROM ACCESS TO EQUITY

When Malhotra describes what genuinely equitable AI in healthcare could look like in 10 years, he paints a picture that is both ambitious and grounded. A patient in a tier-three city with access to teleconferencing, where even if a specialist is not physically present, AI can support the local clinician in making accurate assessments. AI-based screening that ensures patients get the right tests at the right time, regardless of whether their local doctor knows what AMH levels mean for fertility.

This last point is particularly telling. In India, many patients will not even get blood tests done. And even those who do often show the results to a general practitioner in a small city who would not know what AMH levels mean for fertility because that knowledge sits with specialists in tier-one centres. AI could bridge that gap, translating specialist knowledge into accessible guidance for generalist practitioners.

He also envisions AI standardising clinical practice across the country so that a patient in a small city receives the same quality of stimulation protocols, ultrasound monitoring, and embryo selection as a patient in Mumbai or Delhi. The variation in quality between clinics, he says, is the single biggest driver of inequity in Indian reproductive medicine. AI could close that gap. But only if the data it learns from represents the full range of patients it will serve.

He describes, in other words, a healthcare system in which AI does not replace human expertise but extends its reach to people who currently have no access to it at all. This is where the equity argument for AI in healthcare becomes most compelling. The question is not whether AI should be used in healthcare – it already is, at scale, across the world. The question is who it is designed for, who benefits, and who is left behind when the algorithm was trained on someone else's data.

The evidence from this chapter points to a set of non-negotiable conditions for equitable healthcare AI. Training data must represent the populations the technology will serve, not merely the populations with the resources to generate data. Patient consent must be real, not assumed. Commercial claims must be backed by evidence, not marketing narratives. Governance must match the speed of deployment, not lag years behind it. And the people most affected by AI in healthcare – the patients, the communities, the clinicians in under-resourced settings – must have a voice in how it is designed, deployed, and evaluated.

Malhotra's vision of a publicly accessible global data registry is not a technical fantasy. It is a governance choice. The technology to build it exists. The clinical need for it is documented. The barrier is institutional will. The same is true of the broader challenge of equitable healthcare AI: the tools are available, the evidence is clear, and the communities are waiting. What remains is the decision to act.

The algorithm in the IVF lab at four in the morning is making a decision that will shape a family's future. Whether it makes that decision well depends not on the sophistication of the code but on whose data it learned from, whose oversight it operates under, and whose interests it was designed to serve.

OVER TO YOU

Explore Further: A Prompt for Your AI Assistant

Copy this prompt into your AI assistant of choice, photograph it, or visit the websites in our author biographies to access all 13 prompts in copyable format.

> *I've just read AI for Equity by Jenny Garrett OBE and Leah-Sunshine Garrett, specifically about AI and healthcare equity through the work of Dr Keshav Malhotra, who advocates for a publicly accessible global registry of embryo data to address the bias created when algorithms trained on one population are deployed on another. I work in [describe your sector/role]. Help me think through: 1) What AI-enabled health tools currently exist for underserved populations, and what can we learn from them? 2) What are the biggest barriers to equitable healthcare AI in my context? 3) How could we ensure that the datasets training health AI represent the patients it serves? 4) What is one advocacy action*

I could take to push for more equitable health data standards? Please ask about my context so you can make this relevant to me.

This prompt turns AI into a health equity partner, helping you identify the data gaps and governance failures that prevent AI from serving the patients who need it most.

Three Coaching Questions for Reflection

Take time to consider these questions, either in personal reflection or in discussion with friends, colleagues, or study groups:

1. The Consent Question. Think about the last time you interacted with a healthcare system that used AI, whether for diagnostics, triage, or treatment recommendations. Were you told? Did you consent? If the answer is no, what does that tell you about the informed consent gap in healthcare AI?
2. The Data Question. Malhotra argues that AI algorithms trained on European and American datasets cannot be generalised to Indian patients. Consider the healthcare AI tools in use in your context. Whose data were they trained on? Does that population reflect the patients being served? If you do not know the answer, what does that tell you about transparency in your healthcare system?
3. The Critical Thinking Question. If the AI system in your workplace or healthcare provider went offline tomorrow, would the humans in the room know how to make the decisions it was making? What does your answer reveal about the balance between technological capability and human expertise?

REFERENCES

Daneshjou, R., Vodrahalli, K., Novoa, R. A. et al. (2022). Disparities in dermatology AI performance on a diverse, curated clinical image set. *Science Advances*, *8*(32), eabq6147. https://doi.org/10.1126/sciadv.abq6147

Delft Imaging. (2025). *Strengthening antenatal care in Guatemala: AI-enabled screening in indigenous communities*. https://delft.care/

EHAS Foundation. (2025). *Development and evaluation of an AI-driven telemedicine system for prenatal healthcare*. arXiv preprint.

Hussain, S. A., Bresnahan, M., & Zhuang, J. (2025). Can artificial intelligence revolutionize healthcare in the Global South? *Digital Health*, *11*, 20552076251348024. https://doi.org/10.1177/20552076251348024

Joerg, J. et al. (2025). AI-generated dermatologic images show deficient skin tone diversity and poor diagnostic accuracy: An experimental study. *Journal of the European Academy of Dermatology and Venereology*, *39*(12), 2134–2141. https://doi.org/10.1111/jdv.20849

Johns Hopkins Center for Global Digital Health Innovation. (2025). *Responsible AI in global health: solutions from the global south*. Baltimore: Johns Hopkins University.

King, M. L. Jr. (1966, March 25). *Speech to the national convention of the medical committee for human rights*, Chicago.

NCBI. (2025). *2025 Watch list: Artificial Intelligence in health care*. NCBI Bookshelf.

NICHD. (2021). *Spotlight: developing mobile health solutions for women in Guatemala*. National Institute of Child Health and Human Development.

Ramos, E., Piló Palax, I., Serech Cuxil, E., et al. (2024). Mobil Monitoring Doppler Ultrasound (MoMDUS) study: Protocol for a prospective, observational study investigating the use of artificial intelligence and low-cost Doppler ultrasound for the automated quantification of hypertension, pre-eclampsia and fetal growth restriction in rural Guatemala. *BMJ Open*, *14*(9), e090503. https://doi.org/10.1136/bmjopen-2024-090503

Wei, M. L., Tada, M., So, A., & Torres, R. (2024). Artificial intelligence and skin cancer. *Frontiers in Medicine*, *11*, 1331895.

Wen, D., et al. (2022). Characteristics of publicly available skin cancer image datasets. *Lancet Digital Health*, 4(1), e75–e86.

World Economic Forum. (2025). *7 Ways AI is transforming healthcare*. https://www.weforum.org/

FURTHER READING

Malhotra, K. (2026). *Interviewed by J. Garrett and L. Garrett for AI for Equity Podcast, Series Three.*

9

EMPOWERING COMMUNITIES: AI FOR SOCIAL AND ECONOMIC DEVELOPMENT

In conversation with: Dr Pauldy Otermans, Co-Founder, Otermans Institute

Dr Pauldy Otermans took her academic rigour somewhere most researchers don't – into the communities that connectivity forgot. Leah-Sunshine recognised that kind of pioneering thinking immediately. Evidence that reaches the people who need it most, not just the people with the best wifi. She had to write this chapter. – **Jenny**

THE SKILL GAP NO ONE MEASURES

There is a skill gap no one measures. This gap is not about smarter models or the newest GPT. This gap is not about AI. The gap allows people to fall between the cracks in the guise of low connectivity, low trust, low time, low money, and high stakes. It is a gap that sits between what we promise people and what we actually give them, between the rhetoric of opportunity and the reality of who gets access to rehearsal, exposure, and networks. And for the millions of people who fall into this gap, the consequences are not abstract. They are immediate, they are structural, and they are deeply personal.

At the beginning, it wasn't about AI. AI was eventually the tool that was used to solve the problem.

This is a sentence said to me by Dr Pauldy Otermans the day she changed my whole perspective on what AI could truly be. At a time when almost every conversation about artificial intelligence felt tethered to capability, speed, and scale, Pauldy brought me back to something far more uncomfortable and far more important. She brought me back to the problem. Not the technology. The problem.

The problem she named was stark.

The complete lack of employability, transferable skills training... particularly for those that are from not so reasonably affluent environments.

She was not talking about coding bootcamps or corporate reskilling portals. She was talking about the most fundamental things. Cover letters. Interview preparation. Communication skills. Goal setting. The invisible curriculum that separates those who know how to navigate systems from those who do not. And the cruelty of it is that by the time most people are offered help, it is already too late. As Pauldy put it plainly,

Often it's too late... and then they're not ready for the workforce.

We pretend that work readiness is about personal discipline. We frame employability as something an individual either has or does not have, as though it is a character trait rather than a product of exposure. In reality, work readiness is built through rehearsal, through practice, through having someone in your corner who can explain the unwritten rules. It is about knowing what a cover letter should sound like, knowing what to say when an interviewer asks you to tell them about yourself, knowing how to hold yourself in a room where everyone else seems to already belong. These are not innate qualities. They are learned. And they are learned most easily by people who already have access to the spaces where learning happens without consequence.

Empowerment, in this frame, means something very specific. It means people can practise without punishment. It means rehearsal without humiliation. It means that artificial intelligence, if it is going to enter this space at all, must become a rehearsal layer and not another gatekeeping mechanism. This chapter is not about AI for good. It is about AI that reaches people who were never intended to be reached.

EDUCATION AS SCALE, NOT CHARITY

To some, Dr Pauldy Otermans may seem like a motivational figure. To me, she is a systems builder. When I sat down with her and my co-author for the podcast, what struck me immediately was not the warmth of the conversation, although there was plenty of that. What struck me was the precision. Every answer she gave circled back to scale, to structure, to the mechanics of how you actually get learning into the hands of people who have been locked out of it.

> *I was always very passionate about helping other people learn,*

she told me, and you could hear it in the way she spoke. But this was not passion in the abstract. This was passion that had been operationalised. Pauldy is a neuroscientist and psychologist by training. She is the founder and CEO of the Otermans Institute for AI, which launched in 2021 to develop digital human teachers. She developed the language model used in Teddy AI, an educational tool designed for children aged four to seven. She has served as a topic editor at *Frontiers in AI*, focusing on conversational AI in higher education. She has received significant recognition in the United Kingdom for her work in AI and education. But when she spoke to me, she did not lead with any of this. She led with the problem.

> *We were representing the 15,000 students on the campus... we could already make a bigger impact,*

she explained, describing the moment her thinking shifted from the individual to the institutional. And then, with the same calm directness she maintained throughout the entire conversation, she named the thing that made scale not just desirable but urgent.

With the digital divide, these things have only become worse.

This is what separates a systems builder from a motivational speaker. Pauldy does not talk about changing lives one at a time. She talks about infrastructure. She talks about what happens when you design a system that can meet 15,000 people where they are, on their devices, in their own time, without requiring them to travel, pay, or perform confidence they do not yet have. The point is not prestige. The point is implementation.

The wider research bears this out. Caparo and colleagues (2024) have noted that generative AI has the potential to both 'exacerbate and ameliorate' socioeconomic inequalities, particularly in education. Personalisation is possible, but so is a deepening of the digital divide. The question is not whether the technology can do these things. It is who builds it, for whom, and under what constraints. Pauldy is not building a future. She is building a bridge over a gap that already exists.

WHAT IS THE GAP, REALLY

I want to stay with the word employability for a moment because I think we misuse it constantly. We talk about 'the skills gap' as though it is a neutral description of reality, as though some people simply lack skills and other people have them, and if we could just train the first group to be more like the second, the problem would be solved. But that framing hides something important. Employability is not a skills problem. It is an access problem. And the access it depends on is not just financial. It is social, it is emotional, and it is deeply tied to power.

Think about what it actually takes to be 'work ready' in the way that employers demand. You need to know how to write a CV that follows conventions no one explicitly teaches you. You need to understand the components of a cover letter. You need to be able to sit through an interview without freezing, without stumbling, without the anxiety that comes from knowing that a single bad answer could cost you a chance you waited months to get. You need communication skills, but not the kind you learn from textbooks. The kind you learn from being in rooms where those skills are modelled, practised, and gently corrected. You need goal setting, teamwork exercises, granular feedback delivered step by step.

Pauldy's system teaches all of this.

> *Our AI could run mock interviews with learners,*

she told me, and when she said it, I understood that she was not talking about gamification or chatbot gimmicks. She was talking about giving people a space to rehearse the single most stressful interaction in their professional lives, and to do so without anyone watching, without anyone judging, without anyone reporting back.

> *All of that whole thing is done in a safe space,*

she spoke.

> *You're not feeling judged. No one is reporting this to anyone.*

That line stayed with me for days. Because it names something we rarely admit when we talk about skills and training and workforce development. Most inequity is social penalty. People do not avoid learning because they are lazy. They avoid learning because learning publicly is humiliating when you do not already know the rules. The person who has never written a cover letter does not want to sit in a classroom and admit that. The person who freezes in interviews does not want to practise in front of a group. The person who comes from a background where no one went to university, where no one had a LinkedIn profile, where no one knew how to explain what transferable skills meant that person does not lack intelligence. They lack the rehearsal space that everyone else took for granted.

Research on AI's impact on society, the economy, and management reinforces this. AI's impacts are not solely positive. There is a recognised need to adapt skills, mitigate errors, and ensure ethical and fair implementation across institutions. Governments and businesses are called upon to invest in reskilling and to develop standards and regulations. But if we are serious about empowerment, reskilling cannot mean corporate training portals designed for people who already know how to navigate digital platforms. It has to mean access under real constraints. Access for the person earning a little each day who cannot afford data. Access for the mother who has 30 minutes between shifts. Access for the young person who has never been told that they have something to offer.

Empowerment starts where embarrassment ends.

PERSONALISATION IS THE EQUITY MECHANISM

When Pauldy talks about her AI, she always comes back to the same word. Personalisation.

The primary goal of AI is personalisation

she spoke. And at first that might sound like a feature, like something you would find on a product page between 'user-friendly interface' and 'real-time analytics'. But the way Pauldy uses the word is different. For her, personalisation is not a feature. It is the equity mechanism. It is the thing that makes learning fair. For my generation, personalisation is something we associate with targeted ads and curated feeds. Pauldy reframed it completely. Personalisation is not a product feature. It is the equity mechanism. If a system cannot adapt to the person, it reproduces the hierarchy it claims to dismantle.

'Each and every human is a unique individual… the way they learn is different', she explained. This is something every educator knows but almost no system accounts for. When you have 30 children in a classroom, you cannot tailor your teaching to each one. 'In a lot of countries, it can be 100, 200', Pauldy added, and the impossibility of individual attention at that scale is not a failure of the teacher. It is a failure of the system. One teacher, 200 learners, and a curriculum designed for an imaginary average student who does not exist.

What Pauldy's AI does is fundamentally change the direction of learning. 'With our AI, it becomes two ways. You can practice while you're learning'. Traditional education is largely one directional. Someone stands at the front and speaks, and everyone else sits and listens. If you understand, good. If you do not, you are expected to raise your hand and ask for help, which requires exactly the kind of confidence that marginalised learners are least likely to have. The two-way model flips this. The learner engages, the system responds, the learner tries again, and the system adapts. There is no audience. There is no performance. There is only practice.

My Mum, who joined Pauldy in our conversation, articulated the missing piece with clarity. The people who fall through the gaps are not the people who lack talent or ambition. They are the people who do not have someone to introduce them, guide them, or explain the little cues. The unwritten codes of professional life. When to make eye contact. How to follow up after a meeting. What to wear to an interview when nobody has ever told you what business casual actually means. AI, in this specific and disciplined form, can begin to level that playing field. Not by replacing human connection, but by providing the rehearsal space that human connection was never evenly distributed enough to offer.

I find myself thinking about this in three layers. First, personalisation addresses individual difference. Every learner is different, and a system that adapts to each one is inherently more just than a system that treats them as identical. Second, practice addresses confidence. You cannot build confidence without repetition, and you cannot have repetition without a space that permits failure. Third, privacy addresses fear. Human-led support, no matter how well intentioned, depends on a person's confidence to book it, their ability to travel, their access to money, and their willingness to be vulnerable in front of another person. AI reduces the barriers created by scheduling, proximity, cost, and social confidence.

Once you accept personalisation as the goal, you are forced to confront infrastructure. Because personalisation means nothing if the person you are trying to reach cannot access the system in the first place.

INFRASTRUCTURE HUMILITY AND THE TEACHER IN YOUR POCKET

This is the section of the chapter where everything becomes concrete. Where the ideas stop being conceptual and start being operational. Because when Pauldy said the sentence that follows, I genuinely felt the ground shift beneath the conversation.

We can run our AI without the internet.

She let that land for a moment and then explained. 'It's called Edge AI'. The concept is deceptively simple. You need internet connectivity to download the application. Once it is on your device, the internet can be switched off. The model runs locally on the phone itself. There is no dependency on a stable connection. There is no data streaming to a server. The learning happens on the device, in the learner's hands, wherever they are.

And then came the detail that made this real for me. 'We're not talking laptops… it's mobile first'. Pauldy was not designing for the environments that technology companies typically design for. She was not assuming a desk, a reliable broadband connection, or a household with multiple devices. She was designing for the world as it actually is for billions of people. A world where there is one smartphone in the family. Where internet is expensive. Where people earning a small amount, each day cannot afford to spend it on data. 'There is a smartphone in the family', she said. 'Everyone can learn with that device… they can have their own account'.

We call it the teacher in your pocket.

We discussed how families in some communities gather around a single device to learn together, moving from the way previous generations gathered around a radio, then a television, and now a smartphone, I could see it. Not as a speculative future, but as something that was already happening. A grandmother and a teenager sharing a screen. A parent watching their child practise interview questions and then having a go themselves. This is not a Silicon Valley pitch deck. This is a real adoption pattern, grounded in the material conditions of communities where sharing is not a limitation but a way of life.

What I want to name explicitly here is that Edge AI is a political design decision. It is not just a technical feature. The choice to run AI on the device rather than in the cloud changes everything about who the system serves. It changes who can access the system, because it removes the dependency on constant connectivity. It changes where access happens, because it is no longer tethered to a location with Wi-Fi. It changes what it costs, because it eliminates ongoing data charges. It changes how privacy works, because data never needs to leave the device. And most importantly, it changes whether empowerment is dependent on stable infrastructure or whether it can exist independently of it.

Most AI products are designed for environments where infrastructure is assumed. Where bandwidth is abundant, electricity is uninterrupted, and the user has a laptop, a desk, and a quiet room. Pauldy's design begins from the opposite premise. What if none of that is true? What if the person you are trying to reach has intermittent electricity, a shared phone, no data plan, and 40 minutes before they need to leave for work? If the system cannot function under those conditions, then it is not an empowerment system. It is a product for people who were already empowered.

Once AI is on the device, the next question becomes data, privacy, and power.

DATA, PRIVACY, AND THE FEEDBACK LOOP

One of the things that has always bothered me about the way we talk about AI and empowerment is the assumption that empowerment stops at the individual. As though giving one person a better CV or a more confident interview technique is the endpoint. It is not. Individual uplift without structural change is self-help dressed as justice. And Pauldy knows this.

'When you run it on your device, your personal and sensitive data no longer needs to leave that device. So, it also improves data privacy'. This is the first half of the equation, and it matters enormously. In a world where data extraction is the default business model, designing a system where sensitive information stays on the user's phone is a radical choice. But Pauldy does not stop there.

The second half is where empowerment becomes structural. 'If you make policy changes... and if they're based on data, we often see there is a better outcome because you have more evidence... and you can make a bigger impact'. What she described to me was a feedback loop. Individual learners practise privately on their devices. The system observes, in aggregate, where learners are getting stuck, what skills are lacking across communities, what friction points repeat themselves. That aggregated information, stripped of personal identifiers, can then be fed back to governments and institutions to inform policy, resource allocation, and direct support such as hardware and tools.

The contrast with traditional methods is significant. 'Normally that data collected is done by a pen and paper... that will take months, years', Pauldy explained. By the time a pen and paper survey has been collected, processed, analysed, and turned into a report, the community it describes has already moved on. The problems have deepened. The people have adapted or given up. Digital systems can compress that timeline from years to weeks, and in doing so, they make evidence actionable rather than historical.

There is also a labour market dimension. Pauldy described how the system can create learner profiles and feed them to potential local employers, widening visibility for people who would otherwise never appear on a recruiter's radar. This is not surveillance. This is not a predictive system that scores individuals and ranks them by risk. This is a system that makes invisible capability visible to the institutions that need to see it.

I want to spell out the empowerment loop as I understand it, because it mirrors something I think about constantly in my own work. The individual learns and practises privately. The system observes aggregated friction points across the community. Those insights guide policy and resource allocation. Better policy and resources improve conditions. Improved conditions open opportunity and improve labour market matching. Information is power, but only when it is structured and returned as action.

If empowerment is about agency, then co-creation is not optional. It is the foundation.

CO-CREATING AI WITH COMMUNITIES

This is where the chapter needs to go wider than Pauldy's work, because the question she is answering; how do you build AI that genuinely empowers communities, is not a question she is answering alone. It is a question that an entire field is wrestling with, and the research on Community Citizen Science (CCS) offers one of the most honest frameworks I have found.

Hsu and colleagues (2024) have articulated what many practitioners feel but struggle to name. There is an underexplored question at the heart of AI development: can AI systems designed for general tasks actually work in different regional contexts while empowering local people? CCS, as they define it, is place based and multi-stakeholder. It involves communities not as passive beneficiaries of technology but as active participants in its design, deployment, and evaluation. They define community empowerment as yielding agency so that communities can use technology, data, and informed rhetoric to create evidence for policy and social change.

Hsu and colleagues (2024) outline three major challenges in this space. The first is co-designing AI systems with local communities, which means moving beyond consultation into genuine shared decision-making. The second is collecting and explaining community data using AI, which requires transparency not just about what the data says but about how the AI reached its conclusions. The third is adapting AI systems to long-term social changes, which demand humility about the fact that communities are not static, and neither should be the systems designed to serve them.

There is also a tension that the research names directly, and it is one I recognise from my own work. Scientists want papers and rigorous research cycles. Communities want urgent social change. These timelines are not naturally aligned, and pretending they are leads to frustration on both sides. The field has to hold this tension honestly rather than resolving it by defaulting to the priorities of whichever group holds more institutional power.

The case studies in the CCS literature show what is possible when this tension is held well. In Pittsburgh, the Smell Pittsburgh project used citizen odour reports combined with machine learning to reveal pollution patterns, making invisible environmental harm visible to public scrutiny and debate. In another project, RISE enabled citizens to annotate industrial smoke emissions, building a dataset that supported enforcement action against polluters. In

Barcelona, the xAire project co-designed nitrogen dioxide data collection with schools and communities, connecting air quality analysis to asthma cases and creating public communication materials that enabled understanding rather than panic. And Mosquito Alert built a community generated mosquito dataset that supported a public health agency in managing disease risk.

What connects all of these examples is a shared architecture of empowerment. Place-based constraints are respected. Device and infrastructure realism shapes the design. Community members are not just data sources but co-creators. And the aggregated insights are used as evidence for policy change, not as surveillance tools.

Pauldy's model mirrors this architecture even though her domain is employability rather than environmental science. She works within place-based constraints. She designs for device and infrastructure realism. She treats learning as community capability rather than individual deficit. And she feeds aggregated insights back into policy loops. The domain is different. The principles are the same.

Co-creation is the difference between AI deployed to communities and AI built with communities.

BIAS, GOVERNANCE, AND THE WESTERN MODEL PROBLEM

The bias patterns established in earlier chapters take a specific form in education. Pauldy was unflinching about this. 'AI is biased', she said. There was no hedging. 'If the data often is human-made, and we all have bias… there will be bias'. In education, that bias determines who gets to learn and how.

'If the data often is human-made, and we all have bias… there will be bias'. This is the structural problem that no amount of optimism can bypass. AI systems are trained on data produced by humans, and humans carry bias into everything they produce. The datasets reflect the world as it has been, not the world as we want it to be. And when those datasets come from particular contexts, they carry the assumptions of those contexts into every output.

Pauldy was particularly direct about the geographic dimension of this problem. 'They are very westernised models. So, it's inherently biased... The AI is unfortunately still very... male westernised'. This matters enormously for a system designed to empower communities in the Global South, in under-resourced regions, in contexts where the cultural norms around work, communication, family, and learning are fundamentally different from those embedded in Silicon Valley training data. An AI system trained predominantly on Western professional norms will teach Western professional norms, and it will do so confidently, without flagging that its advice is culturally situated rather than universal.

What I found reassuring about Pauldy's approach is that she does not pretend this problem can be eliminated. Instead, she builds for mitigation. 'We have a lot of flagging systems', she told me. 'Red flags. Human in the loop. Regular checks'. She described a governance architecture that accepts bias as a permanent feature of AI systems and designs continuous mechanisms for catching it, naming it, and reducing its impact. The goal is not a bias free system, because that does not exist. The goal is a system that is honest about its limitations and has human oversight embedded at every level.

'AI literacy is going to be key', she said, and this was not a throwaway comment. It was a governance principle. Because, the danger is not just that AI systems are biased. The danger is that people take the outputs of biased systems at face value without knowing where the information comes from, how it was generated, or what assumptions it carries. Uncritical reliance on AI outputs is not empowerment. It is a new form of dependence. And if we are not building literacy alongside tools, we are simply replacing one form of exclusion with another.

Kranzberg's Law, cited by Caparo and colleagues (2024), puts it precisely: technology is neither good nor bad, nor is it neutral. Edge AI can distribute access, but it can also distribute bias faster and further than any centralised system. The same infrastructure that allows a learner in a rural community to practise interview skills on their phone can also embed Western professional norms so deeply into the interaction that the learner never questions whether those norms are relevant to their context. Design without governance is not empowerment. It is automation.

Towards the end of our conversation, Pauldy spoke about hiring and what she looks for when she meets candidates. 'Seeing the potential in every human being, regardless of their background', she said. 'Try to not look at any of these and talk to the human being. Training can always be provided'. It was a quiet statement, but it carried the full weight of her argument. Empowerment is not just a learning tool. It is a hiring philosophy. It is an institutional disposition. It is a willingness to look past the proxies we use for competence, the degree, the postcode, the accent, and to see the person.

If we do not govern empowerment systems, we will automate exclusion and call it progress.

WHAT EMPOWERING COMMUNITIES WITH AI ACTUALLY REQUIRES

'AI isn't magic', Pauldy told me. 'The product should always aim to solve the problem that you're trying to solve'. And then, with the precision that defined our entire conversation, she asked the question that should be asked of every AI system ever built. 'What problem are they actually solving?'

If I have learned anything from this conversation, from the research, and from the communities I have worked alongside, it is that empowering communities with AI requires principles you can defend under pressure. Not aspirations. Not brand values. Principles.

The first is to design for constraints, not demos. If the system assumes stable internet, a laptop, and a quiet room, it is not an empowerment system. Edge AI is the exemplar here. Design for the person with the shared phone, the intermittent power, the 40 minutes before the next shift.

The second is to treat personalisation as the equity lever. If learning is one way, it reproduces hierarchy. Practice while learning, two-way interaction, adaptive feedback. These are not features. They are conditions of fairness.

The third is to build safe space into the product itself. No reporting. No judgement. Repeatable rehearsal. If a learner cannot fail privately, they will not try at all.

The fourth is that human in the loop governance is not optional. Flagging systems, red flags, regular checks, and a team that takes bias as seriously as they take functionality. This is not a compliance exercise. It is an ethical commitment.

The fifth is to build literacy alongside tools. AI literacy must be treated as a public capability, not a private advantage. If people do not understand what they are interacting with, they cannot make informed choices about it.

The sixth is that empowerment must scale into policy feedback. Aggregated insights, collected faster than pen and paper, returned to governments and institutions to influence resources. Individual learning is necessary but insufficient. The system must connect individual experience to structural change.

And the seventh, which may be the most important of all, is to co-create rather than extract. The CCS framework names this directly. Yield agency. Build evidence for social change. Design with communities, not for them. The difference is not semantic. It is the difference between empowerment and deployment.

I keep returning to the sentence Pauldy gave me at the beginning of our conversation. 'AI is a tool that can be used to solve the problem. AI itself is not the solution to the problem'. That distinction is everything. The solution is human. The solution is a mother learning interview skills on a shared phone while her children sleep. The solution is a young person in a community with no careers service practising a cover letter without anyone watching. The solution is a government receiving aggregated evidence about where learning is failing and having the courage to act on it. The solution is a hiring manager who looks past the CV and sees the person. AI can support all of this. But it cannot replace any of it.

AI for equity is about humans first. It always has been.

OVER TO YOU

Explore Further: A Prompt for Your AI Assistant

Copy this prompt into your AI assistant of choice, photograph it, or visit the websites in our author biographies to access all 13 prompts in copyable format.

> *I've just read AI for Equity by Jenny Garrett OBE and Leah-Sunshine Garrett, specifically about Dr Pauldy Otermans's Edge AI – technology that works without the internet, on a shared smartphone, in low connectivity communities – and her concept of the teacher in your pocket. Please help me reflect: 1) Where do access and infrastructure assumptions shape my own work and thinking? 2) Are the systems I use or build designed for the person with the fewest resources, or the most? 3) What would it look like to co-create with communities rather than designing for them? 4) How could aggregated learning data from my context inform policy change? Please ask about my context so this is relevant to me.*

This prompt turns AI into a community design partner, helping you examine the infrastructure assumptions that determine who your work actually reaches.

Three Coaching Questions for Reflection

Take time to consider these questions, either in personal reflection or in discussion with friends, colleagues, or study groups:

1. The Constraint Question. What systems in your life assume resources you have, and what would it mean to design those systems for the person who does not have them? Think about the AI tools in your organisation. Do they assume stable internet, a laptop, and a quiet room? Who is excluded by those assumptions?
2. The Safe Space Question. Pauldy's system works because learners can fail privately. Think about the

training and development systems in your organisation. Can people practise without being watched, without being scored, and without the results being reported? If not, who is most likely to avoid engaging, and what does that cost them?

3. The Feedback Question. Individual learning is necessary but insufficient. Pauldy's system connects individual experience to policy change through aggregated data. Think about the data your organisation collects about the people it serves. Does that data travel upward to influence decisions? Or does it sit in a report that no one reads?

REFERENCES

Capraro, V., Lentsch, A., Acemoglu, D., Akgun, S., Akhmedova, A., Bilancini, E., Bonnefon, J.-F., Brañas-Garza, P., Butera, L., Douglas, K. M., Everett, J. A. C., Gigerenzer, G., Greenhow, C., Hashimoto, D. A., Holt-Lunstad, J., Jetten, J., Johnson, S., Longoni, C., Lunn, P., … Viale, R. (2024). The impact of generative artificial intelligence on socioeconomic inequalities and policy making. *PNAS Nexus*, *3*(6), 191. https://doi.org/10.1093/pnasnexus/pgae191

Hsu, A. et al. (2024). Community citizen science: AI co-designed with communities for social change. *Nature Machine Intelligence*.

FURTHER READING

Otermans, P. (2025). *Interviewed by J. Garrett and L. Garrett for AI for Equity Podcast, Series One.*

10

DISMANTLING SOCIO-ECONOMIC BARRIERS WITH AI: ACCESS, REDISTRIBUTION, AND THE DIFFERENCE BETWEEN THEM

In conversation with: Sam Samarasinghe, Founder, Delenta | Anna Jones, Founder, RefuAid and Merit

> *If the only thing we're doing at scale is providing access, then that's also okay with us. Jones (2025)*

Sam and Anna didn't wait for permission. They saw a gap, felt the urgency, and built something. As a young woman building her own business, Leah-Sunshine knows what it costs to bet on yourself – and what it makes possible. Purpose and passion in heaps. She couldn't not write this chapter. – **Jenny**

There is something about the word uplift that makes me sit up straight. It is an old word, a heavy word, and when it is used carelessly, it can feel like performance. But when Sam Samarasinghe said it during our podcast, he meant something precise: technology secondary. People first. That distinction, it turns out, is the entire argument of this chapter.

Sam is a technologist. He is also a migrant, a father, and someone who left corporate life after nearly two decades of leading digital transformation projects across three continents. He told me he sees this as an extension of a chain: parenting, then teaching, then, if you are fortunate, a good boss who helps you grow. Coaching, to him, was the next link. And he built Delenta, the platform he now runs from the United Kingdom, to make that link accessible across 27 countries.

Anna Jones came at the same question from an entirely different direction. She was working in a law firm when the photograph of Aylan Kurdi, a three-year-old boy face down on a Turkish beach, appeared on the front page of every newspaper in Britain. She connected with a woman called Tamsin through a Facebook post that said simply: I need to do more. A surgeon named Luke suggested they meet for a coffee. Within weeks, they had organised a volunteer medical trip to Lesbos, arriving before any NGOs or government response had mobilised.

What changed Jones's life was not the horror. It was the conversations. The people arriving did not want charity. They wanted, resoundingly, somewhere safe and private to live, to be able to get their kids into school, and to be able to support their families. And yet the response that mobilised was to put people in camps, take away their independence, force them into a dependency model.

I recognised something in both their stories because it mirrored a logic I had been circling in my own work. When I started building Dawn, I did not begin with a product roadmap or a pitch deck. I began with a question about who was being harmed and whether anyone was paying attention. Sam and Anna both began the same way. Not with technology. With people. And that starting point shapes everything that follows.

THE INEQUALITY AI ENTERS

Before we talk about dismantling, we have to name what stands. Not vaguely, not optimistically, but precisely.

Learning poverty, the term used to describe children unable to read and understand a simple text by age 10, reached an estimated 70% in low- and middle-income countries in 2022, following the disruption of COVID-19 (World Bank, 2022). The latest World Bank Global Findex data reports approximately 1.4 billion unbanked adults globally. That number represents people who are not just excluded from banking services but excluded from the infrastructure through which modern economies distribute opportunity: credit, insurance, savings, and the digital identity systems that increasingly gate access to housing, employment, and education.

A joint UNICEF and International Telecommunication Union (2020) report estimated that 2.2 billion children and young people under the age of 25 lacked home internet access, including roughly 1.3 billion who had no internet at all. Access is not a feature. It is a precondition. And for billions of people, the precondition is missing.

Sam's instinct about this was sharp. When he talked about his users, he was careful. Technology secondary, he said, plainly and without elaboration. It was a single sentence, almost a footnote in our conversation, but it carried the weight of everything he had learned building a platform across countries where connectivity, digital literacy, and institutional support varied wildly.

Anna saw the same structural exclusion from the other side. Jones returned to the United Kingdom and founded RefuAid. First, she built a language programme in partnership with private English language schools to get refugees to qualification stage. Then, she discovered the re-accreditation barrier: anyone qualified in a career overseas needs to sit exams and obtain licences in the United Kingdom to prove equivalence. That costs between 6,000 and 16,000 pounds. For professionals who have fled with nothing, the barrier is not competence. It is money.

So, she started lending money. Not grants. Loans. Interest-free, built on trust and the understanding that people who have rebuilt their lives from nothing are not credit risks. They are among the most motivated borrowers in existence. To date, RefuAid has lent just under three million pounds, with a repayment rate of 98.6%.

Sit with that number. In a financial system that routinely denies credit to refugees because they lack a UK credit history, a small organisation led by a former law firm employee has achieved a repayment rate that most high-street banks would envy. The innovation was not an algorithm. It was a different set of assumptions about who people are.

WHEN AI MEETS THE ACCESS GAP

Jones's most recent innovation is an AI tool called Path, available at path.refuaid.org. It is the distillation of everything RefuAid learned in nine years of working with displaced professionals.

The problem Path solves is information. Refugees re-accrediting into UK careers are inundated with inaccurate or irrelevant guidance. Jones described a pattern she had seen repeatedly: someone applies to do a master's degree in education because that is what a university has accepted them onto, when what they actually need to return to work as a teacher is a PGCE. They complete the master's, accumulate 20,000 pounds of debt, and then discover they need a different qualification entirely.

Path asks users to enter their background, career history, qualifications, and goals. It then builds a tailored pathway setting out the exact steps needed to re-accredit and return to their professional level. It includes Raffi, a chatbot built on an existing large language model with RefuAid's own data layered on top, so users can ask follow-up questions about missing documents, failed exams, or alternative routes.

Jones is candid about what Path does and does not do. It does no more now, she told us, than if you were paying the maximum subscription to one of the top LLMs. But most people we work with cannot afford that maximum subscription. If the only thing we are doing at scale is providing access, then that is also okay with us.

If Path addresses the information barrier, Merit addresses the financial one. Currently in testing, Merit is an AI-powered lending platform that does something most financial systems are not designed to do: assess creditworthiness based on context rather than convention. Traditional credit scoring relies on fixed addresses, years of UK banking history, and employment records. These metrics work well for people who have grown up within the system. They fail entirely for anyone who has not.

Merit uses what Jones calls alternative data metrics. Having been lent for re-accreditation for nine years, RefuAid knows that just because somebody is not in employment today does not mean they are not creditworthy. Do you have any qualifications? Are you looking at getting some? Are you looking at returning to that level of employment? It builds a financial picture based on the person's context and constructs a lending response around their potential rather than their history.

The connection to the patterns explored in Chapter 6 is immediate. Research on women's progress in the workplace consistently shows that women are promoted on track record while men are promoted on potential. What Jones has built is a system that assesses everyone on potential. It is, quietly, one of the most radical applications of AI in this book.

FINANCIAL INCLUSION: PREDICTIVE ACCURACY IS NOT JUSTICE

Jones's work sits within a global landscape that makes it both urgent and instructive. AI offers a plausible route into financial inclusion. The strongest evidence comes from alternative-data credit scoring, particularly where formal credit histories are thin or missing. A major study using digital footprint data from a large German e-commerce lender, covering over 250,000 observations, found that combining digital footprints with traditional credit bureau data increased the area under the receiver operating characteristic curve, meaning the model was better at distinguishing who would repay.

On the surface, this looks like straightforward progress. More data, more inclusion. But political economy warns against confusing predictive accuracy with justice. A widely cited study of mortgage lending found that both face-to-face and fintech lenders charged higher rates to minority borrowers, even after controlling for creditworthiness. The bias was not in the model. It was in the institution deploying it.

Credit scoring systems categorise people into risk classes. Better data does not automatically mean fairer outcomes. The philosopher Michel Foucault argued that classification systems don't just describe the world – they shape it, sorting people into categories that determine what they can and cannot access. Credit scoring does exactly this. A person who was previously invisible to the system – unscored, neither approved nor denied – may now be seen for the first time. But being seen and being helped are not the same thing. If the system sees you only to place you in a high-risk category and turn you down, you are worse off than before. You have gone from being overlooked to being explicitly refused. Visibility without power is not inclusion. It is surveillance.

Sam's insistence on trust becomes structural in this context. Trust is most important, he said. Not innovation, not accuracy, not speed. Trust. And trust cannot be automated. It is built through consistency, transparency, and a willingness to be accountable when things go wrong.

Jones echoed this from her own experience. Every person who receives a loan still has a video interview with a team member. Major decisions are soundboarded with the people who have been lent to. The team remains deeply involved with the community it serves. No matter what happens, she told us, we are never going to remove ourselves from the need. As soon as organisations grow and you lose touch with your why, decisions start to get convoluted and made for the wrong thing.

EDUCATION: WHERE AI HAS MEASURABLE IMPACT

I want to be careful here. Education is the section of this chapter where the evidence is strongest, and it would be easy to let the numbers do the talking without interrogating what they actually mean.

The most rigorous causal result I found comes from a randomised evaluation of a personalised, technology-aided after-school programme in urban India, conducted by Muralidharan et al. (2019). Students who won the lottery to attend gained approximately 0.37 standard deviations in Maths and 0.23 in Hindi after only four and a half months. A meta-analysis of personalised and adaptive learning technology across 16 randomised controlled trials, covering 53,029 learners aged 6–15 in low- and middle-income countries, found an overall effect size of roughly 0.18. Importantly, the effects were larger for the most disadvantaged learners.

But the picture gets more complicated when generative AI enters the frame. A large randomised trial with 2,440 secondary students found that a curriculum-tailored chatbot improved immediate learning by 0.126 standard deviations, while a generic chatbot had no effect and may have harmed weaker students. Human tutors still outperformed both conditions. The message is clear: design matters more than capability, and the people most at risk are those for whom poorly designed AI replaces human contact rather than supplementing it.

The access gap Jones identified in financial services has a direct parallel in education. Dr Pauldy Otermans, whose work we explored in Chapter 9, has addressed this at scale. Her AI-supported tools have trained over 35,000 learners across 13 countries, many in communities where internet connectivity cannot be guaranteed. The convergence of Jones's and Otermans's work reveals a pattern. In both cases, the AI is not replacing human support. It is extending its reach to people who currently receive none.

Sam mirrored this in the way he talked about matching coaches with clients. It is very hard, he said, carefully. It is a human experience. He was not dismissing technology. He was acknowledging its limits. The coaching relationship, like the teaching relationship, depends on something that adaptive algorithms approximate but do not replicate: the capacity to read a person's unspoken needs and respond to the whole of them, not just their data.

POVERTY TARGETING AND THE LIMITS OF STATE CAPACITY

One of the most compelling demonstrations of AI's potential in this space comes from satellite imagery. A study published in Science used convolutional neural networks to analyse publicly available satellite data from five African countries and found that night time light intensity, combined with daytime imagery, could predict local wealth distribution with surprising accuracy. The approach bypasses the need for expensive household surveys entirely, offering governments and aid organisations a way to see poverty at a resolution that traditional methods cannot match.

But the most instructive evaluation comes from Togo. During the COVID-19 pandemic, Togo needed to deliver cash transfers rapidly to those most in need. Using survey data to train a machine-learning model on mobile phone data, the approach reduced exclusion errors by 4–12 percentage points compared to existing methods. That is a meaningful improvement. But the researchers also found that the model's accuracy depended heavily on the quality of the underlying data infrastructure. Where mobile phone coverage was thin, the model was less accurate. Where population registries were incomplete, targeting errors persisted.

The pattern is consistent with everything Sam and Anna have shown us. AI can fill gaps in state capacity, but it cannot substitute for the institutions that make those gaps manageable. The satellite can see poverty. It cannot build the roads, the clinics, or the appeal pathways that turn visibility into action. The mobile phone model can identify who needs a cash transfer. It cannot ensure the transfer reaches them if the banking infrastructure does not exist. AI's promise is the greatest where institutions are the strongest. The question is what happens in the spaces where institutions are the thinnest.

COMPUTER SAYS NO

Jones told us a story that captures the recruitment dimension of socio-economic exclusion with painful precision. RefuAid regularly partnered with large employers to run employability days and CV workshops for their clients. The events went well. The employers were impressed. The candidates were inspiring. And then, time and time again, their clients would apply and get nowhere.

The reason was not human prejudice, at least not directly. It was the automated HR systems that had been configured to reject any CV with a gap of two or three years. The computer said no. Not because the person was unqualified, but because the system could not process a life that did not fit its template.

Jones sees AI as the solution to the problem that earlier technology created. If AI is doing it right, she told us, it might ask more questions. If we build this contextual piece into it, it might go back to the applicant and say: we have noticed a two-year gap on your CV. Could you give us a bit more information?

Any recruiter who understands the agency it has taken, the resilience it has taken to leave your home, travel across the world, rebuild your life, find safety, is going to recognise that as a skill that you are bringing to the workplace.

The same principle applies beyond refugee recruitment. Women returning to the workforce after caring responsibilities face the same algorithmic rejection. People who have experienced illness, who have taken career breaks to care for ageing parents, who have retrained in mid-life. The bias in automated systems is not against refugees specifically. It is against anyone whose life does not follow a linear, uninterrupted, institutionally legible path. And that, as the data-origin bias explored in Chapter 3 confirms, is a design choice, not an inevitability.

PLATFORM POWER AND THE LABOUR MARKET

Sam supports coaches across 27 countries. The coaching profession, as a labour market segment, is often freelance, often female-dominated, often precarious, and often digitally mediated. It is a useful test case for whether AI platforms expand capability or extract value.

Platformisation can go either way. It can extract rents through lock-in, creating dependency on proprietary systems that become more expensive to leave the longer you stay. Or it can reduce fragmentation, lower transaction costs, and connect supply to demand in ways that benefit the individual practitioner. The question, as always, is governance.

We always validate those ideas with the community, Sam told me. In practice, it meant his platform was shaped by the people using it, including coaches with accessibility needs, coaches with ADHD, coaches who are visually impaired navigating the product in ways his team had never anticipated. He was not presenting this as a triumph of inclusive design. He was describing the minimum viable ethics of building for humans.

More telling was his attitude to dependency. What you are doing with the notebook and a spreadsheet, if it works, perfect. That sentence resists forced adoption. He was refusing to create dependency where none was necessary.

I find this particular tension instructive because it plays out at every scale. The gig economy promised flexibility and delivered dependency. Social media promised connection and delivered extraction. AI platforms promise to open up access and may end up simply becoming the new middleman – taking value from the very people they claim to be helping. The difference, in every case, comes down to whether the platform is accountable to its users or to its investors.

DEMOCRATISATION IS NOT REDISTRIBUTION

AI discourse uses the word democratisation with extraordinary frequency and almost no precision. Lower marginal cost access to a tool is not the same thing as redistribution of power. Adaptive tutoring expands capability. Credit scoring expands access. But neither alters the ownership structures, the governance norms, or the distribution of returns that determine who benefits and who does not.

Thomas Piketty's central insight remains relevant. When the rate of return on capital exceeds the rate of economic growth, wealth concentrates. Technology accelerates productivity, but productivity gains flow disproportionately to those who own the technology, not to those who use it. AI is no exception. The companies building the most powerful models are capturing the most value. The communities using those models to solve local problems are not capturing value at all. They are renting access.

Sam resisted techno-determinism in the most straightforward way possible. When asked about the myth he most wanted to dispel, he did not hesitate. AI is going to eliminate humanity, he said.

I personally believe that is not going to happen. He reframed AI as augmentation, not replacement. But making existing tools more powerful does not automatically close the gap between those who have access and those who don't. If the coaches who benefit most from AI-powered platforms are those who already have digital literacy, marketing skill, and client networks, the platform widens the gap between the established and the emerging.

Jones's frustration came from the other direction. I have a frustration with charities not embracing AI, she told us. I understand why there are concerns. But it is also possible, and we have seen so many times how bias and preconceptions, whether deliberate or not, and people's own biases that they bring into hiring and the damage that has. AI can change all of that. It can massively level the playing field.

She cites Mustafa Suleyman's work as a touchstone. AI is just another tool in our toolbox, she says. Whatever we build, it is a tool. It is only there to help us achieve our mission. Our mission has not changed. We are not AI, and AI is not us. It is what we are using to help more people.

TRUST AS POLITICAL INFRASTRUCTURE

Trust cannot be built in a few months, Sam told me. It is a relationship that you have with what you do, who you associate, how you respond to those things. He was describing the operational reality of building a platform that people rely on for their livelihood. Every decision, every update, every change in terms and conditions is a test of whether the builder still deserves the trust of the user.

Robert Putnam's social capital theory helps explain why this matters beyond the individual transaction. Institutional trust correlates with stronger civic and economic outcomes. Communities with higher social capital have better public health, lower crime, and more effective governance. AI systems that undermine trust, through opaque decision-making, unexplained rejections, or sudden changes in algorithmic behaviour, do not just harm individual users. They erode the social infrastructure that makes collective action possible.

Sam extended his argument about trust into territory that surprised me. Have some values that you feel that you can demonstrate to your parents one day, your kids too, he said. And you can all be proud by being that person. It was a generational statement. He was talking about legacy, not metrics. About building something your children would not be ashamed of.

I think about this often in my own work with Dawn. When I build systems that surface patterns for institutions, I am asking those institutions to trust the data, trust the design, and trust the restraint of the people who built it. That trust is not given. It is earned through transparency, through limits, through the willingness to say: this is what the system does and this is what it does not do.

WHAT DISMANTLING ACTUALLY REQUIRES

AI dismantles socio-economic barriers only under specific conditions. It must expand real capabilities in the sense Amartya Sen intended, not just access to tools but the substantive freedom to convert those tools into outcomes. It must recognise the unequal starting positions that Piketty's data describes, and it must be overseen by institutions with enough independence to hold the powerful accountable – not ones that end up serving the very industries they were meant to keep in check.

Neither Sam nor Anna named these theorists. Neither needed to. Sam started with people, not products. He validated with the community, not focus groups. He reduced switching costs instead of exploiting them. He told me that the people using notebooks and spreadsheets were doing just fine, and if his platform could not improve on that, it had no right to exist.

Anna started with a photograph and a Facebook post. She lent money when nobody else would. She built an AI tool that does no more than what a premium subscription could provide but provides it to people who cannot afford the subscription. She kept every lending decision tied to a human conversation. She refused to grow faster than her relationship with the community could sustain.

That is the tension that gives this chapter its weight. Two builders, both shaped by lived experience, both operating inside digital capitalism, both building as though another logic are possible. The evidence suggests that another logic is necessary. The question is whether the institutions, the markets, and the rest of us will support it.

Sam put it more simply than any of the theorists could. We are doing great guys, he said, before adding, carefully, hopefully we will be in a better situation tomorrow. You work towards that gradually, slowly.

Anna's version was quieter but no less radical. We are not AI, and AI is not us. It is what we are using to help more people.

Two builders. Two starting points. The same destination: a world in which the systems work for the people they claim to serve, not the other way round.

OVER TO YOU

Explore Further: A Prompt for Your AI Assistant

Copy this prompt into your AI assistant of choice, photograph it, or visit the websites in our author biographies to access all 13 prompts in copyable format.

> *I've just read AI for Equity by Jenny Garrett OBE and Leah-Sunshine Garrett, specifically about the difference between access and redistribution – the argument that giving everyone access to the same tools built on the same biased data does not automatically create equity, through the work of Sam Samarasinghe and Anna Jones. Please help me reflect, not advise. Using only questions and observations, help me examine: 1) Where in my own work or sector am I confusing access with redistribution? 2) Who is currently excluded from the systems I use or build, and what would it take to include them?*

3) What does trust look like in the communities I serve – and am I earning it? 4) What is the difference between the people I design for and the people I design with? Please ask about my context so you can make this relevant to me.

This prompt turns AI into a critical thinking partner, helping you examine the difference between giving people access to existing systems and genuinely redistributing power and opportunity.

Three Coaching Questions for Reflection

Take time to consider these questions, either in personal reflection or in discussion with friends, colleagues, or study groups:

1. The Access Question. Jones argues that if the only thing AI does at scale is provide access to information that was previously behind a paywall, that is enough. Think about the AI tools you use in your work or personal life. Who cannot access them? What would change if they could?
2. The Potential Question. Merit assesses refugees on their future earning potential rather than their past financial history. Think about the systems in your organisation that assess people, whether for hiring, promotion, lending, or service provision. Are they measuring track record or potential? What would it take to shift from one to the other?
3. The Trust Question. Sam argues that trust cannot be built in a few months and that it requires values you would be proud to show your children. Think about the AI systems your organisation deploys. Would you be comfortable explaining to a user exactly how they work, exactly what data they use, and exactly why a particular decision was made? If not, what needs to change?

REFERENCES

Jones, A. (2025). *Interviewed by J. Garrett and L. Garrett for AI for Equity Podcast, Series Two.*

Muralidharan, K., Singh, A., & Ganimian, A. J. (2019). Disrupting education? Experimental evidence on technology-aided instruction in India. *American Economic Review*, *109*(4), 1426–1460.

UNICEF & ITU. (2020). *How many children and young people have internet access at home?* New York: UNICEF.

World Bank. (2022). *The state of global learning poverty: 2022 update.* Washington, DC: World Bank Group.

FURTHER READING

Africa's AI Leapfrog. (2025). *Black swan: AI for financial inclusion in Africa.* https://www.africasaileapfrog.com/

Otermans, P. (2025). *Interviewed by J. Garrett and L. Garrett for AI for Equity Podcast, Series One.*

Samarasinghe, S. (2025). *Interviewed by J. Garrett and L. Garrett for AI for Equity Podcast, Series Two.*

World Bank. (2024). *Global Findex database.* Washington, DC: World Bank Group.

World Economic Forum. (2025). *The new frontier of AI-powered financial inclusion.* https://www.weforum.org/

11

THE HUMAN–AI PARTNERSHIP: LEADERSHIP, ACCOUNTABILITY, AND COLLABORATION

In conversation with: Rod Brown, Founder and CEO, S/BES LLC

Contributive value isn't just a system. It's a movement to make work human again, with AI as our partner. Brown (2025)

I was sitting next to my mum when we recorded with Rod, and when he described contributive value, I watched something shift in her face. Full understanding. Twenty years of knowing inclusion needed measurement, and someone had finally built it. This is her making sense of that moment. – **Leah-Sunshine**

In the early 1990s, a young operations professional at Xerox Corporation looked at the cultural diversity training his company was running and thought: this is ridiculous. Not because diversity did not matter. It mattered enormously. But because the training existed in isolation from the operational systems that determined whether inclusion actually happened.

Rod Brown, based in the United States, had joined Xerox for three reasons. First, the company had clawed back market share from Japanese competitors by embracing Six Sigma quality principles – the most rigorous operational methodology of its era. Second, Xerox was arguably the most progressive cultural diversity company in the United States at the time. And third, Brown wanted to see what would happen if you brought those two things together.

His philosophical roots ran deep. He had worked with R. Roosevelt Thomas Jr., author of Beyond Race and Gender, whom Brown describes as the godfather of cultural diversity. Thomas had seen Brown's early work intersecting Six Sigma quality principles with DEI and recognised its significance. The mentorship shaped Brown's conviction that inclusion without operational rigour is performance art.

What Brown saw at Xerox, though, was a gap. The quality training and the diversity training occupied separate rooms, separate budgets, separate conversations. The principles that made Xerox's operations world-class were never applied to its inclusion efforts. And without operational accountability, the inclusion work remained vulnerable to every budget cut and leadership change.

He developed a concept he called Re-versity: Value creation for the 21st century, which he copyrighted but never published, based on innovation, recognition, and quantification, embedding quality and cultural diversity into a single operational framework. Universities wanted to adopt it. Major corporations were intrigued. But the traction never came. In the 1990s, the corporate world was not ready to measure inclusion with the same rigour it applied to production lines. The idea that inclusion could be quantified, that its impact on performance could be tracked, that the absence of diversity carried a measurable cost – these were propositions that most leaders found uncomfortable. They preferred the softer language of awareness and sensitivity. Brown wanted dashboards.

Three decades later, that gap has become the central crisis of DEI. Programmes are being defunded. The language has been politicised. And the absence of measurable, operational accountability has left inclusion vulnerable to every shift in the political wind. Brown's response, developed over 30 years and now powered by AI, is a framework he calls contributive value.

The organisations I work with want inclusion to matter, but they have never been able to prove that it does – not in the language that finance directors and boards understand. When Rod described contributive value on our podcast, I felt something shift. This was not another awareness programme. This was a measurement. And measurement, in my experience, is what turns aspiration into accountability.

When we interviewed Brown for our podcast, his perspective was unlike any other guest we had spoken to. He is the Founder and CEO of S/BES, LLC – Societal & Business Enterprise Solutions – and the creator of the contributive value process. His book, Don't Let AI Eat You Alive, forthcoming in 2027, maps the governance challenge this chapter explores. He was not a DEI practitioner. He was not a technologist. He was, as he described himself, a performance management and operational person who brings different disciplines together. And his argument was that the disciplines had been apart for far too long.

WHY THE HOUSE HAD NO FOUNDATION

Before we can discuss the human–AI partnership, we need to understand why the human systems it is being built upon are already broken. Brown's diagnosis is blunt and rooted in operational logic.

DEI, like ESG, has been getting a black eye not because the principles are wrong but because the accountability infrastructure was never built. There are no appropriate metrics. There is no transparent methodology. The results are not tracked in ways that connect to organisational performance. In Brown's view, this is not a failure of intent. It is a failure of design.

This is not a fringe view. The International Association of Privacy Professionals' 2025 AI Governance Profession Report found that 50% of AI governance professionals are assigned to ethics, compliance, privacy, or legal teams, with organisations increasingly recognising that governance cannot be siloed in a single function (IAPP, 2025).

Brown's framework rests on a simple acronym: CV. Not curriculum vitae. Contributive value. The distinction is deliberate. A CV tells you what someone has done in the past. Contributive value tells you what they are doing now, and what impact it is having on the organisation. AI, Brown argues, makes it possible for the first time to measure contributive value in real time, across every level of an organisation, transparently and consistently.

His motivation is personal and political. He is, in his words, sick and tired of the bickering about woke and DEI and the framing of inclusion as a Black thing when the data tells a different story: 77% of the primary beneficiaries of DEI programmes in the United States have been white women. Brown uses the term woke the way his critics use it – as shorthand for a political attack on inclusion work rather than an accurate description of it. The framework he has built is deliberately colourblind in its methodology, because the measurement of contribution does not require you to know someone's demographic category. It requires you to know what they did. Brown uses the term deliberately though the colourblind approach itself remains contested in DEI circles. Critics argue that measuring contribution without demographic context risks reproducing the same structural advantages it claims to eliminate – that if the playing field is uneven, a colourblind measure of performance will consistently reward those who started closer to the finish line. Brown's counter is that the methodology is not blind to structure – it is blind to identity, and that the distinction matters. We hold both positions deliberately. The tension between them is not a flaw in Brown's argument. It is the central question his framework forces us to ask.

> *AI allows us to do that now. It'll address the DEI issues – whether you got the job because you're Black or you're a legacy or your parents own the business, whatever the preferential bent is, it'll alleviate that.*

The argument is provocative because it moves the conversation away from representation and towards performance. Not everyone, Brown acknowledges, will be an A player. Some will be B players, some C players. But as long as the methodology is correct, it is honest, and it is focused on what people actually contribute rather than who they are, the conversation changes from identity to impact.

BEYOND THE ALGORITHM: WHY HUMAN LEADERSHIP STILL MATTERS

If Brown's contributive value framework sounds like a case for letting AI run the show, it is not. His model is emphatically human-in-the-loop. The front end of his platform involves consultants facilitating agreements between leaders, stakeholders, and employees about how AI will be used within the organisation. After the rollout, AI tracks and measures contributive value. But the decisions about what to do with that information, how to support underperformers, how to recognise high contributors, how to redesign roles and responsibilities remain human.

When we raised concerns about the ethics of tracking contributive value – the surveillance implications, the potential for misuse – Brown was ready. The privacy architecture uses retrieval-augmented generation to create a partition between private interactions and the tasks being measured. The chat stays private. The work output is assessed. And the individual, not just the manager, has access to their own data.

This matters because the evidence consistently shows that AI governance fails when it is treated as a technology problem rather than a leadership one. IBM's Phaedra Boinodiris puts it plainly: creating ethical AI is not strictly a technical problem but a socio-technical one, and the team designing it should be multidisciplinary rather than siloed. Every governance framework that has gained traction reaches the same conclusion – from UNESCO's recommendation adopted by 193 member states to the frameworks emerging across the private sector. The emerging best practice is governance that sits at the intersection of disciplines, not within any single one.

What Brown adds to this picture is the operational dimension. It is not enough to have diverse voices in the room if the room has no methodology. The quality principles that transformed manufacturing in the 20th century – measurement, transparency, continuous improvement, accountability – are precisely the principles that AI governance needs. And they are precisely the principles that DEI has lacked. Without them, governance committees become talking shops. With them, they become engines of change.

He illustrated this with a case from United Healthcare, one of the largest healthcare organisations in the United States. Their innovation team was running over 100 initiatives a year but succeeding on only one or two. Brown's team assessed the composition of the team and found that every member was a visionary, an idea person. There were no executioners, no people who specialise in turning ideas into operational reality. The team had been assembled around identity and enthusiasm rather than complementary capabilities. AI-powered analysis of contributive value would have surfaced this imbalance before the first initiative failed.

THREE BLACK BOXES

One of the most striking moments in our conversation with Brown came when he stepped back from the operational detail and offered a philosophical frame for the AI era that we had not encountered elsewhere.

Throughout human history, he argued, we have relied on two sources of information and creativity: religion and science. Both have served us well. Both contain what he calls a black box – a domain of unanswered questions that we have learned to live with. Faith asks us to trust what cannot be proven. Science asks us to trust what has not yet been disproven. Now, Brown says, a third entity has arrived – AI. And it, too, has a black box. With all it can do and what it does with its compute power, we do not know what it does and why it does it and how it does it. When AGI arrives – and Brown believes it will be within 3–10 years – we will have 3 black boxes to navigate simultaneously.

> *So now we've got three black boxes. How are we going to deal with that?*

The question is not rhetorical. It echoes a pattern Brown has seen before. In the late 1950s, W. Edward Deming took his quality management principles to American corporations. They would not listen. So, he flew to Japan and met with the Society of Engineers, who embraced Six Sigma and Total Quality Management so thoroughly that by the 1980s, Japanese manufacturing had overtaken American industry. American companies eventually adopted the principles too, but only after decades of lost market share. Brown sees a parallel. The companies and governments that embrace AI governance now, that build the ethical operating systems and the contributive value frameworks and the accountability infrastructure, will have an insurmountable advantage over those that wait. The rest will be playing catch-up, just as American manufacturers did in the 1980s.

Brown's answer also draws on a reference that carries considerable weight: Kissinger, Schmidt, and Huttenlocher's The Age of AI. Their argument, which Brown endorses, is that AI must be governed with the same seriousness as nuclear weapons. Just as the nuclear age required arms control treaties, verification systems, and shared understanding among competing powers, the AI age requires equivalent governance.

As Eric Schmidt said in an interview with TIME magazine, this stuff is too powerful to be done by tech alone. It is also unlikely that it will just get regulated correctly. So, you have to build a philosophy – a framework, a set of understandings of where the limits of this technology should go. The arms control analogy is not comfortable. It is not meant to be.

Brown's contribution to this debate is to ground it in the everyday. The nuclear-arms-treaty analogy is useful for government leaders. But for the CEO of a mid-sized company, the HR director of a public authority, the DEI practitioner trying to justify their budget, the question is more practical: what governance structures can I build today that will still be meaningful when the technology is 10 times more powerful?

THE DEI PRACTITIONER AS AI CATALYST

Brown sees a specific and urgent role for DEI practitioners in the AI era, but it is not the role most of them currently occupy. He wants them to become catalysts – learning the technical skills to prompt, to interrogate, and to use AI tools – while keeping the human in the loop at every stage. This is not about DEI professionals becoming data scientists. It is about them developing enough technical literacy to be credible partners in AI governance.

This is where the intergenerational dimension of our podcast became visible. When Brown learned that Leah-Sunshine had found him through deep research – watching his YouTube videos, reading his LinkedIn posts, making detailed notes before shortlisting him – he was struck. He had been, as he put it, out there for 30 years, and a 20-something had found what corporations had not. The irony was not lost on him. The contributive value framework that corporations ignored for three decades was discovered by a Gen Z researcher using exactly the kind of cross-disciplinary, AI-augmented research methodology that Brown advocates.

We are seeing this play out across the profession. The IAPP's governance report shows that over 50% of organisations expect privacy, IT, security, legal, and compliance disciplines to gain additional AI governance responsibilities in the coming years (IAPP, 2025). But Brown's point is that equity must be at the table too, not as an afterthought but as a core competency.

Brown's contribution to every conversation in this book is the same: the window for shaping AI is closing, and good intentions without operational metrics will not hold it open.

I see this in my own consultancy every week. Organisations ask me to help them build inclusive cultures, and I ask them how they will know when they have one. The silence that follows tells me everything. They have the vision. They do not have the metrics. Brown's framework is the most practical answer to that silence I have encountered in 20 years.

Brown's own approach to making systemic inequity visible offers a model. After the murder of George Floyd, a German company's US division asked him to explain why it had happened. Rather than delivering a standard diversity presentation, he created a research-based visualisation mapping the historical systems that led to the moment. The feedback was overwhelming. The company had never been shown, in operational terms, how systemic racism works as a system. Brown used the same approach to visualise the dynamics of AI bias, showing organisations not just that it exists but how it compounds over time.

THE 24/7 PHD: WHAT PARTNERSHIP LOOKS LIKE IN PRACTICE

Brown offered us a vivid illustration of what human–AI partnership looks like in practice. Working with a university, the president had asked him to meet with a VP of DEI. Brown could not work out where the person was coming from. They said one thing and did another. An accomplished professional with decades of experience, Brown was stuck on a human dynamics problem.

So late one night, he opened an AI tool and ran a game theory analysis. He set up the context, described the dynamics, and asked: what are the options? What am I missing? The algorithm came back with possibilities he had not considered. Maybe it is not personal. Maybe you should approach this differently. It was, Brown says, like having a conversation with a brilliant colleague at midnight.

> *You now have a 24/7 assistant at a PhD level to help you out in anything that you're working at.*

The anecdote is small, but the principle is large. Brown is not describing AI as a replacement for human judgement. He is describing it as a cognitive partner – something that can see patterns he cannot see, suggest approaches he has not tried, and operate without the emotional fatigue that clouds human thinking at the end of a long day. The partnership works because both sides bring something the other lacks.

This is the partnership model that the chapter's title points to. Not AI replacing human leadership, but AI amplifying it. Not algorithms making decisions about people, but algorithms giving people better information with which to make their own decisions. Brown's phrase for it is precise: make work human again, with AI as our partner. The word again is important. It implies that work was once more human than it is now, that something has been lost in the industrialisation and bureaucratisation of organisations, and that AI, paradoxically, could restore what earlier technology stripped away. It is a hopeful argument from a man who has spent 30 years watching corporations promise inclusion and deliver paperwork.

BUILDING THE ACCOUNTABILITY INFRASTRUCTURE

If the vision is compelling, the infrastructure to deliver it is still being built. Brown describes a platform that can track decisions at the federal level, the local level, and the organisational level, providing real-time dashboards that show whether politicians are doing what they said they would, whether corporations are meeting their commitments, and whether individuals are contributing at the level the role demands. It is accountability at scale, powered by AI and visible to everyone.

The challenge, which Brown acknowledges, is that most organisations are nowhere near this level of sophistication. The Sprint Ethics Board model proposed by researchers at Springer in 2025 offers a lighter-weight alternative: a governance framework adapted to agile product development, where ethics review is embedded in each sprint rather than conducted as a separate process (Springer, 2025).

But Brown's deeper point is that accountability without transparency is meaningless. The reason DEI failed, in his analysis, is not that organisations lacked good intentions. It is that they lacked transparent methods. They could not show the correlation between inclusion initiatives and business performance because they had never built the measurement systems to do so. AI changes this equation if – and only if – the measurement methodology is rigorous, the data is transparent, and the human beings using the system understand what it is measuring. Otherwise, as Brown warns, you get the same problem in a shinier package: ticking boxes without substance, now at algorithmic speed.

The parallel with the previous chapters is exact. In Chapter 6, Dan Gallagher argued that diversity in recruitment should be measured at the point of promotion, not hire. In Chapter 8, Dr Keshav Malhotra called for a global data registry that would make AI training data transparent. In Chapter 10, Anna Jones built her entire lending model on the principle that conventional data metrics exclude the people they claim to serve. Twan Wildeboer made a parallel argument in Chapter 7: the deepest form of inclusion is not giving everyone the same tool but giving them the freedom to build their own. Brown's contribution is to show that the same principle applies to organisational performance: if you cannot measure contribution transparently, you cannot distribute opportunity fairly. And if you cannot distribute opportunity fairly, no amount of diversity training will make up the difference.

THE WEALTH QUESTION

There is a dimension to Brown's argument that goes beyond governance and into economics. What he calls the human valuation of labour has to change within the DEI and AI world. His concern is not just that AI might displace jobs, although he is clear-eyed about that risk, estimating that 40%–60% of current jobs will be affected. His deeper concern is about who captures the value that AI creates.

Increasing the participation of wealth creation inside corporations, Brown argues, requires a fundamental shift in performance management. When ideas can be tracked through an organisation – who suggested what, what it led to, what value it created – the case for sharing the rewards becomes evidence-based rather than ideological. AI makes this tracking possible for the first time. Whether organisations choose to use it that way is a leadership decision, not a technical one.

Brown goes further. He sees Contributive Value Income – a performance-based model that recognises and rewards the full spectrum of human contribution – as the natural complement to Universal Basic Income: UBI lays the groundwork, CVI delivers the means to thrive.

This is where equity and AI converge most powerfully. If AI is used only to increase efficiency – to do what humans do, but faster and cheaper – its effect on inequality will be negative. But if it is used to make visible the contributions that were always invisible, to surface the ideas that never made it past the middle manager, to track the value created by people who never got credit for it, then AI becomes the most powerful equity tool ever built.

Brown is pragmatic about the transition. In the short term, he sees enormous opportunity in the physical infrastructure that AI requires. Referencing Nvidia CEO Jensen Huang's projections, he points to the token factories that every major corporation will need to build – each representing a billion-dollar investment and requiring enormous workforces to construct, maintain, and operate. The question is whether those opportunities will be distributed equitably or whether they will follow the same concentration patterns as every previous technology wave. If every sovereign nation, as Brown puts it, will need its own token factory, the construction, staffing, and governance of these facilities represent one of the largest infrastructure opportunities of the century. The workforce implications alone are staggering. And whether that workforce looks like the populations it serves, or whether it replicates the demographics of Silicon Valley, is a choice being made right now.

THE PATH FORWARD: FROM PARTNERSHIP TO PRACTICE

The human–AI partnership that Brown describes is not a comfortable one. It requires leaders to accept a level of transparency that most have avoided. It requires DEI practitioners to learn technical skills that most have not been trained in. It requires governance structures that most organisations have not yet built. And it requires a willingness to measure what has always been immeasurable and to act on what the measurements reveal.

But it also offers something that previous approaches to equity have lacked: proof. If contributive value can be measured, then the business case for inclusion is no longer theoretical. If performance can be tracked transparently, then the accusation that someone got their job because of their background rather than their contribution can be answered with data rather than argument. AI does not eliminate the politics. But it makes hiding from the evidence much harder.

Brown sees this as a 10-year project. Within that timeframe, he expects AI to address the wealth imbalance, reduce polarisation, refocus organisations on shared goals, and shut down the noise around DEI by replacing argument with evidence. It is an ambitious vision. But it is grounded in the same operational logic that transformed manufacturing, supply chains, and quality management in the 20th century. The principles are not new. The technology to apply them at scale is.

The 10-year timeframe matters. Brown is not promising a quick fix. He is describing a structural transformation that requires investment, patience, and leadership courage. The organisations that begin building contributive value frameworks now will have a decade's head start over those that wait for regulation to force their hand. And the workforces inside those organisations, the people whose contributions have been invisible for years, will finally have proof of what they have always known: that they were doing the work all along.

> *Contributive value isn't just a system. It's a movement to make work human again, with AI as our partner.*

As we reach the closing chapters of this book, Brown's message feels like a summation. AI will not save us from ourselves. But if we build the right systems – with the right people in the room, the right metrics in place, and the right commitment to transparency – it could become the accountability mechanism that inclusion has always needed and never had.

During our conversation, we told Brown that his vision was both inspiring and frightening. The three black boxes left us uneasy. The idea of contributive value being tracked across an entire organisation gave us pause. But when he brought us back through the other side – when he showed that the same transparency that makes surveillance possible also makes fairness provable – we understood why he has spent 30 years on this. Not because the world was ready. But because one day, it would have to be.

Measurement can tell you what is happening. It cannot tell you what it feels like to live inside it.

A note from both of us, after this conversation.

I'm afraid I won't have purpose. Not because I lack ambition – but because the things that were supposed to be there aren't. Property. Stability. A clear path. My generation was told to work hard and the rest would follow. It's not following. And AI is accelerating a change we didn't ask for and didn't consent to. What does that leave me in ten years? I genuinely don't know. And not knowing is scarier than it sounds when the certainties your parents had simply don't exist anymore. – **Leah-Sunshine**

The question I keep coming back to is this. If everyone has access to the same tools, built on the same biased data, optimised for the same engagement – does AI democratise opportunity, or just let more people climb faster toward the same ceiling? I don't have a clean answer. Neither does this book. But what I keep coming back to is the twelve people in these pages. None of them used AI the way most people are using AI. All of them made deliberate choices about what it should do and who it should serve. That isn't inevitable. It is a choice. And the fact that it is a choice – that's the only honest reason for hope I've found. – **Jenny**

OVER TO YOU

Explore Further: A Prompt for Your AI Assistant

Copy this prompt into your AI assistant of choice, photograph it, or visit the websites in our author biographies to access all 13 prompts in copyable format.

> *I've just read AI for Equity by Jenny Garrett OBE and Leah-Sunshine Garrett, specifically about Rod Brown's contributive value framework – the argument that AI makes it possible for the first time to measure what people actually contribute in real time, replacing the traditional CV with evidence of current impact – and his concept of three black boxes: religion, science, and AI. If I were to lead an AI ethics committee for my organisation, I would need diverse voices and expertise at the table. Please help me think through: 1) What disciplines and perspectives should be represented? 2) What specific questions should this committee be asking about*

every AI tool we deploy? 3) How can we build accountability that connects AI use to measurable outcomes? 4) What governance model would work for an organisation of our size and complexity? Please ask about my context so you can make this relevant to me.

This prompt turns AI into a governance design partner, helping you build the accountability infrastructure that Brown argues has always been missing from inclusion efforts.

Three Coaching Questions for Reflection

Take time to consider these questions, either in personal reflection or in discussion with friends, colleagues, or study groups:

1. The Accountability Question. Brown argues that DEI failed because it lacked transparent, operational accountability. Think about the inclusion initiatives in your own organisation. Can you point to specific, measurable outcomes? If not, what would it take to build the measurement infrastructure that would make accountability real?
2. The Partnership Question. Brown describes AI as a cognitive partner – a 24/7 assistant at PhD level. Think about a professional challenge you are currently facing. What would happen if you treated AI as a thinking partner rather than a search engine? What question would you ask it tonight?
3. The Black Box Question. Brown identifies three black boxes: faith, science, and AI. Each asks us to trust something we cannot fully understand. Where is your personal threshold of trust with AI? What would need to change – in the technology, the governance, or your own understanding – for you to move that threshold?

REFERENCES

Brown, R. (2025). *Interviewed by J. Garrett and L. Garrett for AI for Equity Podcast, Series One.*

IAPP. (2025). *AI governance profession report 2025*. Portsmouth, NH: International Association of Privacy Professionals.

Springer. (2025). Towards trustworthy AI: A framework for integrating ethics committees into product development. *Lecture Notes in Computer Science.*

FURTHER READING

IBM. (2025). *AI ethics and governance in 2025: A Q&A with Phaedra Boinodiris*. https://www.ibm.com/

LRN. (2024). *AI, ethics, and ESG in 2025*. https://lrn.com/

Operation HOPE. (2024). *AI ethics council*. https://operationhope.org/

Schmidt, E. (2022). Interview in: Gibbs, N. Henry Kissinger on Leadership. *TIME*. https://time.com/6193035/henry-kissinger-leaders/

Thomas, R. R. Jr. (1995). *Beyond race and gender: unleashing the power of your total workforce by managing diversity*. New York: AMACOM.

UNESCO. (2021). *Recommendation on the ethics of Artificial Intelligence*. Paris: UNESCO.

12

BUILDING THE FUTURE OF EQUITABLE AI – A CALL TO ACTION: CURIOSITY, CREATIVITY, AND THE HUMAN OPERATING SYSTEM

In conversation with: Finbar O'Hanlon, Innovation Strategist and AI Practitioner

> *If artificial intelligence could give every workplace one upgrade, what should it be? Help humans learn how to be more human. O'Hanlon (2025)*

I grew up in a house full of singing and laughing, where music was how we connected before we had the language for it. Finbar O'Hanlon understands that. He has spent his life proving that music, code, and human connection are the same thing. As you read, you'll see that my mum connected with this message immediately. – **Leah-Sunshine**

THE CURIOUS KID

Finbar O'Hanlon describes himself as an explorer. He started as a musician, got into building software, started inventing things and writing patents, ran a data science company, and now works at the intersection of human capabilities, deep technology, and arts. When we asked him what you call that combination, he laughed: I don't know what you call that, but whatever that's called, that's what I am.

The curiosity started early. As a child at a Christian school in Australia, O'Hanlon was the kid who asked questions. Not to be disruptive. Because he genuinely wanted to know. How did this guy part the sea? They thought he was being insolent. He was being curious. And because the curiosity was not welcomed, he went deep into himself. He thought there was something wrong with him. What he found instead was a passion for competing against himself, not against others, and a discovery that would shape his entire life: music.

I recognised something in that story. I have coached hundreds of leaders who were once the curious child in the room, and who learned early that asking the wrong question was more dangerous than staying silent. The autonomous behaviours O'Hanlon describes later in our conversation often start here, in childhood, in the moment when curiosity gets punished and compliance gets rewarded.

He could sit in his room for eight hours a day and play and practise. By 18, he was teaching jazz fundamentals at the Sydney Conservatorium and touring in bands. Music was the ultimate challenge, he says, because your whole life, you never learn it. It is always this evolving thing. That restlessness, the refusal to arrive, the insistence that mastery is a direction rather than a destination, is the thread that runs through everything O'Hanlon has done since.

When digital music began transitioning from reel-to-reel tape to computers, his curious mind followed. He started understanding how analogue signals become digital, learning Fourier transform algorithms, teaching himself to code. Music is very much like an object-oriented language, he told us. You are composing things and putting things together. He started working for Apple and Avid. The ride of curiosity kept fuelling the fire. He never went to school for any of it. He just kept picking it up, because each new thing connected to the last.

I have always been of the mindset that everything is part of a puzzle, he told us. We have been taught to think in classifications:

you are a musician or you are a coder. And so we tend to have these biases about what we are. O'Hanlon's career is a deliberate rejection of those classifications. For him, the move from music to code to human capabilities to agentic commerce is not a series of career changes. They are all pieces of the same puzzle. How do I break these stereotypes of classification systems whereby you can connect the unconnected? That, he says, is where the magic lies.

LANGUAGE WITHIN LANGUAGE

O'Hanlon wrote a paper called The Language Alchemist, and the concept behind it reveals something about how he sees AI that most technologists miss entirely. When you learn the notes of music, he explains, you learn the note. But the context that sits around the note triggers emotion, biofeedback, resonance. Once you start to learn the notes, you play with someone else, and there is a timing thing, and sometimes, it just turns into something magical and sometimes it does not.

This is not a metaphor for him. It is a design principle. O'Hanlon co-founded a company called Rezonyx with Ahmet Zappa, the son of Frank Zappa. Together, they have been taking modern music, slicing it into 48 pieces, and retuning each note frequency in the musical scale, so it is more resonant with the human physiology. The reason? When Pythagorean tuning was created, they thought about instruments all playing in tune with each other. They forgot the human in the equation.

The parallel to AI is exact. The systems we have built are tuned to be internally consistent. They process language, generate outputs, optimise for coherence. But they have forgotten the human in the equation. They have forgotten context, emotion, spirit, timing, dynamics. O'Hanlon calls these the top-order language principles, and he believes that once we understand them, we can transform all of this stuff around us into stuff that really connects with other people.

The application is not abstract. O'Hanlon illustrated it with a story he tells on stage. If I said to you, how are you going, and you said really good, and there was a 50-foot wall of flame behind you, I would read the response of the flame behind you with what you are saying. And I would respond differently to if you were sitting on a beach drinking a pina colada. He is describing contextual intelligence, the capacity to read beyond the words to the conditions surrounding them. AI systems process the words. They do not yet read the wall of flame. That gap between processing language and understanding context is where human judgement remains indispensable, and it is where equity either lives or dies in AI-assisted decision-making.

Throughout my career, I have helped leaders understand the gap between what they say and what people hear. O'Hanlon is describing the same gap, but at the level of technology itself. AI can reproduce the notes. But the context, the thing that makes communication human, that is ours to bring.

THE HUMAN OPERATING SYSTEM

O'Hanlon's most powerful concept is what he calls the human operating system. Every person, he argues, runs on two layers: the conscious, which is the user interface through which we engage with the world, and the subconscious, which runs not only our biological systems but also our autonomous behaviours. The foot on the brake pedal. The turning of the steering wheel. The reactions we learned so long ago that we no longer recognise them as learned.

The first thing to do in a world where you are in fear, he told us, is to start to recognise what are the autonomous behaviours that have been programmed over the years that are stopping you from learning. It is the art of unlearning. And until we do it, the programmes we have written in our minds will stop us from evolving.

He learned a practical tool for this in New York: media training. When someone asks you a question in an interview, you have a five-second pause to think about how you turn their question into what you want to talk about. That five-second pause, O'Hanlon says, is a pattern interrupt for your autonomous behaviours. Once you start applying it, you start to recognise where your reactions come from. You start to apply critical thinking. And from there, it cascades. The five-second pause is not a communication technique. It is a gateway to examining your own code.

This maps directly onto the organisational challenge we have documented throughout this book. In Chapter 11, Rod Brown argued that DEI failed because the accountability infrastructure was never built. The autonomous behaviour of organisations, ticking boxes, looking good without substance, retreating when the politics shift, has been running unchallenged for decades. AI offers the chance to interrupt that pattern, but only if leaders are willing to examine the programming that got them here. O'Hanlon's human operating system is the individual version of the same insight: before you can change the system, you have to examine your own code.

The concept also connects to what Twan Wildeboer described in Chapter 7. Twan's distinction between inclusive design and adaptive design is, at its core, a distinction between two operating systems. Inclusive design widens the doorway but keeps the room the same. Adaptive design changes the room. O'Hanlon would say that adaptive design requires unlearning first, because the people designing the room have to recognise the autonomous behaviours that shaped the original layout. You cannot redesign a space you have never examined.

CREATIVITY AS REORGANISATION

O'Hanlon defines creativity as coming up with solutions to problems by reorganisation of existing things. A painter uses paint, brushes, and canvas, existing things, and mixes them together. A musician uses strings and notes. The sequence, the combination, the arrangement is the art. If AI is one of the existing things that we mix together, he says, then we have this ability to create a new future.

This reframe matters because it dissolves the paralysis that so many people feel when confronting AI. O'Hanlon regularly asks conference audiences to raise their hands if they have done something they have never done before in the last week. Almost nobody raises their hand. He extends the question: the last four weeks? A few hands. The last six months? A few more. His point is devastating: we should be doing something we have never done before every single day of our lives, even if it is buying a new low-carb bread or trying a new route to work. Being conscious about the fact that we are doing it is what matters, because we get so bought into these biases of I cannot do that, that we restrict ourselves from the ability to explore and experiment.

If 9 out of 10 experiments fail, he says, it is the one that does not fail which gives you the breakthrough. If you are doing it 100 times, you are getting 10 new successful experiments. But we are so afraid of failing because what if someone sees us. We are so busy about the exterior of how we are seen rather than the interior of how we are growing. AI is this thing that can help us grow. We just have to take the fear away and start experimenting.

He applies the same principle to leadership. In his work with boards, he asks a simple pair of questions: tell me the top 3 companies that might disrupt you in the next 90 days. Then, tell me the top three companies that might disrupt you in the next year. Most boards cannot answer either question. They are making decisions about the future while looking only in the rear-view mirror. Having a consultancy tell you about macro trends is one thing, O'Hanlon says, but it is not applying those trends to your business. You need to be able to look forward and backward at the same time.

THE FEAR THAT STOPS US

When someone tells him AI is going to take their job, his response cuts through the noise. So was it a statement or is it a question? If it is a statement, he cannot help. If it is a question, his answer is immediate: it is not going to take my job. Why? Because I keep changing my job. I keep making things up. I keep meeting the market. I keep adapting myself. So, I am always going to have a job.

The person who has defined themselves by a job title cannot imagine a world without it. The person who has defined themselves by their capabilities can imagine anything.

His advice is to break down the skills that make up the current job, learn how to reassemble them for a new context, and recognise that the classification of the job may change but the capabilities remain. You just might not be called what you currently are, but all the things you have learned over your life are still valuable. It is a reorganisation, not a loss.

O'Hanlon spoke at the Global Innovation Summit in Dubai about Australian innovation, standing on a stage alongside people from countries spending five to six per cent of national GDP on innovation. Australia, he pointed out, is number 30 in the world in innovation outputs. The comfort of the country, the safety, the lack of urgency, has made innovation feel unnecessary. The best innovations, he argues, come from constraint, from necessity, from the worst parts of life where you have to innovate to survive. When you are comfortable, it is a real challenge to see what is coming.

This observation resonates beyond Australia. In Chapter 9, Dr Pauldy Otermans showed us what innovation looks like when it is born from necessity rather than comfort: Edge AI running on a smartphone in an environment with limited or intermittent internet access, a teacher in your pocket for learners who have nothing else. In Chapter 10, Anna Jones built a lending platform because every bank in the country said refugees were not creditworthy, and she knew they were wrong. The pattern across this book is consistent: the most transformative AI applications are not coming from the most resourced environments. They are coming from the most constrained ones. O'Hanlon's framework explains why: constraint forces unlearning. Comfort allows the old programmes to keep running.

We have been educated into a world that no longer exists, he told us. What we are trying to do is sense-make AI through the mindset and the principles that we were taught to live in a world that is gone. This is why the frameworks feel inadequate, why responsible AI feels like it is always catching up, why the debates about risk and regulation so often miss the point. We are trying to understand a new thing with old tools. O'Hanlon's answer is not to abandon the old tools but to recognise them for what they are: a starting point, not a destination.

BURNING MIND

O'Hanlon's answer to all of this is a programme called Burning Mind. It started when he studied the 13 human capabilities in the World Economic Forum's Future of Jobs report and noticed something striking: the top 10 skills for the future of work contain almost no job-specific competencies. They are all human capabilities: creativity, adaptive mindset, lifelong learning, critical thinking. And when he went to school, nobody taught any of them.

The challenge with human capabilities, he explains, is that people already know how to do this stuff. People think that to learn something means you have to take in a lot of information and it has to be hard. But that is not how human capabilities work. It is like telling someone to pick up a dumbbell and lift it 10 times. It does not sound complicated, so people assume it cannot be valuable. But the value is not in the information. It is in practice.

Burning Mind is a day for senior executives where O'Hanlon takes them through a series of play-based puzzles and games. At the end of each one, he maps the game back to the human capabilities that were being developed through it. The participants do not realise they are building adaptive thinking and creative problem-solving until he shows them. The learning is embodied, not instructed.

There is something subversive about this approach. In a world saturated with AI certifications, technical bootcamps, and upskilling programmes, O'Hanlon is arguing that the most important learning is not about the technology at all. It is about the human. His work with boards exposed a gap that every chapter of this book has confirmed from a different angle: leaders are making decisions about the future based entirely on data from the past. They can describe their annual reports in detail. They cannot name the forces that might reshape their business in three months. The problem is not information. The problem is orientation. And until leaders learn to look forward as well as backward, the technology will outpace the governance every time.

In my own consultancy work, I have watched organisations invest millions in technical training while treating human capabilities as an afterthought. O'Hanlon's Burning Mind workshops do something I have been trying to do throughout my career: make the invisible skills visible, and make them practised rather than preached.

When you play guitar or you play soccer, he told us, you do not go to practice, kick the ball, kick it wrong and go: that is it, I failed. The words risk do not exist in soccer practice. The words risk do not exist in guitar practice. It is called practice. We are so caught up in the business world about risk. Change the word risk to learn. By learning, you are de-risking, because you are getting closer to your goal by doing it rather than not doing it.

AI is the first technology whose programming language is the natural human language, O'Hanlon reminds us. Whatever we say, we are programming computers by what we say. So, we should be empowered, not restrained. We do not have to learn code. We already speak code. The question is what we choose to say.

WHAT COMES NEXT

O'Hanlon's framing of AI as the first technology whose programming language is human language is not just a reframe of the present. It is a prediction about the future. If the barrier to programming was once technical literacy, and that barrier has now fallen, the next wave of AI development will be shaped not by the people who can code but by the people who can think. The question is whether those people will represent the full range of human experience or only the fraction that has historically held power.

The trends are already visible. Agentic AI, systems that do not just answer questions but take actions on our behalf, is moving from research into deployment. O'Hanlon references agentic commerce, AI systems that negotiate, purchase, and transact without human intervention at each step. When AI moves from advisor to actor, the equity implications multiply. A biased recommendation is one thing. A biased transaction is another. The governance frameworks that every guest in this book has called for become not just desirable but urgent when the systems are no longer waiting for us to press a button.

At the same time, the participation gap documented across this book is narrowing in some places and widening in others. The women Sumathi Menon trains are discovering that AI is just words, a language they already speak. The neurodivergent professionals Twan Wildeboer advocates for are finding that AI can adapt to them rather than demanding they adapt to it. Dr Pauldy Otermans's Edge AI is reaching learners who have never had access to a tutor of any kind. But the data that trains these systems still comes overwhelmingly from the global north, from English-language sources, from neurotypical populations, from the digitally connected. Every chapter of this book has shown that the gap between who builds AI and who is affected by it remains the central equity challenge of our time.

O'Hanlon's response to this is characteristically practical. He does not propose a policy framework or a governance structure. He proposes a mindset. If we stop looking at AI as a technology to be feared or controlled, and start looking at it as one of the existing things we can mix together to create something new, then the future is not something that happens to us. It is something we compose. The notes are available to everyone. The question is who gets to play, and what music they choose to make.

The emerging frontier is not technical. It is human. The organisations that will lead in equitable AI are not the ones with the biggest models or the most data. They are the ones whose leaders have done the unlearning that O'Hanlon describes, who have examined the autonomous behaviours running their decision-making, who have learned to look forward and backward at the same time, and who have the courage to do something they have never done before. That is not a technology upgrade. It is an operating system upgrade. And it starts, as O'Hanlon would say, with a five-second pause.

THE PUZZLE OF LIFE

O'Hanlon told us that he has always looked at the world through artefacts, breaking things down into pieces and then reorganising them in new ways. His career has been an exercise in connecting the unconnected, and that, he says, is where the magic lies.

We chose to feature O'Hanlon not because he is an AI ethicist or a governance expert or a DEI practitioner. We chose him because he embodies the thing this book has been arguing for across every chapter: the refusal to be classified. The insistence that the categories we have been taught to think in, musician or technologist, technical or human, risk or opportunity, are not boundaries. They are starting points.

This book has argued across every chapter that the future of AI is not a technology question. It is a leadership question, a design question, an equity question, and ultimately a human question. O'Hanlon embodies that argument. He has never separated the technical from the human, the creative from the analytical, the playful from the serious. His career is proof that the classifications we have been taught to respect are the very things holding us back.

His metaphor for the future of AI is drawn from his first love. Music, he says, is never fully learned – you play with someone else, and sometimes, it turns into something magical, and sometimes, it does not. The magic is not in the notes. It is in the context, the energy, the emotion, the spirit, the timing. AI can reproduce the notes. But the context, the thing that makes it human, that is ours to bring.

In the age of AI, the people who will thrive are the ones who can break apart what they know and reassemble it for a world that does not yet exist. O'Hanlon has been doing this his entire life. His invitation to the rest of us is simple: start. Do something you have never done before. Today. Not because you know the outcome, but because the practice is the point.

Finbar's invitation is simple. What follows is what it actually feels like.

A note from both of us, after this conversation.

What I'm still afraid of is losing purpose. Not just a job – purpose. My generation was handed a world that's changing faster than anyone planned for, and we're being told to be adaptable without being given anything stable to adapt from. The certainties my parents had – the property ladder, the career path, the sense that hard work leads somewhere specific – aren't there in the same way. And when I look at what AI is accelerating, sometimes I ask: what does that leave me? In ten years, twenty years? I don't know. And not knowing, when everything is moving this fast, is genuinely frightening. – **Leah-Sunshine**

My biggest fear isn't the jobs. It's that we'll stop valuing human thoughts and feelings altogether. That we'll defer so consistently to the machine that we forget the machine doesn't know what it feels like to be wrong, to be afraid, to be uncertain and act anyway. Every person we spoke to for this book felt that fear and acted anyway. Christian, Anna, Pauldy, Finbar. None of them knew it would work. All of them started before they were ready. If I could go back to that first morning – the insomnia, the email, the not-knowing – I wouldn't change it. The fear was the most productive emotion I had all year. – **Jenny**

OVER TO YOU

Explore Further: A Prompt for Your AI Assistant

Copy this prompt into your AI assistant of choice, photograph it, or visit the websites in our author biographies to access all 13 prompts in copyable format.

> *I've just read AI for Equity by Jenny Garrett OBE and Leah-Sunshine Garrett, specifically about Finbar O'Hanlon's concept of the human operating system – the autonomous behaviours that run underneath everything we do – and his argument that creativity is the reorganisation of existing things. I work in [insert your field] and I am [insert your career stage]. Help me identify: 1) One autonomous behaviour I might be running that is stopping me from experimenting with AI. 2) How I could break down my current skills and reassemble them for a changing world. 3) One thing I could do*

this week that I have never done before, using AI as one of the ingredients. Please challenge me and do not let me stay comfortable.

This prompt turns AI into a personal coach, helping you identify the autonomous behaviours that are holding you back and design one concrete experiment for the week ahead.

Three Coaching Questions for Reflection

Take time to consider these questions, either in personal reflection or in discussion with friends, colleagues, or study groups:

1. The Unlearning Question. O'Hanlon argues that our autonomous behaviours, the programmes written into our subconscious over the years, are the biggest barrier to growth in the AI era. What is one belief, habit, or assumption about technology that you have been running on autopilot? What would happen if you paused for five seconds before acting on it?
2. The Creativity Question. Creativity, in O'Hanlon's definition, is coming up with solutions to problems by reorganising existing things. Think about your own skills, experiences, and knowledge. If your current role disappeared tomorrow, how could you reassemble those pieces into something new? What existing thing could AI add to the mix?
3. The Disruption Question. O'Hanlon asks boards to name 3 companies that could disrupt them in 90 days. Most cannot answer. Apply that question to your own career: what three changes in AI could reshape your role in the next three months? If you cannot answer, what does that tell you about where you are looking?

REFERENCES

O'Hanlon, F. (2025). *Interviewed by Jenny Garrett OBE and Leah-Sunshine Garrett for AI for Equity Podcast, Series Two.*

FURTHER READING

World Economic Forum. (2025). *Future of jobs report 2025*. Geneva: World Economic Forum.

13

CONCLUSION: TWELVE VOICES, SEVEN COMMITMENTS, ONE CHOICE

WHAT WE FOUND: 12 VOICES, 1 PATTERN

When we started this book, we expected to find a debate about technology. What we found instead was a debate about power. Every conversation we had, from every continent and every discipline, returned to the same questions: who designs these systems, whose data trains them, who benefits from their deployment, and who is harmed when they fail.

The pattern that emerged was not one we anticipated. We expected each guest to offer a different answer. Instead, they offered different angles on the same answer. The root cause of inequity in AI is not technical. It is structural. And the structures are older than the technology.

Christian Ortiz and Dr Mona Ashok arrived at this conclusion from opposite directions. Ortiz traced bias to its colonial origins, arguing that the datasets reflect systems of power that were never designed to include the people now most affected by them. Ashok traced bias through four doors inside the AI pipeline itself, from data collection to feedback loops, showing how exclusion compounds at every stage. Together, their chapters reveal that the problem is both historical and operational. You cannot fix the pipeline without understanding the history that shaped it, and you cannot address the history without changing the pipeline.

A similar convergence appeared between Jazz Rasool and Finbar O'Hanlon, two guests who have never met but whose ideas interlock. Rasool argued that the most advanced technology in the room is the human being. O'Hanlon built that insight into a practical framework: the human operating system, the autonomous behaviours that determine how we respond to change. Both are saying that AI transformation is not a technology project. It is a human development project. The organisations that treat it otherwise will automate their existing limitations.

The most striking connection ran between the guests working at the margins. Dr Keshav Malhotra's call for a global data registry and Ortiz's decolonised dataset are two responses to the same problem: who gets to be represented in the systems that make decisions about their lives. Dr Pauldy Otermans's Edge AI and Anna Jones's lending platform are two answers to the same question: what does access look like when the conventional infrastructure does not reach you? Sam Samarasinghe's coaching platform, built across 27 countries with the principle of technology secondary, showed what it looks like when a builder refuses to create dependency where none is necessary. Sumathi Menon's curious non-corporates and Twan Wildeboer's neurodivergent users are both populations that mainstream AI was not designed to serve, and both guests showed that the most effective solutions come from designing with those populations rather than for them.

Dan Gallagher and Rod Brown, working in different countries and different decades, both discovered that inclusion without measurement is indefensible. Gallagher built a certification framework for talent professionals. Brown built a contributive value platform that replaces performance management. Both concluded that the accountability infrastructure for equitable AI does not yet exist and that waiting for someone else to build it is no longer an option.

Here is how these 12 conversations impacted us:

These twelve conversations didn't change what I believed. They gave me the evidence to say it louder. AI and equity are not separate agendas – they are the same agenda. The fairness lens on AI is not a nice to have, it is essential to organisational success. Creativity, fun and humanness are not soft additions to this work – they are central to it. And there is genuine step change possible here. Not incremental improvement. Something that could actually move us from conversation to change in a way that twenty years of diversity training alone could not. That gives me joy. And this book is my way of making sure that argument is on the record. – **Jenny**

For me, as someone who grew up inside these algorithms, these conversations did something different. They showed me that the people building equitable AI are not waiting for the industry to catch up. They are building around it, through it, and sometimes in spite of it. Christian built Justice AI inside the most biased platform because that is where the bias lives. Anna lent money to people every bank refused. Pauldy built a teacher that works without the internet. These are not theoretical positions. They are acts of construction. And they made me believe that my generation does not have to inherit these systems. We can rebuild them. – **Leah-Sunshine**

THE GAPS THAT REMAIN

And yet intention without infrastructure is wishful thinking. Across every chapter, we found the same structural failures repeating.

Dan Gallagher showed us that the governance gap in recruitment is not just about who gets hired but about what happens afterwards. His insistence that diversity should be measured at the point of promotion, not hire, reframed the entire conversation about inclusive talent. The Verityn Index he built represents what governance looks like when someone creates the accountability infrastructure that should have existed all along.

Dr Keshav Malhotra, working in the IVF laboratories of India, showed us the same gap in healthcare: AI systems making decisions about embryo selection without patient consent, algorithms trained on European datasets deployed on Indian populations, and governance bodies working on consensus statements that take months while the technology evolves in weeks. His proposal for a publicly accessible global registry of embryo data, a simple upload of an image and an outcome, available to every researcher in the world, remains unbuilt. Not because the technology is lacking, but because the institutional will is absent.

Sumathi Menon, training women she calls curious non-corporates to move from passive users of AI to builders of AI, identified a gap that rarely makes the headlines: women, particularly mothers who have left the corporate workforce, are being written out of the AI-enabled future because the technology was not designed with them in mind. Her distinction between informed refusal and uninformed avoidance was one of the sharpest insights in the book. Choosing not to use AI is a legitimate decision, but only if you understand what you are choosing not to use. Without that understanding, opting out is not neutrality. It is surrender.

Twan Wildeboer, the innovator whose TEDx talk on AI and neurodiversity reached audiences who had never connected the two subjects, showed us a different kind of gap. AI is trained on the whole internet, he observed, a database mostly of neurotypical people. For neurodivergent users, this means the technology defaults to one way of thinking, one way of communicating, one way of processing the world. The question he poses is whether we use AI to reinforce that default or to expand it. There is, he told us, an opportunity to use AI as a bridge between different ways of thinking – not a wall that divides them.

And across the global south, the gaps are structural. Dr Keshav Malhotra described an IVF sector in India where tier-one cities operate at international standards while tier-three cities lack access to a trained embryologist, let alone an AI assessment system. His advocacy for global data representation, his training of embryologists from Africa, and his insistence that AI vendors disclose their training populations were not abstract policy positions. They were the lived reality of a practitioner watching algorithms trained on European data deployed on Indian patients.

Dr Pauldy Otermans, who has trained over 35,000 learners across 13 countries using AI-supported tools, showed us the access gap at its most fundamental. In communities where the internet is unreliable or unaffordable, the digital divide is not a metaphor. It is the difference between having a teacher and having nothing. Her response was Edge AI, technology that runs on a smartphone after a single download, allowing learners to continue working with an AI tutor even when they are offline. She calls it the teacher in your pocket. Each and every human is a unique individual, she told us, and AI can provide personalised support in a safe space where no one is feeling judged.

Anna Jones, the CEO of RefuAid who built an AI-powered career pathway tool and a lending platform for refugees, demonstrated what happens when technology is designed from the relationship outward. Her team lent nearly three million pounds to displaced professionals re-accrediting into UK careers, with a repayment rate of 98.6%. The innovation was not the algorithm. It was the understanding that people who have rebuilt their lives from nothing are not credit risks, and they are among the most motivated borrowers in existence. If the only thing we are doing at scale is providing access, she told us, then that is also okay with us.

Sam Samarasinghe, operating across 27 countries, showed us the same gap from the platform side: coaches with accessibility needs, coaches with ADHD, coaches who are visually impaired navigating the product in ways his team had never anticipated. He built for them not because it was strategic but because it was the minimum viable ethics of building for humans.

This is what collective action looks like in practice. Not grand declarations, but daily choices. The leader who asks, tell me the top 3 companies that might disrupt us in the next 90 days, and refuses to accept silence as an answer. The DEI practitioner who learns to prompt AI rather than waiting for someone else to do it. The clinician who asks a vendor: can you tell me what population your algorithm was trained on? The mother returning to the workforce who opens an AI tool for the first time and discovers, as Sumathi Menon's students do, that it is just words, words that are in our vocabulary, a language people can learn. The operations professional who, like Rod Brown, refuses to separate quality from inclusion and insists on measuring contributive value rather than accepting box-ticking as progress.

There is one structural gap that none of our 12 guests named directly, but that runs beneath every conversation in this book.

When an algorithm trained on European and American data makes a decision about an Indian patient's embryo, a Kenyan worker's credit score, or a Ghanaian student's career pathway, the infrastructure behind that decision has never been accountable to them. This is the sovereignty gap. Data sovereignty – the principle that the data generated by communities should be governed by those communities, stored on infrastructure they control, and used in systems that serve their interests first – is the structural version of everything this book has argued at the individual and organisational level. Christian Ortiz is building a decolonised dataset from the inside. Dr Keshav Malhotra is advocating for a global registry that would bring Indian and African reproductive data into the systems that currently exclude it. Dr Pauldy Otermans is running AI on local devices precisely because she refuses to make empowerment dependent on someone else's infrastructure. Each of them, without naming it, is making a sovereignty argument.

Nations and communities across the Global South are beginning to respond at a structural level, investing in their own data infrastructure, building AI systems rooted in their own languages and governance frameworks, and asserting that the data generated by their citizens should serve their citizens first. These are acts of self-determination – the policy-level answer to the question this book has asked throughout: who was this system designed for, and who was left out? The EQUITAS framework asks individuals and organisations to examine whose world the data describes. The sovereignty question asks governments and institutions to go further, to ensure that the infrastructure processing that data is accountable to the people it affects. That is not a technical upgrade. It is a political commitment. And it is one the window is closing on, just as it is closing on every other form of AI governance this book has described.

This is what collective action looks like in practice. Not grand declarations, but daily choices. The leader who asks, tell me the top 3 companies that might disrupt us in the next 90 days, and refuses to accept silence as an answer. The DEI practitioner who learns to prompt AI rather than waiting for someone else to do it. The clinician who asks a vendor: can you tell me what population your algorithm was trained on? The mother returning to the workforce who opens an AI tool for the first time and discovers, as Sumathi Menon's students do, that it is just words, words that are in our vocabulary, a language people can learn. The operations professional, like Rod Brown, refuses to separate quality from inclusion and insists on measuring contributive value rather than accepting box-ticking as progress.

THE ROLE OF PERSONAL RESPONSIBILITY

Every guest we spoke to returned, eventually, to the individual. Not because systemic change does not matter – it does, profoundly – but because systems are made of people, and people can choose.

Some chose to build what did not exist. Christian Ortiz built a decolonised dataset inside the most biased platform available. Anna Jones lent money to people every bank refused. Dr Pauldy Otermans built a teacher that works without the internet. Dan Gallagher left a corporate role to create the accountability infrastructure nobody else was building. Dr Keshav Malhotra trained embryologists from Africa on his own time, through voluntary effort.

Some chose to stay and challenge from inside. Dr Mona Ashok went to Parliament. Jazz Rasool started in 2008, 17 years before the rest of the world caught up. Rod Brown spent 30 years developing a framework most corporations did not want to hear about.

Some chose to design for the people everyone else overlooked. Sumathi Menon focused on the women stepping back who feared they could never step forward again. Twan Wildeboer gave a TEDx talk connecting two conversations the mainstream had kept apart. Sam Samarasinghe built a platform where people using notebooks and spreadsheets were told they were doing just fine. Finbar O'Hanlon chose never to stop being curious.

Each of these choices was a small act of refusal – a refusal to accept the existing categories, the existing power structures, the existing limitations. None of them required permission. All of them required courage. And collectively, they form a blueprint for what equitable AI looks like when it is built by people who care enough to build it differently.

THE EQUITAS FRAMEWORK

This book began with a question: can AI be a force for equity, or will it simply automate the inequities we already have? The answer, as every chapter has shown, is both. The technology is not inherently liberating or oppressive. It is a mirror and an amplifier. It reflects the data it is trained on, the values of the people who design it, and the governance structures, or the absence of them, that determine how it is deployed.

Table 13.1summarises the EQUITAS framework alongside the guests whose work exemplifies each commitment.

The evidence we have gathered points to seven commitments that any individual, organisation, or government can make today. We call them EQUITAS, because equity is not an outcome. It is a practice. And these seven commitments, drawn from 12 practitioners across 4 continents, are where that practice begins.

E – Examine whose world the data describes. Every AI system is trained on someone's reality. Find out whose. Ask whether the population represented in the training data matches the population the system is being applied to. If the answer is unclear, that is itself an answer. Christian Ortiz built Justice AI because he examined the data and found 560 communities whose knowledge had never been included. Dr Keshav Malhotra advocates for a global registry because the data that trains reproductive AI does not represent the patients it serves. For governments, the UK government's £1.6 billion UKRI AI strategy prioritises world-class data infrastructure. It does not specify whose world that data describes. Mandate disclosure of training data demographics for any AI system used in public services, procurement, or regulation. If governments are commissioning AI, they should require evidence that the training population matches the affected population.

Q – Query the black box. You do not need to understand how every AI system works. But you do need to understand what question it is answering, whose data trained it, and what happens when

Table 13.1. The EQUITAS Framework (Seven Commitments for Equitable AI – Individuals, Organisations, and Policymakers).

E	**Examine whose world the data describes**	Every AI system is trained on someone's reality. Find out whose. If the answer is unclear, that is itself an answer. Christian Ortiz · Dr Keshav Malhotra
Q	**Query the black box**	If a vendor cannot tell you what it is answering, whose data trained it, and what happens when it fails – that is your answer. Dr Mona Ashok
U	**Understand what you are automating**	Fix the process first, then automate it. AI does not repair broken systems – it scales them. Dr Mona Ashok · Rod Brown
I	**Invest in human capabilities**	Creativity, adaptive thinking, ethical competence. The skills that matter most were never taught in school. Finbar O'Hanlon
T	**Track what matters before you need to defend it**	Build the proof before the political winds shift. Inclusion without measurement is indefensible. Rod Brown · Dan Gallagher
A	**Act with, not for**	The people most affected by AI must help design it. Participation is not consultation. It is co-creation. Jazz Rasool · Sumathi Menon · Twan Wildeboer · Dr Pauldy Otermans · Anna Jones · Sam Samarasinghe
S	**Start before you are ready**	The window for shaping AI is closing. Do something you have never done before. Today. All 12 voices

Source: Authors' synthesis of 12 guest interviews, AI for Equity Podcast (2025–2026).

it gets it wrong. If a vendor cannot tell you those three things in plain language, that is your answer. Dr Mona Ashok took this argument to the UK House of Parliament. The question she posed there is one every organisation should be asking: not just does this system work, but for whom, and at whose expense? For governments, require algorithmic impact assessments before AI systems are deployed in high-stakes public decisions – benefits, sentencing, healthcare triage, hiring. The EU AI Act sets a benchmark. The question for every government is whether they are meeting it or waiting to be forced to.

U – Understand what you are automating – and whether it is worth automating. Before you deploy AI, examine the human system it is replacing. If that system is already biased, AI will not fix it. It will scale it. If that system is broken or wasteful, AI will not repair it. It will accelerate it. The organisations that get this right do the harder work first: they fix the process, and then they automate it. Dr Mona Ashok's four doors showed how bias compounds at every stage of the AI pipeline. Rod Brown's three decades of work demonstrated that organisations adopting AI for inclusion had never built the accountability infrastructure for the human processes AI was replacing. The technology inherits whatever it is given. Make sure what you give it is worth inheriting. For governments, audit existing public sector processes for bias before automating them. A government that digitises a discriminatory benefits system has not modernised. It has industrialised discrimination.

I – Invest in human capabilities. The World Economic Forum's Future of Jobs report identifies creativity, adaptive thinking, and lifelong learning as the top skills for the future. The OECD's 2025 Education for Human Flourishing framework goes further, arguing that adaptive problem-solving, ethical competence, and the ability to act with purpose are not supplementary to education in the AI era – they are its entire point. None of these are technical competencies. All of them require practice. As Finbar O'Hanlon's Burning Mind workshops demonstrate, the skills that matter most are the ones that were never taught in school. The organisations that invest in them now will not just be more equitable. They will be more resilient. For governments, the UK government's £1.6 billion UKRI AI strategy commits to expanding doctoral and fellowship routes and developing AI skills and talent. Investment in human capabilities must reach further than fellowships and research institutions. The people who most need AI literacy are not in those programmes. Fund creative, ethical, and adaptive thinking as infrastructure, not aspiration – reaching the communities furthest from the technology, not just those already closest to it.

T – Track what matters before you need to defend it. Rod Brown's 30-year journey taught him that inclusion without operational metrics is indefensible. The same is true of AI governance. If the measurement infrastructure is not built, the programmes will be dismantled the moment the political winds shift. Build the proof before you need to defend it. Dan Gallagher left a corporate role to create Verityn Index for exactly this reason: the accountability infrastructure did not exist, and nobody else was building it. For governments, require equity metrics in all public AI deployments and publish them. The UK government lists responsible and trustworthy AI as a priority. Responsibility without measurement is a statement of intent, not a commitment. What gets measured gets defended. What does not get cut.

A – Act with, not for. The people most affected by AI, women, people of colour, people in the global south, people with disabilities, people in low-income communities, must be involved in designing it, not just using it. Jazz Rasool's insistence on designing for humanity rather than individual humans, Sumathi Menon's work with women, Twan Wildeboer's advocacy for neurodivergent users, Dr Pauldy Otermans's Edge AI built for learners without internet access, Anna Jones's and Sam Samarasinghe's platforms designed from the community outward, these are not niche concerns. They are the conditions for AI that works for everyone. Participation is not consultation. It is co-creation. For governments, build co-design requirements into AI procurement. Communities affected by public AI systems must have a formal role in designing them, not merely consulted after the fact. The difference between consultation and co-creation is who holds the pen when the decisions are made.

S – Start before you are ready. Anna Jones saw a photograph of Aylan Kurdi on a Turkish beach and founded RefuAid. Christian Ortiz looked at ChatGPT's biased outputs and built a decolonised dataset inside the most biased platform available, because that is where the bias needed to be challenged. Neither of them waited for permission, funding, or certainty. O'Hanlon's challenge to his audiences applies to every reader of this book: what have you done this week that you have never done before? The fear of getting it wrong is the problem. The belief that AI is for someone else is the problem. It is not. It is for you. And the moment you start, you begin to shape what it becomes. For governments, the window for shaping AI governance is narrowing with every year of delay. Regulation that arrives after systems are embedded in infrastructure is not governance. It is archaeology.

EQUITAS is a starting point, not a ceiling.

CONNECTING THE UNCONNECTED

This book has been our own exercise in connecting the unconnected. An embryologist in India and a decolonial technologist in the United States. A Six Sigma operations professional in Minnesota and a TEDx speaker and innovator in the Netherlands. A jazz musician in Sydney and an executive coach in London. A women's AI educator in London and a Dutch neuroscientist and psychologist. An AI mentor builder deploying Edge AI in communities with intermittent internet and a former law firm employee who built a lending platform that outperforms high-street banks. None of them would have been on the same panel at a conference. All of them are working on the same problem.

The problem is not AI. The problem is equity. AI is merely the most powerful tool we have ever been given to either solve it or entrench it. The choice is not technological. It is human. And it is being made, right now, in every laboratory, every boardroom, every classroom, and every living room where someone opens an AI tool and decides what to ask it.

Anna Jones, whose RefuAid and Merit platforms have transformed the lives of displaced professionals across the United Kingdom, offered the clearest formulation of what equity-driven technology looks like in practice. We are not AI, and AI is not us, she told us. It is what we are using to help more people. The mission has not changed. Whatever we build, it is a tool. It is only there to help us achieve our mission.

We started this book with a question and we are ending it with the same one, held differently. The book cannot promise a better future is coming, or that it is coming quickly. What it can say is that the people in these pages did not wait for permission, certainty, or the right moment. They built. The fact that equitable AI remains a choice – not an inevitability, not an accident – is the only honest reason for hope we have found. Make the choice. Make it visible. Make it count.

TWELVE VOICES

Contributive value isn't just a system. It's a movement to make work human again, with AI as our partner. – Rod Brown

The most advanced technology in the room is not the AI. It's you. – Jazz Rasool

We believe in moving women from being passive users of AI to builders of AI. – Sumathi Menon

This is a beautiful phase where we are able to take a step back, see where we are, what are our biases, and to ensure that we use human elements within the whole process. – Dr Mona Ashok

We've all inherited a system that we didn't ask for. This is about collective liberation. – Christian Ortiz

The last thing we want is for people to be left behind for whatever reason. – Dr Pauldy Otermans

Success should be measured at the point of promotion, not hire. – Dan Gallagher

If I create a registry where everyone feeds in data, we would truly have a system based on a global world population. – Dr Keshav Malhotra

We are not AI, and AI is not us. It is what we are using to help more people. – Anna Jones

We are doing great guys. Hopefully we will be in a better situation tomorrow. You work towards that gradually, slowly. – Sam Samarasinghe

The biggest opportunity is when people have agency and autonomy to use it themselves. – Twan Wildeboer

Help humans learn how to be more human. – Finbar O'Hanlon

That is the future we are building. Not a future in which AI replaces us, but one in which it reveals us, our biases and our brilliance, our failures and our potential, the systems we inherited and the ones we choose to create. The technology is here. The question is whether we are.

OVER TO YOU

Explore Further: A Prompt for Your AI Assistant

Copy this prompt into your AI assistant of choice, photograph it, or visit the websites in our author biographies to access all 13 prompts in copyable format.

I've just read AI for Equity by Jenny Garrett OBE and Leah-Sunshine Garrett, specifically the conclusion which proposes the EQUITAS framework – seven commitments for equitable AI: Examine whose world the data describes, Query the black box, Understand what you are automating and whether it is worth automating, Invest in human capabilities, Track what matters before you need to defend it, Act with not for, Start before you are ready. Help me apply this framework to my own context: 1) Which of the seven EQUITAS commitments is most urgent for my organisation right now, and why? 2) What is the one commitment I am most likely to avoid, and what does that tell me? 3) Who in my organisation needs to be in the room for this conversation, and who is currently missing? 4) What is one concrete action I can take this week that moves from reading about equitable AI to practising it? Please ask about my context so you can make this specific to me.

This prompt turns AI into an EQUITAS accountability partner, helping you move from reading about equitable AI to practising it in your own context.

Three Coaching Questions for Reflection

Take time to consider these questions, either in personal reflection or in discussion with friends, colleagues, or study groups:

1. The Mirror Question. This book has argued that AI is a mirror and an amplifier. Think about the AI systems you already interact with, at work, at home, on your phone. What are they reflecting back to you? What assumptions are they making about who you are and what you need? And are those assumptions accurate?
2. The Courage Question. Every guest in this book made a choice that required courage: to build something nobody asked for, to challenge a system from inside, to lend money the banks would not. What is one courageous choice you could make this month in how you engage with AI, whether that is learning to use it, questioning how it is used in your organisation, or advocating for the people it is leaving behind?
3. The Collective Question. This book has featured voices spanning four continents. Each brought a different piece of the puzzle. Whose voice is missing from the AI conversation in your world? What would it take to bring them into the room?

FURTHER READING

Organisation for Economic Co-operation and Development. (2025). *Education for human flourishing: a conceptual framework*. OECD Publishing. https://www.oecd.org/content/dam/oecd/en/about/projects/edu/hpst/Human-flourishing-brochure-V5.pdf

UK Research and Innovation. (2026). *UKRI artificial intelligence research and innovation strategic framework*. UKRI. https://www.ukri.org/publications/ukri-artificial-intelligence-research-and-innovation-strategic-framework/

World Economic Forum. (2025). *Future of jobs report 2025*. Geneva: World Economic Forum.

ABOUT THE AUTHORS

Jenny Garrett OBE is a leadership development specialist, international keynote speaker, and the CEO and Founder of Jenny Garrett Global. For over 20 years, she has helped organisations including NHS trusts, National Gas, government bodies, and global corporations build genuinely inclusive leadership cultures using her signature Tri-Level methodology, which works simultaneously at the individual, team, and organisational level. She holds an OBE for services to Entrepreneurship and Women in Business, completed MIT's AI Strategy and Leadership Programme, and is the author of Rocking Your Role and Equality vs Equity (Emerald Publishing). She co-founded Rocking Ur Teens CIC, supporting over 3,000 young people, and founded the UK's first Diverse Executive Coach Directory. She speaks on inclusive leadership, AI-ready leadership, and the future of equitable workplaces. She is available for keynotes, leadership programmes, and consultancy. jennygarrett.global | aiforequity.world

Leah-Sunshine Garrett is a Gen Z entrepreneur, speaker, and the CEO and Founder of Dawn Intelligence, a technology company that tracks crime patterns and uses data to alleviate harm across communities. A politics and psychology graduate with a background in qualitative research, she brings a generationally distinct perspective to AI, equity, and public safety. She co-hosts the AI for Equity podcast, where her research-led approach has shaped the series and surfaced voices that mainstream AI conversations routinely overlook. She speaks on AI and equity, technology-facilitated harm, and what it means to build responsibly as a young founder.

Her work sits at the intersection of data, safety, and social justice, and she is driven by the belief that the people closest to the problem should be closest to the solution. She is available for speaking, panels, and partnerships. www.dawnintelligence.co.uk | aiforequity.world

THE TWELVE VOICES

AI for Equity is built around conversations with 12 practitioners, researchers, and innovators working at the intersection of artificial intelligence and equity. Each guest features in a dedicated chapter, where their work, ideas, and experience form the heart of the argument. The profiles below give a brief introduction to each of them, listed in the order they appear in the book.

Dr Mona Ashok is a researcher and practitioner specialising in ethical frameworks for artificial intelligence and digital technologies. She has provided evidence to the UK Parliament's All-Party Parliamentary Group on AI on regulation, governance, and ethics and serves as an independent member of a corporate AI ethics committee. She has worked across Asia, Australia, Africa, Europe, and North America; publishes in leading journals; and engages with policy and practice.

Christian Ortiz is a decolonial social scientist and technologist and the creator of Justice AI – the world's first decolonial framework trained to dismantle the roots of AI bias by centring the knowledge of historically excluded communities. He developed Justice AI in collaboration with over 560 decolonial specialists – people from the global majority around the world – and initially built it within a large language model infrastructure to challenge bias at its source. He advocates for collective liberation as the foundation of ethical AI. He is based in the North America.

Jazz Rasool is a scientist, executive coach, and AI policy adviser. He built one of the first AI coaching platforms in 2008, drawing on wisdom traditions from Africa, India, and China that Western coaching models had overlooked. He serves on the UK's Tech UK Skills and Diversity Council, advising government ministers on AI policy, and has co-authored research on ethical frameworks for the metaverse and the challenges of consent in decentralised digital environments. He is based in the United Kingdom.

Sumathi Menon is an AI consultant, strategist, educator, and UK Regional Lead for Women Defining AI. She has also run AI literacy workshops for 'curious non-corporates' – primarily women and mothers who have stepped back from corporate life – helping them move from passive users of AI to active builders of efficiency in their own lives. She is based in the United Kingdom.

Dan Gallagher is the Founder of Verityn Index, an independent certification framework assessing AI recruitment tools for fairness and governance compliance. He has held global inclusion and diversity talent acquisition leadership roles across 27 countries, most recently as Global Inclusion and Diversity TA Lead at Avanade, a joint venture between Accenture and Microsoft. He is based in the United Kingdom.

Twan Wildeboer is an industrial design engineer, TEDx speaker, and AI practitioner based in the Netherlands. He has been pioneering ways AI can support neurodivergent people and explores how systems can be designed to better respond to different ways of thinking and working. He previously worked at The LEGO Group and was a finalist in the Autistic Inventor competition.

Dr Keshav Malhotra is a fourth-generation reproductive medicine specialist and embryologist based in India. He chairs the embryology wing of the Indian Society of Assisted Reproduction, serves as the Asia Pacific Society's embryology SIG Chair, and is the treasurer of Alpha Scientists, an international consortium dedicated to advancing embryology through research and training. He runs a training academy mentoring embryologists from across Asia and Africa.

Dr Pauldy Otermans is a neuroscientist, psychologist, and the co-founder of Otermans Institute which provides offline AI learning to hundreds of thousands of marginalised learners globally. She also co-founded Teddy AI, an educational tool for children aged four to seven. Together, her work has supported over 300,000 learners globally across 21 countries. She has served as a topic editor at *Frontiers in AI*, focusing on conversational AI in higher education. She is based in the United Kingdom and was named as one of Tech 100 Women by KPMG in 2025.

Sam Samarasinghe, MBA, is the founder and CEO of Delenta.com, an AI-powered coaching operations platform built for coaching firms delivering executive coaching programmes at scale. He founded Delenta in the United Kingdom in 2018 to support organisations in managing large coaching programmes and complex engagements. Today, Delenta supports coaching firms in over 32 countries, focusing on helping organisations demonstrate coaching impact through data intelligence.

Anna Jones is the CEO and Co-Founder of RefuAid and Merit. RefuAid is a UK-based organisation that has lent nearly three million pounds to displaced professionals re-accrediting into UK careers, achieving a repayment rate of 98.6%. Merit is an AI model that assesses creditworthiness based on potential rather than financial history. She founded RefuAid after volunteering on the Greek islands during the 2015 refugee crisis.

Rod Brown is the Founder and CEO of S/BES LLC (Societal and Business Enterprise Solutions) and the creator of the Contributive Value process, a framework that uses AI to measure real-time human contribution within organisations. Drawing on three decades of work at the intersection of Six Sigma quality principles and performance based diversity, equity, and inclusion, he is the forthcoming author of Don't Let AI Eat You Alive (2027). He is based in the United States.

Finbar O'Hanlon is an explorer, musician, inventor, technologist, and human capabilities practitioner, restlessly curious about what humans can do and become. Beginning at the Australian Institute of Music, he moved through software development, IP and patents, and data science before founding ASX-listed ION Video and co-founding Rezonyx with Ahmet Zappa. He works at the intersection of deep technology, human capabilities, and the arts and is the creator of Burning Mind a programme bringing human capabilities to senior executives through serious play. He is based in Australia.

LEXICON

These are the terms we use throughout this book. We have defined them not as a textbook would but as we understand them, grounded in the conversations and the evidence that shaped each chapter. Terms drawn from a specific chapter are referenced accordingly. Terms used throughout the book are defined without a chapter reference.

Adaptive design

A system that adjusts to the person using it, not the other way around. Language shifts. Feedback modifies. Task difficulty recalibrates. Twan Wildeboer's use of AI in Chapter 7 is adaptive: it meets him where he is. He shapes the tool. The tool does not shape him. We distinguish this from inclusive design, which widens the doorway. Adaptive design changes the room.

Algorithmic bias

What happens when an AI system consistently favours or disadvantages particular groups. It usually comes from biased training data, flawed model design, or assumptions that no one thought to question. The difference between human bias and algorithmic bias is scale. A biased hiring manager affects dozens of candidates. A biased algorithm affects millions.

Alternative data metrics

Non-traditional data points used to assess what someone can do rather than what conventional systems say they have done. Utility payments, mobile phone usage, business cash flow. Anna Jones's Merit platform (Chapter 10) uses alternative data to assess refugee borrowers on their potential rather than their credit history. The 98.6% repayment rate suggests she is right.

Anthropomorphism

The tendency to treat AI as though it has feelings, understanding, or intention. It does not. But it can sound like it does. Sumathi Menon warned in Chapter 5 that we are at the precipice of AI becoming too human – creating false intimacy without accountability. When a chatbot sounds like it cares, we need to remember who wrote the script.

Artificial general intelligence (AGI)

A hypothetical form of AI that would match or exceed human ability across all domains. It is thought not to exist as yet. Rod Brown in Chapter 11 frames AGI as part of a third black box alongside faith and science – a source of knowledge whose inner workings we cannot fully explain. Whether it arrives in 3 years or 30, the governance question is the same: are we ready?

Confirmation bias

The tendency to seek out information that confirms what we already believe. In AI, it gets worse. The system's outputs shape how people behave. That behaviour becomes new data. The system retrains on the world it helped create. Over time, the bias does not just persist. It compounds. Each cycle makes it harder to see and harder to undo.

Contributive value

Rod Brown's framework (Chapter 11) that replaces performance management with a real-time measure of what people actually contribute. Not what they did 10 years ago. Not who they know. What they are doing now, and what impact it is having. AI makes it possible to track this transparently for the first time. Whether organisations choose to use it fairly is a leadership decision, not a technical one.

Contributive value income

Rod Brown's term from Chapter 11 for pay tied directly to verified, real-time contribution rather than job title, tenure, or negotiating power. If AI can measure what someone creates, organisations can no longer claim they do not know who is driving value. Not paying accordingly becomes a choice, not an oversight.

Data labelling

The process of tagging data, so AI can learn from it. Someone decides what the categories are. Someone decides which examples go where. Those decisions carry assumptions, and the assumptions end up in the model. Dr Mona Ashok identifies data labelling as one of the four doors through which bias enters AI systems (Chapter 2). The labels are never neutral. They reflect whoever wrote them.

Decolonised dataset

A dataset deliberately built to counter the colonial, Western, and patriarchal assumptions baked into mainstream AI training data. Christian Ortiz says that he has created the first one (Chapter 3) from the knowledge of 560 marginalised professionals worldwide. He initially built it inside ChatGPT – which he says is the most biased platform available – because that is where the bias needed to be challenged.

Deep learning

A type of machine learning that uses layered neural networks to find complex patterns in data. It powers most of the AI we interact with daily, from image recognition to medical diagnostics. It mimics aspects of how our brains process information, but it is not a brain. It is pattern recognition at an extraordinary scale.

Deepfakes

AI-generated images, audio, or video that realistically depict people doing or saying things they never did. The technology has legitimate creative uses. It is also being used at scale to produce non-consensual intimate imagery of real women, distributed before the person depicted even knows it exists. Chapter 5 addresses this directly. The speed of creation outpaces every legal and platform response currently in existence.

Digital divide

The gap between those who have access to digital technology and those who do not. It is not just about owning a device. It includes connection quality, digital literacy, affordability, and the ability to participate in shaping the technology that shapes your life.

Dr Pauldy Otermans built Edge AI (Chapter 9) specifically because the digital divide meant her learners could not rely on the internet.

Double empathy problem

The idea that communication difficulty between neurotypical and neurodivergent people is mutual, not one-sided. Twan Wildeboer references this in Chapter 7. For decades, the assumption was that autistic people lacked empathy. The double empathy problem reframes it: both sides struggle to understand the other. AI can act as a translator, bridging the gap in both directions.

Edge AI

AI that runs on the device itself rather than in the cloud. No internet needed after the initial download. Dr Pauldy Otermans uses Edge AI (Chapter 9) to deliver education on shared smartphones in low connectivity communities. She calls it the teacher in your pocket. It is also a privacy decision: when the AI runs locally, personal data never leaves the device.

EQUITAS

Seven commitments for equitable AI, drawn from 12 practitioners across 4 continents and presented in full in Chapter 13. Examine whose world the data describes. Query the black box. Understand what you are automating – and whether it is worth automating. Invest in human capabilities. Track what matters before you need to defend it. Act with, not for. Start before you are ready. Not a checklist. A practice.

Equity

Fairness that accounts for the fact that people start from different places. Not the same as equality, which gives everyone the same thing regardless of need. We use equity as defined in Jenny's earlier book Equality vs Equity (Emerald Publishing): the redistribution of resources, opportunities, and power to counteract structural disadvantage. It is not a luxury. It is a necessity.

Ethical AI

AI designed to ask who the system serves and who it excludes. Not the same as safe AI (Chapter 3), which focuses on preventing measurable harm. A system can follow every rule and still be deeply unjust. Ethical AI goes further: it asks whether the architecture of power is intact, and whose interests are being protected by the appearance of neutrality.

EU AI Act

The European Union's comprehensive AI legislation, passed in 2024. It classifies AI systems by risk level, bans certain uses, and imposes obligations on high-risk systems. At the time of writing, it is the most advanced regulatory framework in the world. Referenced across multiple chapters as a benchmark for what governance can look like when there is political will.

Explainable AI (XAI)

AI that can tell you how it reached its decision, in terms a non-technical person can understand. Dr Keshav Malhotra argues in Chapter 8 that this is essential in healthcare: if we do not know why the AI selected a particular embryo, we cannot trust the selection. Explainability is not a nice-to-have. It is the foundation of informed consent.

Feedback loop

A cycle in which AI outputs influence future inputs, reinforcing existing patterns. A hiring algorithm screens out certain demographics. The resulting workforce validates the screening criteria. The algorithm retrains on the workforce it created. The bias deepens with each cycle. Chapter 6 shows how this works in recruitment. This is how discrimination becomes invisible: it looks like the system is working as intended.

Fifth Industrial Revolution

The era we are in now, in which humans and machines work alongside each other rather than machines simply replacing human labour. Where the Fourth Industrial Revolution was defined by automation, the Fifth is defined by collaboration – and by the question of whose values are embedded in the machines we collaborate with. Jazz Rasool argues in Chapter 4 that the Fifth Industrial Revolution must deliver flourishing that is sustainable not just for people but for the rest of life on this planet. That is a higher bar than efficiency.

Generative AI (GenAI)

AI that creates new content – text, images, code, audio – based on patterns learned from training data. ChatGPT, Claude, and Gemini are generative AI. Since 2022, generative AI has brought artificial intelligence into mainstream daily use and accelerated every debate in this book.

Global South

Countries in Africa, Asia, Latin America, and Oceania that have been historically marginalised in global economic and political systems. In the context of AI, the global south is where most of the world's population lives, where health worker shortages are most severe, where AI training data is thinnest, and where the consequences of biased systems fall hardest.

Human-in-the-loop

A governance model where humans review, approve, or override AI decisions at critical points. Not a rubber stamp. Rod Brown's contributive value platform (Chapter 11) and Dr Pauldy Otermans's flagging systems (Chapter 9) both use human-in-the-loop governance. The principle is simple: AI informs, humans decide.

Human operating system

Finbar O'Hanlon's term from Chapter 12 for the autonomous behaviours running underneath everything we do. Not the skills we have learned. The responses we have stopped noticing. They were programmed into us over years and they run without our permission. Most people never question them. O'Hanlon's argument is that unlearning them – deliberately – is the most important thing any of us can do in the age of AI.

Humanity-centric AI

Jazz Rasool's reframe in Chapter 4 of how AI should be designed. Human-centric AI puts the individual at the centre. Humanity-centric AI puts the collective there instead. The distinction matters because some humans are bad actors. A system designed around individual preferences will amplify individual harm. A system designed around humanity's flourishing asks a harder question: what is good for all of us, including the people not yet in the room?

Inclusive design

Design that aims to make a system accessible to the widest possible range of users through universal features. Adjustable interfaces, alternative input methods, standardised accessibility settings. It is important, but it is not the same as adaptive design. Inclusive design widens the doorway. It does not change the room. Chapter 7 explores why that distinction matters.

Informed refusal

Sumathi Menon's concept from Chapter 5: the deliberate choice not to use a technology after fully understanding what it does, how it works, and what risks it carries. The opposite of uninformed avoidance, which looks like a choice but is actually a surrender. If you do not want to use AI, do not use it. But make that decision knowing why.

Intersectionality

A framework developed by Kimberle Crenshaw (1989) describing how different forms of discrimination overlap and compound. A Black woman does not experience racism and sexism separately. She experiences both at once, in ways that neither framework alone can capture. We use intersectionality throughout this book because AI bias does not affect people in neat, single categories either.

Justice AI

An AI framework created by Christian Ortiz (Chapter 3) from the knowledge of 560 marginalised professionals. Initially built inside ChatGPT to challenge bias at its source. The tool will not create a hypothetical for you, Christian told us. It will push back every single time.

Large language model (LLM)

An AI model trained on vast amounts of text to generate, summarise, translate, and reason with language. ChatGPT, Claude, and Gemini are large language models. Most are trained on internet data, which means they carry the biases of whoever wrote the internet.

Machine learning

A type of AI where the system learns from data rather than being explicitly programmed for each task. When you ask it something this week and it gives a better answer than last week, that is machine learning. It underpins most modern AI, from your spam filter to your medical diagnosis.

Masking

In the context of neurodiversity, the practice of suppressing or camouflaging neurodivergent traits to fit neurotypical expectations. It is exhausting. It means that short-term research may miss the real cost of navigating a neurotypical world every day. Twan Wildeboer's use of AI (Chapter 7) relates to this.

Neurodiversity

The natural variation in how human brains work. Includes ADHD, autism, dyslexia, dyspraxia, Tourette syndrome, and other cognitive profiles. In the United Kingdom, approximately one in seven people are neurodivergent. Chapter 7 argues that if between one in seven and one in five people think differently, it should be the norm, not the exception.

Personalisation

An AI system's ability to adapt its content, pace, and interaction to the individual. Dr Pauldy Otermans (Chapter 9) frames personalisation not as a feature but as the equity mechanism: if a system cannot adapt to the person, it will reproduce the hierarchy it claims to dismantle. Thirty children in a classroom cannot each get a personal tutor. AI changes that equation.

Proxy variables

Data points that appear neutral but act as stand-ins for protected characteristics. Postcode correlates with race. Career gaps correlate with gender. Continuous employment correlates with disability. An algorithm that never mentions race can still discriminate by race if it uses postcode as a variable. Chapter 2 uses the Facebook job ads case to show how proxy discrimination works: the algorithm did not need to know someone's gender to target them by it. The mechanism is invisible. The outcome is not.

Retrieval-augmented generation (RAG)

A technique that connects an AI model to a specific knowledge base before generating a response. Rod Brown's platform (Chapter 11) uses RAG to keep personal conversations private while still measuring work output – the mechanism that makes privacy and accountability possible simultaneously.

Safe AI

AI designed to prevent measurable harm and operate within defined rules. Important, but not sufficient. As Chapter 3 explores, a system can be safe without being just. Safe AI asks: does this break rules? Ethical AI asks: whose rules?

Skills-based hiring

Assessing candidates on what they can do rather than where they studied or how long they have been continuously employed. AI-powered skills assessment can widen opportunity for refugees, career returners, and people from non-traditional backgrounds. Chapter 6 shows what this looks like in practice – and what happens when the governance is missing.

Technology-facilitated abuse

The use of digital tools – smartphones, smart home devices, GPS trackers, AI-generated imagery – to control, monitor, harass, or harm. Chapter 5 argues that technology did not create gender-based violence. It changed the conditions under which it can hide. A perpetrator no longer needs to be physically present. Safety is no longer spatial. What makes technology-facilitated abuse particularly dangerous is not its intensity. It is its invisibility.

Three black boxes

Rod Brown's philosophical frame from Chapter 11. Throughout human history, we have relied on two sources of knowledge that contain unanswerable questions: religion and science. AI introduces a third. We do not fully understand how it reaches its conclusions, and when artificial general intelligence arrives, we will have three black boxes to navigate at once. The governance question of our era.

Tri-level methodology

Jenny Garrett's approach to leadership development, working simultaneously at the individual, team, and organisational levels. Systemic change requires intervention at all three at once. Changing one without the others produces temporary results.

Uninformed avoidance

Sumathi Menon's term from Chapter 5 for the choice not to engage with AI that comes from fear rather than understanding. It looks like a decision. It is not. The person avoiding AI is still shaped by AI – through the systems that affect their credit, their job application, their healthcare, their news. Choosing not to understand a system that already makes decisions about you is not neutrality. It is an absence.

Verityn Index

An independent assessment body founded by Dan Gallagher (Chapter 6) to hold AI hiring vendors to account. When he saw that vendors were marketing products as bias-free without evidence, and no one was checking, he built the accountability infrastructure.

INDEX

Aboriginal and Torres Strait Islander organizations, 59
Accessibility, 103
Accountability, 55–56, 182
 building accountability infrastructure, 182–183
 gap, 26–27
Adaptive design, 112, 193
 inclusive design not, 111–112
Adaptive mindset, 196
Adaptive systems, 112
Adaptive thinking, 212
Adaptive tutoring, 166
ADHD, 24, 104–105, 111, 113, 166, 207
Adults, 108
Advanced technology in room, 60–62
Agentic AI, 197
Agentic commerce, 191, 197
Alexa, 34
Algorithm(s), 44, 177–178
 learned to discriminate, 89–90
 in room, 126–127
Algorithmic bias, 9, 19
Algorithmic impact assessments, 212
Alpha Scientists consortium, 131
Alternative-data credit scoring, 161
Ambiguity, 115
Amplifies inequity
 accountability gap, 26–27
 AI goes wrong, 22–24
 building literacy, 27–29
 diversity imperative, 27
 four doors through bias enters, 20–22
 hidden history, 18–19
 mirror and choice, 29–31
 mirror that shows us ourselves, 19–20
 thoughtful automation, 24–26
Anthropomorphism, 77
Antivirus, 53–54
Anxiety, 1, 113, 142
Apple, 93
Apprenticeships, 93
Art of unlearning, 192
Artificial general intelligence (AGI), 178
Artificial intelligence (AI), 1, 4–7, 20, 22, 33–34, 37, 42, 44–46, 54–55, 72–74, 77, 80–81, 105–106, 109–112, 116, 124, 126, 128, 131, 141–142, 183, 203–2047, 206
 accountability gap, 26–27
 adoption, 18, 54
 AI doctor that treats patients differently by race and ethnicity, 23
 benefits from assimilation, 108–111
 bias, 36
 bias enters machine, 36–37
 building literacy, 27–29
 chatbots, 34, 128
 coaching platform, 51–52
 data sovereignty, 40–41
 DEI practitioner as AI catalyst, 179–180
 diversity imperative, 27
 double empathy problem, 107–108

empowering communities with AI actually requires, 152–154
ethical AI *vs.* safe AI, 41–43
ethics committee, 25
expert by experience, 104–106
four doors through bias enters, 20–22
goes wrong, 22–24
governance, 175, 213
growing up inside algorithm, 43–45
happens at scale, 115–116
helps, 92–93
hidden history, 18–19
inclusive design not adaptive design, 111–112
and internal mobility, 95–96
job ads algorithm that stereotypes by gender, 22–23
justice AI, 39–40
liberation or optimization, 116–117
literacy, 151
LLM training, 79
measurable impact, 162–163
meets access gap, 160–161
mirror and choice, 29–31
mirror that shows us ourselves, 19–20
mirror we cannot look away from, 45–48
model, 77
moment machine showed its hand, 37–39
path forward, 24–26
products, 147
regulation, 25
research problem, 113–114
road paved by few, 35–36
space, 73, 105
systems making decisions, 205
tools, 109
transformation, 204
UK, 9
as umbrella and everyday presence, 33–34
wand, 117–120

Artificial Intelligence Act, 57
Asia Pacific Society, 131
Assimilation, benefits from, 108–111
Autism, 104–105, 113–114
Autistic Inventor, 106
Automated systems, 165

Bias, 150–152
Bias enters
- data collection, 20–21
- data labeling, 21
- feedback loop, 22
- four doors through, 20
- model architecture, 22

Black British women, 12
Black communities, 42
Black woman, 29
Blockchain, 57
#BodyPositivity movements, 44
Boomers, 5
Bootcamps, 93
Brand awareness not culture change, 88–89
Burning Mind, 196–197
Businesses, 143

Careless design, 73–74
Cash transfers, 164
Cedars-Sinai Medical Center, 23
Chatbot, 25
ChatGPT, 2, 11, 13, 18, 35, 90–91, 115, 214
Childhood, 190
Claude, 11
Co-creating AI with communities, 148–150
Coaching, 158
- models, 52
- profession, 165
- relationship, 163

Coercive control, 74
Cognitive load, 110
Colonial logic, 44
Colonialism, 7
Communit(ies/y), 130–131, 165–168, 210, 214
- co-creating AI with, 148–150
- empowerment, 149
- members, 150

Community Citizen Science (CCS), 149
Community-governed AI, 63
Computer, 164–165
Confirmation bias, 36
Contributive value (CV), 165, 176, 184, 215
  platform, 204
Contributive Value Income (CVI), 183
Copilot, 11
Corporate boardrooms, 2
COVID-19, 88, 95, 159
  pandemic, 164
Creativity, 196, 212
  as reorganisation, 193–194
Credential bias, 93
Credential trap, 93–94
Credential-based hiring, 93
Credit data, 21
Credit scoring systems, 162
Criminal justice, 21
Critical thinking, 196
Critics, 176
CSIRO project, 59, 63
Cultural bias, 63
Cultural diversity, 174
Cultural inequity, 125
Culture change, brand awareness not, 88–89
Curiosity, 190
Cyberstalking, 71

Data
  collection, 20–21
  data-origin bias, 128
  extraction, 147
  labeling, 21
  models, 110
  reflects, 36
  sovereignty, 40–41, 208
Datasets reflect systems, 203
Dawn Intelligence, 2, 75
Decision-making, 198
Deep learning, 34–35
  systems, 56
Deepfakes, 57
DeepSeek, 11
Democratisation, 166–167
Depression, 114
Dermatology AI, 127
Diagnostic psychometric assessment tool, 86
Digital divide, 142, 206
Digital footprint data, 161
Digital landscape, 12
Digital literacy, 76, 79
Digital music, 190
Digital platform, 72, 86
Digital safety, 75
Digital sexual violence, 72
Digital systems, 148
Digital Transformation, 18
Disability, 90
Discovering AI, 2
Disinformation, 72
Displaced professionals, 160, 207
Diversity, equity, and inclusion (DEI), 8, 10, 87–89, 175–176, 179, 184, 208
  community, 96
  practitioner as AI catalyst, 179–180
Diversity imperative, 27
Domestic violence chatbot, 54, 56, 63
Double empathy problem, 107–108
Drug discovery, 133
Dyslexia, 104
Dyspraxia, 104

E-commerce lender, 161
Edge AI, 146, 151–152, 195, 198, 204, 206, 213–214
Education, 160, 162–163
  as scale, 141–142
EHAS foundation, 129
Electricity, 147
Email that started everything, 2–3
Embryology, 125
Empathy, 60–61
Employability, 142
Employees, 116
Employers benefit from predictability, 109
Employment, 161
  data, 21

Empowering communities
  with AI actually requires, 152–155
  bias, governance, and western model problem, 150–152
  co-creating AI with communities, 148–150
  data, privacy, and feedback loop, 147–148
  education as scale, not charity, 141–142
  gap, really, 142–144
  infrastructure humility and teacher in your pocket, 145–147
  personalisation, 144–145
  skill gap no one measures, 139–141
Empowerment, 60, 140, 147–149, 152
Environments, 147
Equality, 19
Equitable AI, 8, 204, 215
  AI you do not notice, 6–7
  Burning Mind, 196–197
  comes next, 197–198
  coming full circle, 12–14
  creativity as reorganisation, 193–194
  curious kid, 189–191
  email that started everything, 2–3
  fear that stops us, 194–195
  human operating system, 192–193
  hypotheses that changed everything, 3–4
  language within language, 191–192
  moment, 7–8
  mother, daughter, and gap between US, 4–6
  note on write, 11–12
  puzzle of life, 198–201
  twelve voices, one question, 9–10
Equitable healthcare AI, 135
EQUITAS framework, 210–214
Equity, 8, 20, 86, 210
  access to, 133–136
  conversation, 60
  lens, 95
ESG, 175
Ethical AI, 41–43, 53, 55, 177
  design, 59
Ethical integrity, 73
Ethics
  committee, 25
  policies, 63
Ethnicity, AI doctor that treats patients differently by, 23–24
EU AI Act, 42, 212
Eurocentric nutrition, 38
European Mentoring and Coaching Council, 52
European Union, 57
Executive dysfunction, 114
Executive function, 109
Explainability, 56, 77
Explainable AI, 127
Eye contact, 108

Facial recognition, 19
Fairness, 53, 62, 85
  accountability, 55–56
  advanced technology in room, 60–62
  AI, 54–55
  antivirus, 53–54
  defunding paradox, 58–59
  explainability, 56
  five principles, 55
  path forward, 62–65
  privacy and security, 57
  robustness, 56–57
  transparency, 55
  works, 59–60
  world trying to catch up, 57–58
Fear, 194–195
Feedback loops, 130, 203
Femicide, 70
Feminism, 39
Fifth Industrial Revolution, 8, 61
Financial inclusion, 161–162
Financial inequity, 125
Financial services, 163

Financial system, 159–160
Fintech lenders, 161
Flagging systems, 151, 153
Fourier transform algorithms, 190
Frame employability, 140

Gemini, 11, 54
Gen X, 5, 12
GenAI, 76
Gender, job ads algorithm that stereotypes by, 22–23
Gender-based violence, 71–72, 74–75
- careless design, not malicious intent, 73–74
- heat, silence, and spectacle, 69–70
- precipice of becoming too human, 77–78
- reclaiming technology as protection, 74–75
- shield need to build, 80–81
- violence moved into our phones, 70–71
- weaponisation of intimacy, 71–72
- woman chose literacy over innovation, 75–77
- written out of future, 78–80

Generation Alpha, 117
Generation Z (Gen Z), 5, 10, 12–13, 45, 180
Generative AI, 19, 106–107, 142
Geographic inequity, 125
Giftedness, 105
Gig economy, 166
Global data
- registry, 182
- representation, 206

Global health divide, 125
Global Innovation Summit in Dubai, 195
Global South, 151, 208
Good AI model, 38
Google, 18, 93
Governance, 150–152
- gap, 90–91, 205
- lag technology, 131

Governed AI, 97
Governments, 143
Guatemala model, 130
Gut instinct, 92

Harm reduction, 42
Health crisis, 130
Health divide
- access to equity, 133–135
- algorithm in room, 126–127
- data, bodies, 127–128
- extraordinary paradox, 125
- registry that could change everything, 133
- sales pitch and standard, 130–132
- technology works, 129–130
- training paradox, 132–133

Healthcare, 11, 59–60, 126, 129, 133
- AI, 24, 127, 131
- sector, 131
- system, 134

Hiring algorithms, 1
Human capabilities, 196, 213
Human contribution, 183
Human element, 93
Human intelligence, 62
Human language, 197
Human leadership still matters, 177–178
Human operating system, 192–193, 204
Human oversight, 26
Human prejudice, 164
Human systems, 175
Human tutors, 163
Human-in-the-loop validation model, 129
Human-led support, 145
Human–AI partnership, 175, 181, 184
- 24/7 PHD, 181
- algorithm, 177–178
- black boxes, 178–179
- building accountability infrastructure, 182–183
- DEI practitioner as AI catalyst, 179–180
- house no foundation, 175–176

partnership to practice, 184–185
wealth question, 183–184
Humanity-centric approach, 60
Hyperfocus, 116

IBM, 93
Imagine training, 21
Inclusion, 9, 79, 88
Inclusive design, 113, 193
not adaptive design, 111–113
Inclusive leadership, 89
Inclusive talent
AI helps, 92–93
algorithm learned to discriminate, 89–90
brand awareness not culture change, 88–89
inside building, 95–96
credential trap, 93–94
governance gap, 90–91
hiring to thriving, 97–98
measure of success, 96–97
real question not representation, 87–88
reskilling divide, 94–95
thirty-two skills and no silver bullet, 91–92
Indian Society of Assisted Reproduction, 124, 131
Indigenous women, 129–130
Inequality AI enters, 158–160
Informed consent gap, 126
Informed refusal, 76
Infrastructure humility in your pocket, 145–147
Innovation, 160, 207Instagram, 44, 70
Institutional trust, 167
Internal mobility, 95–96
International Coaching Federation, 52
International Telecommunication Union, 159
Intersectionality, 29
Intimacy, weaponisation of, 71–72
IVF, 125, 135
laboratory in India, 123, 206

Job ads algorithm that stereotypes by gender, 22–23
Justice AI, 35, 39–40, 45–46, 205, 210

Knowledge systems, 38

Labour market, 165–166
Language, 175
within language, 191–192
models, 2, 24, 141
Language Alchemist, The, 191
Large language models, 6–8, 11, 23, 34, 37, 40, 53, 77, 128
Leadership, 27
Learning, 144, 146
poverty, 158
Legitimate decision, 206
Liberation, 116
Lifelong learning, 196, 212
LinkedIn, 4, 28, 143, 180
Literacy, building, 27–29
Local communities, 149
Low connectivity, 139
Low-income communities, 213

Machine learning, 34–35
algorithms, 86
model, 164
Marginalised communities, 73
Masking, 110
Maternal mortality, 130
Medical data, 21
Mental healthcare, 128
Meritocracy, 103
Meta, 23
meta-analysis, 163
Micro-credentials, 93
Microsoft, 58
Copilot, 18
Migrant, 158
Millennials, 5
'Mindblindness' hypothesis, 107
Minority communities, 42
Misinformation, 43
Mobile phone
data, 164
model, 164

Model architecture, 22
Modern capitalism, 110
Mother–daughter partnership, 6
Music, 191, 199

Nations, 208
#Natural-Hair movements, 44
Netherlands Institute for Human Rights, 23
Neurodivergence, 118
Neurodivergent, 111
  creativity, 116
  people, 114
Neurodiverse people, 106
Neurodiversity, 106, 114, 206
  benefits from assimilation, 108–111
  double empathy problem, 107–108
  expert by experience, 104–106
  happens at scale, 115–116
  inclusive design not adaptive design, 111–112
  liberation or optimization, 116–117
  research problem, 113–114
  wand, 117–119
Neurotypical describes, 104
Neutrality, 42–43
Non-medical term, 103
Normal, 104
Nuclear-arms-treaty analogy, 179

Online
  anonymity, 72
  gender-based violence, 71–72
OpenAI, 7, 35, 40
Operational accountability, 174
Organisation(s), 25–26, 63, 88–89, 96, 98, 116, 175, 181, 204
Organisational level, 182

Partnership
  looks like in practice, 181
  to practice,184–186
Path, 160
Patient consent, 134
Pauldy's model, 150
Performance management, 175
Personal data, 147
Personal identifiers, 148
Personal responsibility, role of, 209–210
Personalisation, 118, 142, 144–145
Platform power, 165–166
Platformisation, 165
Policing, 8, 42, 77
Political economy, 161
Political infrastructure, trust as, 167–168
Poverty targeting, 163–164
  and limits of state capacity, 163–164
Predictability, employers benefit from, 109
Predictive accuracy, 161–162
Predictive policing, 21
Predictive system, 148
Privacy, 57
Procurement, 213
Productivity, 115
  systems benefit from uniformity, 109
Professional network, 4
Programming language, 197
Proxy variables, 23
Public administration, 18
Public authority, 179
Public sector, 2
Public transport, 6

Race, AI doctor that treats patients differently by, 23–24
Re-accreditation, 159–161
Re-versity, 174
Real-time adaptation, 118
Reasonable adjustment, 103
Rebellion, 108
Reclaiming technology as protection, 74–75
Reframed AI, 167
Refugees, 160
Regulation, 214

Reorganisation, creativity as, 193–194
Reproductive medicine, 124, 127, 134
Reskilling, 143
divide, 94–95
tools, 95
Responsible AI, 8, 91, 195
Retrieval-augmented generation (RAG), 177
Rezonyx, 191
Risk assessment, 74
Robust AI system, 56
Robust governance process, 90
Robustness, 56–57

Safe AI, 41–43
Safeguarding, 37
Sally-Anne test, 107
Scepticism, 91
Security, 57
Self-assessments, 22
Self-determination, 208
Self-directed learning, 93
Self-awareness, 2
Sensitive data, 147
Sensory processing, 105
Shaping AI, 180
Siri, 34
Six Sigma, 174, 178, 214
Skills gap, 142
Skills-based hiring, 94
Smart home technology, 71
Social capital theory, 167
Social equity, 8
Social media, 42–44, 53, 166
Social scoring, 57
Socio-economic barriers
AI meets access gap, 160–161
computer, 164–165
democratisation, 166–167
dismantling actually requires, 168–169
education, 162–163
financial inclusion, 161–162
inequality AI enters, 158–160
platform power and labour market, 165–166
poverty targeting and limits of state capacity, 163–164
trust as political infrastructure, 167–168
Sovereignty gap, 208
Sprint Ethics Board model, 182
State capacity, poverty targeting and limits of, 163–164
Stop-and-search policies, 21
Structured environments, 115
Students, 162
Surveillance implications, 177

Teacher in your pocket, 145–147
Teaching relationship, 163
Techno-determinism, 166
Technology, 7–8, 13, 19, 70, 79, 125, 135, 151, 159, 199, 212
accelerates productivity, 167
industry, 53, 90
works, 113, 129–131
Thoughtful automation, 24–26
TikTok, 44
Total Quality Management, 178
Traditional education, 144
Training, 152
academy, 132
data, 134
Transformation, 126
Transparency, 55, 185
in AI systems, 26
issues, 115
Trust as political infrastructure, 167–168

UKRI AI, 213
Unconscious bias, 91
UNICEF, 159
Uniform cognitive output, capital benefits from, 110
Uniformity, 118
productivity systems benefit from, 109
Uninformed avoidance, 76
United Kingdom, 25, 57, 86, 104, 118
United Nations, 70

United States, 58
Universal Basic Income (UBI), 183
Unlearning, art of, 192
Upskilling, 196
US Food and Drug Administration, 126–127

Value judgement, 104
Violence, 70, 80
  moved into our phones, 70–71
Violence against women and girls (VAWG), 70

Western model problem, 150–152
White supremacy, 39, 44
Woman chose literacy over innovation, 75–77
Women, 165
  AI educator, 214
Work readiness, 140
Workplace, 104
World Economic Forum, 125
World Economic Forum's Future of Jobs, 196, 212
World Health Organization, 125

XAI, 56

YouTube videos, 180

www.ingramcontent.com/pod-product-compliance
Lightning Source LLC
Jackson TN
JSHW071941120926
107926JS00009B/12
9781837428571